Despite a master narrative of cultural and racial homogeneity, Japan is home to diverse populations. In the face of systematic exclusions and marginalization, minority groups have consistently challenged the subordinate identities imposed by the Japanese majority. *Japan's Minorities* addresses a broad range of issues associated with the six principal minority groups in Japan.

- Ainu
- Burakumin
- Chinese
- Koreans
- Nikkeijin
- Okinawans

The contributors to this volume show how an overarching discourse of homogeneity has been deployed to exclude the historical experience of minority groups in Japan. The chapters provide clear historical introductions to particular groups and place their experiences in the context of contemporary Japanese society.

Michael Weiner is Director and Senior Lecturer, East Asia Research Centre, School of East Asian Studies, University of Sheffield.

This book may be re...

Sheffield Centre for Japanese Studies/Routledge Series
Series editor: Glenn D. Hook
Professor of Japanese Studies, University of Sheffield

This series, published by Routledge in association with the Centre for Japanese Studies at the University of Sheffield, will make available both original research on a wide range of subjects dealing with Japan and will provide introductory overviews of key topics in Japanese studies.

Japan's Minorities

The illusion of homogeneity

Edited by Michael Weiner

ROUTLEDGE

London and New York

First published 1997
by Routledge
11 New Fetter Lane, London EC4P 4EE

Simultaneously published in the USA and Canada
by Routledge
29 West 35th Street, New York NY 10001

Reprinted 1998

Typeset in Times by
BC Typesetting, Bristol

Printed and bound in Great Britain by
T J International Ltd, Padstow, Cornwall

British Library Cataloguing in Publication Data
A catalogue record for this book is available from the British Library

Library of Congress Cataloguing in Publication Data
A catalogue record for this book is available from the Library of Congress

1001378435

ISBN 0-415-13008-5 (hbk)   T
ISBN 0-415-15218-6 (pbk)

This book is for my children, Jessica and Leah

Contents

Tables

Contributors

Millie Creighton is Associate Professor of Anthropology in the Department of Anthropology and Sociology at the University of British Columbia. Among her most recent publications are: 'The Shifting Imagery of Childhood Amidst Japan's Consumer Affluence', in H. Eiss, ed., *Images of the Child* (1994); 'Japanese Craft Tourism: Liberating the Crane Wife', Annals of Tourism Research, 22: 2 (1995); and 'The Non-Vanishing Ainu: A Damning Development Project, Internationalization and Japan's Indigenous Other', in *American Asian Review*, 13: 2 (1995). Her current research addresses issues of ethnicity and marginality in contemporary Japan.

Ian Neary is Professor of Politics and Director of the Contemporary Japan Centre, the University of Essex. He is the author of numerous articles and books including: *Political Protest and Social Control in Pre-war Japan: Origins of Buraku Liberation* (1989); and *Intervention and Technological Innovation: Government and the Pharmaceutical Industry in the UK and Japan* (1995). His current research, funded by the Economic and Social Research Council, focuses on issues of human rights in East Asia.

Yoko Sellek is Lecturer in Sociology, the School of East Asian Studies, at the University of Sheffield. Her most recent publications include: 'Migrant Workers: the Japanese Case in International Perspective' (with M. Weiner), in G.D. Hook and M. Weiner, eds, *The Internationalization of Japan* (1992); and 'Illegal Foreign Migrant Workers in Japan: Change and Challenge in Japanese Society', in J.M. Brown and R. Foot, eds, *Migration: the Asian Experience* (1994). Her current research focuses on migration in contemporary Japan.

Richard Siddle is Lecturer in History, the School of East Asian Studies, at the University of Sheffield. His publications include: 'With Shining Eyes: Ainu Social and Political Movements 1918–1937', in *Asian Cultural Studies*, 21 (1995); 'The Ainu: Construction of an Image', in J. Maher and G. Macdonald, eds, *Diversity in Japanese Culture and Language* (1995); and *Race, Resistance and the Ainu of Japan* (1996). He is currently involved in a collaborative research project on the construction of indigenous identities in Okinawa and Taiwan.

Koji Taira holds joint appointments as Professor in the Departments of Economics and the Institute of Labor and Industrial Relations at the University of Illinois. His numerous publications include: *Economic Development and the Labor Market in Japan* (1970); *Labor Markets: Readings* (in Japanese, 1990); and 'Dialectics of Economic Growth, National Power, and Distributive Struggles', in A. Gordon, ed., *Postwar Japan as History* (1993). His current research interests focus on international labour migration, Japan's role in the 'new' World Order, and Ryukyuan studies.

Andrea Vasishth is a Ph.D. candidate in Japanese History at the University of Sheffield. She holds degrees from Adelaide and Jawaharlal Nehru Universities, has studied at Kobe University and the Beijing Language Institute. She is currently engaged in research at Kobe University under a grant provided by the Japan Foundation Endowment Committee.

Michael Weiner is Senior Lecturer in Japanese History and Director of the East Asia Research Centre at the University of Sheffield. His publications include: *The Origins of the Korean Community in Japan: 1910–1923* (1989); *The Internationalization of Japan* (with G.D. Hook, 1992); and *Race and Migration in Imperial Japan* (1994). His current research, funded by the Economic and Social Research Council, is concerned with labour and refugee migration in East Asia. He is Managing Editor of *Japan Forum* and Series Editor for *Monographs on East Asia*.

Introduction

Michael Weiner

Early in the twentieth century, in *The Souls of Black Folk*, W.E.B. Du Bois predicted that issues of 'race', or, in his terms, the 'Colour Line' would be the defining problem of the twentieth century (Du Bois 1961: 23). Given both the historical context within which the prediction was made and the evidence which marches across our television screens on a daily basis, there can be little doubt that 'race' remains a primary determinant of social relations. Nevertheless, while the invidious imagery of 'biological' superiority and inferiority certainly informs some contemporary forms of racism, there is reason to doubt the universal explanatory power of a colonial inspired paradigm of 'race'. In the first place, emphasis on the 'Colour Line', as conceptualized by Du Bois, runs the risk of reifying skin colour, of ignoring the fact that the visibility of somatic difference is itself a social construct. Of course, the existence of physical differences between human populations is not disputed here. Of far greater relevance are the processes of signification which attribute meaning to those differences. Historically, moreover, a wide range of both physiological and cultural characteristics, either real or imagined, have been employed as natural or 'racial' signifiers. The assumption that one historically specific instance of signification can provide an adequate explanation for all forms of 'racial' exclusion, ignores evidence which illustrates that other populations (the Jews in central Europe, Koreans, Chinese, Burakumin, Ryukyuan/Okinawan and Ainu in Japan) have been signified as distinct and inferior 'races' without reference to the colour stigmata. Indeed, as one of the contributors to this volume argues, the construction of 'Otherness' can be projected on to either real or imagined populations. Here, parallels can be found in the recrudescence of anti-Semitism in parts of central Europe where the Jewish presence was eliminated some fifty years ago.

Although there is a temptation to offer a global definition of 'race', there are compelling reasons not to do so. Firstly, 'race' is a social construct, fluid in content, whose meaning is determined by historical and national context. Of far greater value as a subject of inquiry are the processes which have led to groups not previously defined in 'racial' terms being defined as 'races'. Processes within which the state has functioned as both a primary site of racial articulation and contestation, and as an arena where minority voices have been constrained and suppressed. Secondly, while 'racialized' notions of citizenship, inclusion and exclusion undoubtedly exist in, for example, the United States, Britain, France and Japan, the historical experience of the excluded and 'racialized' Others in each of these countries reveals clear differences and discontinuities. Unlike the United States, where 'racial' identities were initially produced within the institutions of slavery, and were reproduced during the course of several centuries of territorial expansion and immigration, both voluntary and involuntary, the 'racialization' of identities in Japan is of more recent origin and lacks the 'pedigree' of plantation slavery. 'Racialized' minority populations are also distinguished by their relative size, settlement pattern, length and status of residence, degree of social economic and political integration, or by a combination of these factors. Finally, any attempt to generate a global definition of 'race' for comparative purposes, at various levels of discourse, runs the risk of either distorting the historical/national context, or of imbuing the notion of 'races', as natural and distinctive groups, with even greater explanatory power.

Thus, while there exists an extensive literature on 'race' and 'race' relations, it tends to be country-specific. This is not, however, to suggest the complete absence of continuities, or similarities. The minority experience in each of the societies referred to here has been characterized by the existence of multi-layered racisms, systematic exclusions and relative disadvantage, economic, political and social. Rather than addressing issues of 'race', as such, the point of departure for this book is an analysis of the historically specific factors involved in the appearance and maintenance of 'racialized' relations in Japan. By this, I refer to processes of attribution, inclusion and exclusion, all of which are determined by historical context.

Although there have been divergencies in the representation of 'Self', expressed variously in terms of 'race', ethnicity or culture, all have been grounded in notions of an essentialized identity which distinguishes the Japanese from other populations (Masuda 1967; Ishida 1974; Ueyama 1990; Kawakatsu 1991). To a certain extent, recent conceptualizations of Japanese uniqueness reflect an attempt to avoid the genetic consequences of the Second World War. In the broadest sense, cultural determinants (religious values, language, patterns of social and economic organization), rather than genetic or physiological markers, have been deployed to signify the existence of an immutable and homogeneous Japanese identity. Within this literature the Japanese present is transformed by an idealized past, heterogeneity ignored, and historical memory suppressed. The resilience of this narrative was succinctly expressed in Japan's initial submission to the Human Rights Committee of the United Nations in 1980 which denied the existence of minority populations.

The dominant paradigm of homogeneity has, however, been challenged by a number of recent studies which have sought to locate the construction of this identity within the appropriate historical context/s (Yoshino 1992; Befu 1993; Amino 1994; Weiner 1995; Morris-Suzuki 1995). But the social construction of 'Self' in Japan has also presumed its opposite, the excluded 'Other', against whom notions of Japanese homogeneity and purity could be measured. Publications which focus upon the historical formation of minority populations, though more extensive, have tended to address the situation of a particular population in isolation from other groups which have been subjected to comparable exclusions (DeVos and Wagatsuma 1972; Pak 1978; Lee and DeVos 1981; Pak 1988; Neary 1989; Weiner 1989, 1994). In contrast to these studies, the intention here is to provide a historically contextualized analysis of 'Otherness' in Japan with reference to its principal minority populations: Ainu, Burakumin, Chinese, Koreans, Okinawans, and, of most recent origin, *Nikkeijin*.

Despite a master narrative of 'racial' and cultural homogeneity, which precludes the existence of minorities, Japan is home to diverse populations. Of these, only the Burakumin, descendants of the Eta and Hinin outcasts of the Tokugawa period, could be described as indigenous. Both Ainu and Ryukyuan/Okinawan populations were only incorporated during the late nineteenth century. While the historical evidence of earlier migrations from the Asian mainland is not in doubt, the present-day Korean and Chinese communities are largely a consequence of Japanese imperialism during the twentieth century. In contrast to these well-established, though by no means fully integrated, populations, we also include for discussion the *Nikkeijin*, primarily Latin. Americans of Japanese descent, whose emergence as a distinct minority population coincided with the demand for inexpensive, low-level labour in Japan during the 1980s.

In light of the above, state encouragement for the recruitment of *Nikkeijin* is an especially significant phenomenon since it also provides an opportunity to reconsider the claim that the Japanese nation-state has evolved as an expression of the enduring purity of a homogeneous people, whose distinctive qualities remain undiluted by the incorporation of alien elements. The myth of a homogeneous people is most clearly illustrated by current immigration laws, which, with the exception of *Nikkeijin*, prohibit the entry of foreign migrant labour.

The objectives of this volume are therefore threefold. Firstly, to critically evaluate both the historical construction and contemporary manifestations of a 'racialized' Japanese identity, the corollary of which has been the exclusion of other populations on the basis of characteristics assumed to be inherent. Secondly, to provide a historical analysis of the formation of Japan's principal minority populations. Thirdly, to consider aspects of minority life within the contemporary context of the 1990s. In the case of the Burakumin, Koreans and, to a somewhat lesser extent, the Ainu, about whom there already exists a substantial literature, the emphasis has been placed on contemporary issues of integration, exclusion and identity. Due to the virtual absence from the literature of accounts of the Ryukyuan/Okinawan and Chinese populations, Chapters 5 and 6 emphasize the historical processes which led to the formation of these minority communities. Since the *Nikkeijin*, the subject of Chapter 7, are a phenomenon of the past decade, the status of this community can only be considered within a contemporary and comparative framework.

The point of departure is the period 1868-1945. Although there is a substantial literature which covers the economic, political and institutional aspects of Japan's transformation from an isolated semi-feudal state on the Asian periphery to a modern imperial power, relatively less attention has been given to the ideological contours of this process. In Chapter 1, the construction of a Japanese identity, incorporating both the naturalization of selected cultural characteristics and the grafting of pseudo-scientific notions of biological determinism borrowed from the West, is considered. Although the categories of 'race' and nation are often regarded as analytically distinct, the argument advanced is that in the pre-1945 context there was a high degree of overlap between them, and that this was a critical element in the 'racialization' of the national community.

The appearance of Ainu representatives at the United Nations and other international fora in recent years contrasts sharply with mainstream Japanese perceptions of the Ainu as assimilated and culturally extinct. Following on from an overview of the incorporation and subsequent marginalization of the Ainu, the focus of Richard Siddle's contribution shifts to contemporary issues of Ainu identity and nationalism. Rather than a revival of vestigial tribal identities, Siddle argues that the resurgence of ethnicity, expressed as Ainu nationalism, represents a reconstruction of ethnic identity in response to deprivation and structural inequalities. In Chapter 3, Ian Neary's discussion of the Burakumin focuses upon the activities of the Buraku Liberation League (BLL) and the extent to which the introduction of post-war legislation has facilitated an improvement in the social, political and economic position of Buraku communites. Given that the material circumstances of many Burakumin have undoubtedly been improved by the introduction of the Special Measures Law and subsequent *Dōwa* projects, Neary addresses the question of how the BLL is seeking to redefine itself in the 1990s. As in the case of the Ainu, the Burakumin struggle to end inequality has also developed an international dimension in recent years. Finally, Neary asks what else can be done to eliminate discrimination and what role Buraku organizations can play in that process. Chapter 4, by contrast, is primarily concerned with the politics of historical memory in post-war Japan as reflected in the treatment of Korean victims of the atomic bomb. It also represents an attempt to map a particular terrain in which conflicting representations of the past and present coexist. As in the case of the Ainu and Burakumin, this chapter also provides a summary analysis of the historical formation of the Korean community. This is followed by a description of Korean settlement in Hiroshima and Nagasaki and the consequences of the atomic bombings for Korean residents of both cities. For many Japanese, the atomic bombings were the defining moments in their nation's modern history. At a discursive level, however, the atomic bombings have been situated within a post-war master narrative of peace and internationalism. It is a narrative which not only enhances a well-constructed image of Japan as a, if not the, victim of the Pacific War, but has relegated other dissonant histories to the periphery of public consciousness. In this chapter, we consider issues of compensation within the broader context of the decades-long struggle by Koreans for recognition and medical treatment.

There are a number of factors which, at least on the surface, distinguish Chinese residents from other minority communities. From a comparative perspective, far less is known about this community, a fact which has served to perpetuate an image of the Chinese as highly assimilated, economically successful, and largely disinterested in the political activism associated with their Korean or Burakumin counterparts. From this perspective, Chinese residents fill a role structurally analogous to certain 'model' minority populations in Europe and North America. It is perhaps due to this apparent lack of controversy, and a very limited understanding of the pre-1945 experience, that the Chinese community has attracted so little scholarly interest. In Chapter 5, Andrea Vasishth traces the development of this community from its origins during the Edo period when a Chinese commercial community was established in Nagasaki through the 1990s. Although often mistakenly perceived as a single homogeneous grouping, Chinese residents have historically been distinguished, and have defined themselves, on the basis of lineage, province of origin and, more recently, by political affiliation. These factors, as Vasishth observes, have influenced not only areas of settlement and occupation, but Japanese perceptions of the community as well.

In 1879, the Japanese state forcibly absorbed the Ryukyu Kingdom. Until that time, the status of Ryukyu had been defined both by its traditional tributary relationship with Qing China and by its increasing political and economic subservience to the daimiate of Satsuma. These ambiguities were ultimately resolved by Japan's victory in the Sino-Japanese War, 1894-5, and the subsequent Japanization of Ryukyuans as citizens of Okinawa Prefecture. For more than a quarter of a century after the Pacific War Okinawa remained under American occupation, with reversion to Japan not taking place until 1972. Chapter 6, by Koji Taira, is essentially a historical analysis of the evolution of Ryukyuan society, its responses to modern Japan, the Japanization of Ryukyu as an internal colony, the post-war responses to American occupation, and more recent efforts to re-assert an Okinawan/Ryukyuan identity distinct from that of Japan proper.

Chapter 7, by Yoko Sellek, considers the phenomenon of 'return migration' and the establishment of *Nikkeijin* communities within the framework of current labour flows to Japan. As noted at the outset, current immigration laws have been designed to prevent the entry of unskilled labour. The exception to this are the *Nikkeijin*, foreign workers primarily of Latin American origin but of Japanese descent. Following on from a discussion of both current patterns of migration and the response of the state to the entry of migrant labour, Sellek provides a detailed analysis of *Nikkeijin* settlement, areas of employment and relations between the newcomers and the host communities. Although regarded as Japanese in terms of lineage, this view is not shared by the majority of *Nikkeijin*, whose links with Japan prior to migration were tenuous at best. Sellek questions the viability of policies which have encouraged *Nikkeijin* settlement, assesses the social costs involved and the possible emergence of a 'new' minority at a future date. In the concluding section, the ideological significance of *Nikkeijin* migration is addressed.

In Chapter 8, Millie Creighton's primary concern is with the ways in which images of the 'Other' are deployed in 'mood' advertising to circumvent social conventions within Japan, while reinforcing images of a homogeneous Japanese identity. A second strand of analysis, supported by extensive interviews, delineates both majority and minority responses to these same representations. Rather than addressing the specifics of a particular minority group, the discussion is expanded to include media representations of purely external Others – Blacks and Asians in particular.

With the exception of the *Nikkeijin*, a critical aspect of the minority experience in modern Japan has been resistance to 'racialized' exclusions, exploitation and oppression. Although often cast in the role of victim, Japan's minorities, at both the individual and organizational levels, have contested the imposition of structural inequalities. Oppositional strategies have assumed a variety of forms, most recently through the establishment of international links with indigenous and diasporan communities in North America and Australia in particular. In a society which remains wedded to the myth of racial and cultural homogeneity, which denies the existence of minority populations, and where minority access to economic, political and social opportunities is restricted, it is difficult to offer generalizations about contemporary developments. It is, however, the hope of the contributors that this volume will in some way assist in the struggle for human rights and dignity in Japan.

BIBLIOGRAPHY

Amino, Y. (1994) 'Nihon Minzoku to iwareru mono no Seitai', *Chūō Kōron*: February.

Befu, H. (ed.) (1993) *Cultural Nationalism in East Asia*, Berkeley: University of California Press.

DeVos, G. and Wagatsuma, H. (1972) *Japan's Invisible Race: Caste in Culture and Personality*, Berkeley, University of California Press.

Du Bois, W.E.B. (1961) *The Souls of Black Folk*, New York: Fawcett World Library.

Ishida, E. (1974) *Japanese Culture: A Study of Origins and Characteristics,* Tokyo: University of Tokyo Press.

Kawakatsu, H. (1991) *Nihon Bunmei to Kindai Seiyō,* Tokyo: NHK Books.

Lee, C. and DeVos, G. (1981) *Koreans in Japan: Ethnic Conflict and Accommodation,* Berkeley: University of California Press.

Masuda, Y. (1967) *Junsui Bunka no Jōken, Nihon Bunka wa Shōgeki ni dō Taetaka,* Tokyo: Kōdansha.

Morris-Suzuki, T. (1995) 'The invention and reinvention of "Japanese culture"', *The Journal of Asian Studies* 54, 3: 759–80.

Neary, I. (1989) *Political Protest and Social Control in Pre-War Japan: The Origins of Buraku Liberation,* Atlantic Highlands: Humanities Press.

Pak, K. (1978) *Zainichi Chōsenjin Undōshi Kaihō mae,* Tokyo: San'ichi Shobō.

—— (1988) *Zainichi Chōsenjin Undōshi Kaihō go,* Tokyo: San'ichi Shobō.

Ueyama, S. (1990) *Nihon Bunmeishi no Kōsō: Juyō to Sōzō no Kiseki,* Tokyo: Kadokawa Shōten.

Weiner, M. (1989) *The Origins of the Korean Community in Japan 1910–1923,* Atlantic Highlands: Humanities Press.

—— (1994) *Race and Migration in Imperial Japan,* London: Routledge.

—— (1995) 'Discourses of race, nation and empire in pre-1945 Japan', *Ethnic and Racial Studies,* 18, 3: 433–56.

Yoshino, K. (1992) *Cultural Nationalism in Contemporary Japan,* London: Routledge.

1 The invention of identity

'Self' and 'Other' in pre-war Japan[1]

Michael Weiner

Nationalisms are rarely consistent in content; what remains permanent are their bases in national consciousness. Depending upon the
specific historical context, nationalism has most often been expressed
in terms of economic or territorial expansion, the establishment of
political sovereignty, or social and cultural norms of behaviour. In
contrast, national consciousness, which serves as a precondition to
the development of nationalism implies the existence of historically
embedded and culturally transmitted assumptions concerning the
imagined community of the nation and its citizens. The modality of
nationalism which emerged in the context of post-restoration Japan
was one which idealized cultural and 'racial' homogeneity as the
foundation of the nation-state.

What had been a political, economic and social rupture was redefined to connote linkages with an ancient past, thus locating the
events of 1868 within a continuous and unbroken chain of events
culminating in the restoration of imperial rule. Paralleling this were
the increasingly organized efforts by the new Meiji state to infuse a
heterogeneous population with a sense of homogeneity and community (Fujitani 1993: 77–106). Along the way, powerful, but selective,
cultural empathies were mobilized, while regional identities were
either suppressed or subjected to a process of cultural redefinition
whose objective it was to bring reality into line with ideology.
Within this framework the *kazoku kokka* (family state) was projected
as an enduring essence, which provided the state with an elevated iconography of consanguineous unity, enhanced the legitimacy of new
economic, social and political relations, and provided the Japanese
people with a new sense of national purpose and identity. It was a
national identity forged from both indigenous and imported elements, and which rested upon the assumed unique qualities and capacities of the Japanese *minzoku* (Weiner 1995: 433–42). The argument

pursued here is that rather than existing as independent categories of inclusion and exclusion, 'race' and nation inhabited the same ideological space, with each functioning to define the parameters of the other. Set within the dominant paradigm of *minzoku*, both 'race' and nation were regarded as naturally occurring phenomena, further reinforcing their credibility as explanatory factors in social, political and economic relationships (Yoshino 1992: 25).

In erecting a set of new symbolic boundaries around Japan, the language, imagery and iconography of nationalism suggested that the nation was the modern manifestation of a primordial community of which the citizenry had always been a part (Yasuda 1992: 63). Set against the background of a radically transformed environment, the efforts of state propagandists, the selective revival of ancient institutions, as in the case of *Jingikan* (Department of Shinto Affairs), the transformation of local or folk shrines (as in the case of Ise) into sites of national memory and pilgrimage, and the invention of commemorative structures, linking an imagined imperial past with present accomplishments, were designed to connote, diffuse and sustain a particular landscape. The naturalization of culture, of which these processes formed an integral part, re-cast the meaning of 'Japaneseness' in powerful images of the enduring purity and homogeneity of the nation, the family, and Japanese way of life. The nation was projected as an extended family, and the emperor established as semi-divine father to the national community and head of state. Ultimate sanctification of the imagined community was thus located at the sacred level, in Shinto, while reverence for the emperor as *minzoku no ōsa* (head of the people) and loyalty and obedience to the state were rendered equivalent (Gluck 1985: 91–3).

The conflation of cultural and 'racial' criteria by which membership within the imagined community of the nation could be identified has assumed various guises. Anticipating the later genre of literature associated with the *Nihonjinron* and *Nihon Bunka-ron*, Takakusu Junjiro, in a 1938 publication, argued in favour of the existence of a dominant Yamato or stem 'race' which had assimilated various prehistoric racial groupings. The consanguineous unity, or, 'culture of the Japanese blood', to which Takakusu referred, had subsequently been preserved through the 'virtuous rule of succeeding emperors'. The putative relationship between blood and culture is made more explicit in Kada Tetsuji's *Jinshu Minzoku Sensō* (Jinshu, Minzoku and War), published in 1940. While the title implies a conceptual distinction between *jinshu* ('race') and *minzoku* (ethnicity; people; nation), Kada consistently reaffirms the biological basis of *minzoku*.

Indeed, for Kada, the origins of *minzoku* can only be found in the distinctive *jinshuteki* (racial) and *seishinteki* (spiritual) qualities of people. 'We cannot consider *minzoku*', he concludes, 'without taking into account its relation to blood' (Kada 1940: 70–1). In arguing a biological or genetic basis for the distinctiveness and superiority of the Japanese people, Kada was also reinforcing what one writer termed *ketsuzokushugi* (the ideology of the blood family) (Hayashida 1976: 82). Parallels can also be drawn between the 'racial' literature of the inter-war years and, for example, Hozumi Nobushige's *Ancestor Worship and Japanese Law* which was originally published in 1901 (Kikuchi 1972: 24–5). Here, the imagined community of the nation was conceived as a consanguineous community comprised of three primary constituent elements (the Imperial family, the regional clan and the family unit) (Ito 1982: 31–3).

The argument advanced here is that social structures and attitudes in Japan have historically been imbued with 'racial' meaning, and that these meanings are themselves dynamic and contingent. That is to say, both 'racial' meanings and 'racialized' identities are historically specific, and can only be understood in relation to other factors – economic and political – and in relation to the international environment within which they emerged and have since been reproduced (Gilroy 1990: 264–5). In developing this argument, I also suggest that the construction of a Japanese national identity has also entailed the transformation of culture through an overarching discourse of 'race', into a 'pseudobiological property of communal life' (Gilroy 1990: 267).

A further area of concern here is to identify the various strands of 'racialized' discourse which were developed during the period 1868–1945, and the channels through which European imperialist perspectives on 'race' and native populations were domesticated within the Japanese context. In tracing the relationship between ideologies of 'race' and nation in the construction of the modern Japanese identity, I seek also to identify the discursive elements which have informed perceptions of the excluded 'Other' (both external and internal) against whom this identity has been produced and reproduced at particular historical junctures.

New ideologies and configurations of social power do not emerge unchallenged within an empty space (Greenfeld 1992: 399–403). As in Europe and North America, ideas of 'Self' and 'Other' in Japan were moulded both by the broader international context in which they evolved and through the appropriation of indigenous themes in Japanese history. The 'experts in legitimation' who contributed to the diffusion of 'racial' knowledge and the dissemination of scientific 'racism' in Japan were themselves aware of and deeply influenced by European scholarship in particular (Shimao 1981: 93–8). The scientification of knowledge, of which these processes were an integral part, also provided the means by which the civilized 'Self' could be distinguished from the uncivilized 'Other'. Just as Meiji industrialization was dependent upon the prior existence of well-established market relations and the importation of Western technology, in their construction of a national identity, Japanese ideologues drew inspiration from both the West and through the appropriation and manipulation of indigenous myths. The search for a usable past engaged the resources of academics, educators, journalists, politicians and government officials alike. Their interests and concerns frequently overlapped; politicians were frequent contributors to newspapers, while academics were often called upon to advise on matters of public policy and education. Although there was no master narrative to which they all subscribed, nor a smoothly orchestrated discourse imposed upon a passive audience, their efforts would assist in the dissemination of 'racial' knowledge and the production of 'Otherness'.

The intention thus far has been to suggest a high degree of functional equivalence between cultural and 'racial' categories within prewar 'racial' discourse. If, as is argued here, culture is regarded as the manifestation of a primordial or innate essence, reliance on cultural or ethnic criteria in distinguishing between peoples functions in the same way as biological determinism (Miles 1993: 101). The essential distinction to be drawn is not between assumed cultural or physiological characteristics, but how these criteria are signified and subsequently acted upon. Rather than making the marginalized the focus of analysis, the subject of our inquiry should become the historical processes through which groups or nations have been constructed on the basis of these assumed innate qualities and subsequently located within specific material and power relations. In this sense, the dichotomy between the Yamato *jinshu* ('race') or Yamato *minzoku* (ethnicity/people/nation) is more apparent then real. Barshay's observation that, in the pre-1945 context, the ideological terrain defined by *minzoku* 'overcame universality' and itself became 'absolute', is particularly salient (Barshay 1988: 230).

Throughout the final decades of the nineteenth century in particular, attempts to establish the criteria for what constituted 'Japaneseness' occupied the energy and resources of statesmen, bureaucrats and unofficial publicists alike. It was a preoccupation which reflected a recognition that the muscular nationalism of the Western powers would have to be met by an equally assertive Japanese national identity if sovereignty were to be preserved (Pyle 1969: 75). The contours of this identity, which invoked powerful images of communal solidarity and exclusivity, were further refined through the lens of scientific 'racism' embodied in the writings of Haeckel, Lamarck and Spencer (Shimao 1981: 93–102; Nolte 1987: 44). A Japanese translation of Spencer's evolutionary theory first appeared in 1884, and in total some thirty translations of his works had appeared by the turn of the century. The provision of a classificatory grid which located the Japanese within a clearly defined hierarchy of 'race', while offering a scientifically reasoned yet easily accessible explanation for both the complexities of a modern society and national survival, found a receptive audience among academics, journalists and politicians alike. Set within the colonial context, to which we shall return later in this chapter, the diffusion of social-Darwinism also made it possible to demonstrate 'scientifically' that some cultures were advanced and civilized while others remained backward and uncivilized (Weiner 1989: 14–22).

For the young intellectuals associated with the newspaper *Nihon* and the journal *Nihonjin*, the nation was increasingly identified with *minzoku* – a term first popularized by Shiga Shigetaka in the 1880s. In common with other terms like *kokusui* (national essence) and *kokuminshugi* (civil nationalism), *minzoku* was a critical element in the development of a popular nationalism which arose partly in response to what was regarded as the over-Westernization of the previous decades. As articulated by Shiga and his contemporaries, *minzoku* reflected what were assumed to be the unique characteristics (historical, geographical and cultural) of the Japanese nation (Gluck 1985: 110–15). This sense of nation, as expressed by *minzoku*, was subsequently appropriated by constitutional scholars like Hozumi Yatsuka, for whom the *kokutai* (national polity) was identified with the imperial line and the network of beliefs which sustained it: principally ancestor worship. In common with Inoue Tetsujirō, Katō Hiroyuki and other family state theoreticians, Hozumi conceived of the Japanese *minzoku* as a manifestation of common ancestry rather than shared culture. A parallel line of argument was pursued by Ueda Kazutoshi in *Kokugo to Kokka to* published in 1894. In this seminal piece, Ueda emphasized that the Japanese polity had been, and would continue to be, sustained by the Japanese race, and argued that the Japanese language itself was a manifestation of the inherited qualities of its people (Yun 1993: 16). Although he originally challenged the legitimacy of a *kokutai* which located sovereignty in the person of the emperor, Katō Hiroyuki's early enthusiasm for and advocacy of the 'natural rights' of man and representative government was replaced by a firm commitment to Darwinian theories of social evolution (Katō 1955: 111–12; Irokawa 1986: 253). With the publication of *Shinkagaku yori kansatsu shitaru nichiro no unmei* in 1905, Katō applied Darwinian inspired notions of *seizon kyōsō* (struggle for survival) and *yūshō reppai* (survival of the fittest) to an analysis of the current struggle between Japan and Russia. He concluded that a Japanese victory was inevitable due to the superiority of a homogeneous polity which had been thoroughly integrated within the emperor system (Kawamura 1990: 67).

The dissemination of social-Darwinism was also encouraged by early Japanese encounters with the various racisms prevalent in the United States and in the European colonies. These date from an 1860 mission to the United States and extend through to the Iwakura mission of 1871–3. In addition to the official reports, which were unavailable to the public, individual envoys and their attendants published personal accounts, often in diary form. Yanagawa Kenzaburo, a member of the 1860 mission, for example, seems to have uncritically imbibed the prejudices of his American hosts. Yanagawa's reference to the inherent stupidity and inferiority of blacks is paralleled by comparisons between blacks and the Eta outcast drawn by Kimura Tetsuya. Morita Kiyoyuki, too, commented on the ugliness and uncivilized behaviour of the Hawaiian 'natives' (Leupp 1995: 7). Far more expansive was Kume Kunitake, later professor of history at Tokyo University, and one of two official secretaries who accompanied the Iwakura mission to Europe and the United States a decade later. Kume's two-volume account of the mission, first published in 1878, contains lengthy references to both the origins and distinctive characteristics of the various peoples encountered by the mission. In contrast to the British, for example, whose inherent industriousness Kume regarded as the basis of their country's wealth and power, Spain's decline as a world power had come about as a result of the equally inherent indolence of its people (Kume 1985: Vol. 2, 39).

The conflation of physiological and cultural characteristics is also apparent in an earlier passage where Kume assesses the inevitable decline of the 'Indian' population of North America. Like Kimura a decade earlier, Kume also draws a direct physiological comparison between certain North American 'Indians' and the *senmin* (literally 'lowly people') of Japan, a category which during the Tokugawa period had incorporated the Eta and Hinin outcast groups (Kume 1985: Vol. 1, 132–5). The Darwinian imprint is equally evident in

Takahashi Yoshio's *Nihon Jinshu Kairyōron* (Improvement of the Japanese Race), published in 1883 (Ishii 1937: 38–9). Takahashi was by no means alone in advocating intermarriage with Westerners as the preferred means of enhancing the inferior physical and intellectual capacities of the Japanese. Four years later, an identical course of action was proposed by Katō Hiroyuki in a short piece entitled *Nihon Jinshu Kairyō no Ben* (A Justification for the Improvement of the Japanese Race) (Yun 1993: 15). The then prime minister, Ito Hirobumi, sought a second opinion from Herbert Spencer, who subsequently advised against interbreeding with Europeans on the grounds that hybridization between disparate 'races' would, as it had in Latin America, produce disastrous consequences for both (Stepan 1982: 105).

The impact of 'racial' as well as related theories of geographical or climatic determinism was also evident in contemporary textbooks (Tanaka 1993: 39–40). Along with history, geography formed an integral part of the national curriculum in Meiji schools, as well as providing a conduit for knowledge of the outside world generally. Early texts like Fukuzawa Yukichi's *Sekai Kunizukushi* (World Geography [1869]), of which more than a million copies were sold, ranked countries within an evolutionary hierarchy of barbarian, semi-civilized, and civilized states. While all civilized states were European in character, not all European nations were civilized. Echoing the views of Kume Kunitake, Fukuzawa wrote of Spain as a nation whose decline as a world power had come about as a result of inherent deficiencies in the character of its people. Japan, by comparison, was depicted as a country in transition from semi-civilized to civilized status.

Scholarly enthusiasm for and interest in deterministic theories of social evolution also ensured that the assumed relationship between geography and *kokka ishiki* (national consciousness) featured prominently in secondary school textbooks. Increased ministerial control over textbook content in the years following the Imperial Rescript on Education (1890) did little to dampen enthusiasm for deterministic theories of social evolution. On the contrary, 'racial' differences between and within individual nations featured even more prominently. In that part of the 1893 edition of *Bankoku Chiri Shoho* (Geography for Beginners) which charts relations between the native American and Caucasian populations of the United States, the destitution of the former is portrayed as a consequence of their 'primitive and simple nature' (Takeuchi 1987: 9).

Although intellectuals and journalists performed an important role as channels of legitimation, institutions of the state were the primary sites of ideological articulation. By the end of the first decade of the twentieth century, state-inspired nationalism had penetrated all strata of society and offered the Japanese people an easily accessible explanation of their social, political, and economic position, both domestically and in terms of the wider international context. It was a nationalist ideology whose central motif was that of the *kazoku kokka* (family state), itself the product of a re-working of the concepts of citizen and nation in accordance with myths of common ancestry. The existence of a Yamato *minzoku*, sharing a common ancestry, history and culture had become as canonical and 'natural' to the Japanese as it was to their European counterparts. While the physical and historical evidence of migrations to the Japanese islands could not be ignored, these were deemed to be of such antiquity that they had long since formed a single 'race' and culture (Yun 1993: 27). Cultural indebtedness to China was also acknowledged, but this too was relegated to the distant past. As represented in school textbooks after 1910, it had become axiomatic that responsibility for the regeneration of Asia had fallen to the Japanese by virtue of their innately superior qualities (Tanaka 1993: 201).

In defining the Japanese nation as a collective personality, characterized by uniformity and homogeneity, the family state was itself conceived as a reflection of the inherited qualities and capacities of its people. The immutable characteristics which distinguished the Yamato *minzoku* provided what Balibar has termed 'a historical backbone; a concentration of qualities that belong "exclusively" to the nationals: it is in the race of "its children" that the nation can contemplate its true identity at its purest' (Balibar 1990: 284). As enshrined in the national school curriculum, and projected through a variety of channels, both formal and informal, the criteria for membership in this uniquely powerful national collectivity were construed as both 'racial' and cultural. A corollary of this construction of a Japanese 'race' would be the simultaneous categorization of other populations as members of equally distinct but subordinate 'races'.

The articulation of an ideology in which the categories of 'race' and nation so clearly overlapped was not unique to Japan. The reification of the nation as an organic entity had clear parallels in contemporary Europe where the conceptualization of nations as 'naturally occurring groups identified by cultural *differentiae*' implied that the 'symbols of "nation" were themselves grounded in race'

(Miles 1993: 62; Lauren 1988: 40). This was certainly the case in Czarist Russia where:

> The Russian national idea consisted in the following: the nation was (1) defined as a collective individual, (2) formed by ethnic, primordial factors such as blood and soil, and (3) characterized by the enigmatic soul or spirit.
>
> (Greenfeld 1992: 261)

Given that Japan was consciously modelling its behaviour in other spheres of activity on that of its European and North American contemporaries, it is hardly surprising that Japanese 'racial' discourse was inspired by and developed in response to that of the most advanced Western nations.

THE 'EXCLUDED OTHER'

The notion of a civilized Japan presumed its opposite, the existence of which provided both a measure by which Japanese accomplishments could be judged and a reminder of the fate which awaited those who failed to become civilized. But modern narratives of inclusion and exclusion, like those of the Tokugawa period, were not limited to those 'Others' who lived beyond the spatial confines of Japan. New social and economic relations within Japan were also commonly viewed through a parallel and equally deterministic framework of the 'survival of the fittest.' These 'racisms' of the interior affected not only traditional outsider populations, as in the case of the former outcasts and the Ainu, but the urban and rural poor in general. In each case, particular groups were identified not only by their material deprivation, but by certain assumed physical or cultural characteristics. In late nineteenth- and early twentieth-century Japan, members of *kasō shakai* (lower class society), were excluded from mainstream society by virtue of both the material conditions of their existence and what were perceived as inherent moral deficiencies. Although such groups were also referred to as *tennō no sekishi* (children of the emperor), evoking images of a seamless family state, they existed for the most part beyond the pale of civilized society. Early accounts of the urban poor often read like 'adventure stories in faraway lands'. That such reports were often compiled by officials engaged in the task of civilizing the savage interior was itself significant, since it was dependent upon the prior identification and exclusion of certain groups within the boundaries of the state. The urban slum was represented in contemporary newspapers and journals as the symbolic opposite of *bunmei* (civilization); its inhabitants depicted as the descendants of 'remote foreign races' upon whom were projected images of savagery and barbarism. In an 1897 account of Osaka slum dwellers, for example, the area is described as otherworldly, inhabited by 'countless deaf, crippled, limbless, and pygmies, all wrapped up in worse rags, wriggling like worms with griefs filling the air' (Chubachi and Taira 1976: 391–437).

Such contemporary accounts are broadly comparable to those applied to the peasantry, whose 'physiognomy', like the odour peculiar to animals, made them readily identifiable (Hane 1982: 35). In Mayama Seika's *Minami Koizumi-mura*, published several years after the Russo-Japanese War, peasant life was depicted as one of unspeakable misery, and the peasantry likened to 'insects that crawl on the ground'. The author found it inconceivable that 'the blood flowing in those miserable peasants also flows in my body' (Irokawa 1986: 223, 244). In each case, parallels can be drawn across time, to the negative images of commoner and peasant held by the samurai elites of the Tokugawa period, and across space to the imagery employed against the 'lower orders' in the industrializing nation-states of late nineteenth- and early twentieth-century Europe and North America.

The Meiji period also witnessed the establishment of a colonial order in Hokkaidō. Employing institutional and administrative mechanisms very similar to those which would later be deployed in Korea and Taiwan, the Meiji state moved to exploit the island's strategic and economic potential. The destitution which rapidly came to characterize the lives of the indigenous Ainu population was attributed not to the specifics of colonial policy, but to the innate inferiority of the *dojin* (native) population. The dehumanization of the Ainu, of which this was an integral part, began with the view that the Ainu were either not there, or savages, or both. In a process which would be repeated elsewhere in the empire, the Ainu were gradually constructed as a primitive and 'racially' immature 'Other' in a discourse which justified and rendered the colonial project inevitable. The colonial relationship with the Ainu, and their categorization as primitive savages, also provided an initial context in which images of indigenous inferiority could be contrasted with those of a modern, civilized Japan.

It was within the context of the political, economic and social processes which developed under colonial rule in Hokkaidō, Korea and Taiwan that the new Japanese identity was most fully expressed. If a strongly collectivistic nationalism allowed the Japanese to partake of a modern and progressive identity, the existence of empire confirmed their own manifest superiority *vis-à-vis* the peoples of Asia. Likewise, if industrial and technological progress were the indices of civilization and enlightenment, then a lack of material development provided indisputable evidence of inferiority. It was this very lack of both a martial spirit and the institutions of modern industry which persuaded many in Japan that the peoples of East Asia could only achieve a civilized state through exposure to the work habits and martial values which had produced a powerful Japan. The presumed correlation between economic development and the inherent and differing capacities of human societies led Fukuda Tokuzō, in 1902, to conclude that the transformation of Korea from a pre-industrial to a modern capitalist society could only be accomplished through Japanese intervention (Hatada 1972: 34–5; Yamabe 1978: 262). Other commentators, however, were less sanguine about the civilizing impact of Japanese rule. Thirty years later, and despite more than two decades of imperial benevolence, Koreans would still be regarded as by nature 'unsuited for work in a modern industrial society' (Osaka-shi 1933: 32–3; Zensei 1930: 176–7).

Core narratives of progress and civilization, of which social scientific discourse formed an important part, further assisted in the ordering of popular knowledge of the excluded 'Other'. An extremely popular vehicle for the celebration of modernity, civilization and, subsequently, imperial expansion were the *hakurankai* (national expositions). Modelled after the first international exposition held at Crystal Palace in 1851, Japanese variants were held in 1877, 1881, 1890, 1895 and 1903. Designed by the noted anthropologist, Tsuboi Shogoro, the *Jinruikan* (Hall of Mankind) was designed as the centrepiece of the Fifth Industrial Exposition held in Osaka in 1903. Tsuboi's plan to exhibit the 'races' of the world in their 'natural' settings for the education of the general public encountered rigorous opposition from Chinese, Koreans and Ryukyuans who objected to representations of their cultures as frozen in the past. The stark imagery of an irrational and primitive Asia, in contrast to a modern, civilized Japan, was, however, retained in the form of exhibits detailing the lives of Ainu, Taiwanese aboriginals and the Malays.

The popular discourse of the primitive 'Other' was also sustained by the imagery of the Japanese civilizing mission. Everything else was relegated to the background, with the indigenous populations of Hokkaidō, Taiwan and Korea classified as stagnant, degenerate and incapable of appreciating the resources they possessed. Representations of this type were evident at both the *Takushoku Hakurankai*

(Colonial Exposition) of 1912 and at the Natural History Museum in Sapporo. The latter contained life-size waxwork reproductions depicting the Japanese 'exploration' of Hokkaidō in 1870. Here, the impression conveyed was of an entire territory unappreciated and unused by its original inhabitants. The 'new' history of Hokkaidō, cast in images of a redemptive Japanese project and tethered to invidious stereotypes of racial infantilism and primitivism, was there for all to behold. The set of deterministic assumptions concerning the capacities of subordinate populations which informed the *hakurankai* and museum exhibitions of this type fused popular and socially scientific understandings of the 'Other' within an overarching discourse of 'race'. By providing detailed and scientifically verified information about the 'racial' character, behaviour and habits of the 'Other', the social sciences offered both a further justification for paternalistic control and an archival resource which colonial administrators could draw upon. Within the colonial context itself, 'racialized' discourses informed both policy formulation and administrative practice. Inequality was attributed to differences in national or 'racial' characteristics; differences which marked some peoples as unfit to survive the struggle for survival in a modern industrial society. As such, their exclusion from the national community was adjudged natural and inevitable. In *The Japanese Nation*, written in 1912 soon after his appointment as Professor of Colonial Studies at Tokyo Imperial University, Nitobe Inazo described the 'hairy Ainu' as a stone age population (Nitobe 1912: 86–7). Nitobe's depiction of the Ainu as somehow existing beyond the confines of human history, and therefore doomed to extinction, paralleled conclusions drawn some years earlier by Basil Hall Chamberlain: 'so little have they [Ainu] profited from the opportunities offered to them during the last one thousand years or two thousand years, that there is no longer room for them in the world' (Chamberlain 1887: 43).

Nitobe's assessment of the Ainu also bears comparison with a similar account of the Korean people written after a visit to the peninsula. In representing the inhabitants as moribund and incapable of adapting to current realities, Nitobe draws a clear distinction between the neglect and forlornness of the Korean 'present' and, at least by implication, the promise of a progressive future under Japanese governance:

> The very physiognomy and living of these people are so bland, unsophisticated and primitive, that they belong not to the twentieth or the tenth – nor indeed to the first century. They belong to a

prehistoric age . . . the Korean habits of life are the habits of death. They are closing the lease of their ethnic existence. The national course of their existence is well-nigh run. Death presides over the peninsula.

(Nitobe 1909: 214–16)

As either colonial subjects or migrant labour drawn to the metropolitan core, the marginalization of subordinate populations was interpreted almost exclusively within an overarching discourse of 'race'. Kawamura Minato has argued in this context that by the late 1920s mass orientalism, in which images of colonial and other inferior populations were contrasted with a progressive and modern Japan, had become an integral part of common-sense understanding. Imagery of this type would later become a regular feature in both novels and children's comic strips, the most popular of which was Shimada Keizō's *Bōken Dankichi* (Dankichi the Adventurer), which, between 1933 and 1939, serialized the adventures of a Tintin-like protagonist among the primitives of the South Seas. Whereas the savagery of the islanders in *Bōken Dankichi* was offset by their comically exaggerated features, in the exploits of the common soldier, *Nora-kura* (Black Mutt), the (Chinese) enemy was degraded to the level of barnyard animals (Kawamura 1993: 119).

It was also in the sphere of international relations, particularly between Japan and the other imperial powers, that a 'two-tiered' and apparently contradictory narrative of 'race' was articulated (Shimazu 1989: 93). It was a conceptualization which, on the one hand, assumed a common destiny for the peoples of Asia and was predicated on an inevitable conflict between the white and yellow 'races' (Oyama 1966: 341). The Japanese were thus identified as sharing the same 'racial' origins as Chinese and Koreans. None the less, this European-derived narrative of 'race' did not preclude the existence of a further definition which identified 'race' with nation, and which distinguished imperial Japan, in equally deterministic terms, from its Asian neighbours. This perspective, founded upon the assumed incapacity of a subordinate population to manage their own affairs, reaffirmed a sense of national purpose and 'racial' superiority among the Japanese people, irrespective of their class position at home. The subdivision of the human species, which these assumptions affirmed, also imposed a set of obligations on Japan as *Tōyō no Meishu* (The Leader of Asia). These included not only raising colonial peoples to a level commensurate with their 'natural' abilities, but preserving the essential and superior qualities of the Japanese within a carefully delineated hierarchy of 'race' (Takeda 1938: 121).

NOTE

1 An earlier version of this chapter first appeared in *Ethnic and Racial Studies*, vol. 18, no. 3, 1995.

BIBLIOGRAPHY

Balibar, E. (1990) 'Racisme et nationalisme', in E. Balibar and I. Wallerstein (eds) *Race, Nation, Classe*, cited in M. Edwards (trans.), 'Paradoxes of universality', in D.T. Goldberg (ed.) *Anatomy of Racism*, Minneapolis: University of Minnesota Press.
Barshay, A. (1988) *State and Intellectual in Imperial Japan: The Public Man in Crisis*, Berkeley: University of California Press.
Chamberlain, B.H. (1887) *The Language, Mythology and Geographical Nomenclature of Japan, Viewed in the Light of Aino Studies*, Tokyo: Tokyo Imperial University.
Chubachi, M. and Taira, K. (1976) 'Poverty in modern Japan: perceptions and realities', in H. Patrick (ed.) *Japanese Industrialization and its Social Consequences*, Berkeley: University of California Press.
Fujitani, T. (1993) 'Inventing, forgetting, remembering: toward a historical ethnography of the nation state', in H. Befu (ed.) *Cultural Nationalism in East Asia*, Berkeley: University of California Press.
Gilroy, P. (1990) 'One nation under a groove: the cultural politics of "race" and racism in Britain', in D.T. Goldberg (ed.) *Anatomy of Racism* Minneapolis: University of Minnesota Press.
Gluck, C. (1985) *Japan's Modern Myths*, Princeton: Princeton University Press.
Greenfeld, L. (1992) *Nationalism, Five Roads to Modernity*, Cambridge, Mass.: Harvard University Press.
Hane, M. (1982) *Peasants, Rebels, and Outcastes: The Underside of Modern Japan*, New York: Pantheon Press.
Harada, T. and Kang, J. (1985) *Kōza Sabetsu to Jinken [4] Minzoku*, Tokyo: Yūzankaku.
Hatada, T. (1972) *Nihonjin no Chōsen Kan*, Tokyo: Keiso Shobō.
Hayashida, C.T. (1976) 'Identity, race and the blood ideology of Japan', unpublished Ph.D. thesis, University of Washington.
Irokawa, D. (1986) *The Culture of the Meiji Period* (M. Jansen ed. and trans.), Princeton: Princeton University Press.
Ishii, R. (1937) *Population Pressure and Economic Life in Japan*, Chicago, Chicago University Press.
Ito, M. (1982) *Kazoku Kokka no Jinruigaku*, Tokyo: Minerva Shobō.
Kada, T. (1940) *Jinshu Minzoku Sensō*, Tokyo: Keio Shobō.

Kato, H. (1955) 'Kokutai Shinron', in *Meiji Bunka Zenshu*, Tokyo: Nihon Hyōron Shinsha.

Kawamura, M. (1993) 'Taishū Orientarizumu to Ajia Ninshiki', in M. Kawamura (ed.) *Kindai Nihon to Shokuminchi [7]; Bunka no naka no Shokuminchi*, Tokyo: Iwanami Shōten.

Kawamura, N. (1990) 'Sociology and socialism in the interwar period', in J.T. Rimer (ed.) *Culture and Identity: Japanese Intellectuals During the Interwar Years*, Princeton: Princeton University Press.

Kikuchi, I. (1972) 'Hozumi Nobushige to Shakai Ken' *Nihon Gakushi-in Kiyo* 30, 1: 21–42.

Kume, K. (1935) *Kyūjyūnen Kaikoroku*, Tokyo: Waseda Daigaku Shuppanbu.

—— (1985) *Tokumei Zenken Taishi Beiō Kairan Jikki*, Tokyo: Iwanami Shōten.

Lauren, P.G. (1988) *Power and Prejudice, The Politics and Diplomacy of Racial Discrimination*, Boulder: Westview Press.

Leupp, G. (1995) 'Images of black people in late mediaeval and early modern Japan', *Japan Forum* 7, 1: 1–13.

Miles, R. (1993) *Racism After 'Race Relations'*, London: Routledge.

Nitobe, I. (1909) *Thoughts and Essays*, Tokyo: Teibi Publishing Company.

—— (1912) *The Japanese Nation: Its Land, Its People, Its Life: With Special Consideration to its Relations with the United States*, New York: G. Putnam's Sons.

Nolte, S.H. (1987) *Liberalism in Modern Japan*, Berkeley, Calif.: University of California Press.

Osaka-shi, Shakai-bu, Rōdō-ka (1933) Shakai-bu Hokoku dai 177, 'Chōsenjin Rōdōsha no Kinkyō', Osaka.

Oyama, A. (ed.) (1966) *Yamagata Aritomo Ikensho*, Tokyo: Hara Shobō.

Pyle, K.B. (1969) *The New Generation in Meiji Japan*, Stanford, Calif.: Stanford University Press.

Shimao, E. (1981) 'Darwinism in Japan', *Annals of Social Science* 38: 93–102.

Shimazu, N. (1989) 'The Japanese attempt to secure racial equality in 1919', *Japan Forum* 1, 1: 93–100.

Stepan, N. (1982) *The Idea of Race in Science: Great Britain 1800–1960*, London: Macmillan.

Takeda, Y. (1938) 'Naichi Zaijyū Hantōjin Mondai', *Shakai Seisaku Jihō* 213: 99–136.

Takeuchi, K. (1987) 'How Japan learned about the outside world: the views of other countries incorporated in Japanese school textbooks' 1868–1986', *Hitotsubashi Journal of Social Sciences* 19: 1–13.

Tanaka, S. (1993) *Japan's Orient, Rendering Pasts into History*, Berkeley: University of California Press.

Weiner, M. (1989) *The Origins of the Korean Community in Japan, 1910–1923*, Atlantic Highlands: Humanities Press.

—— (1995) 'Discourses of race, nation and empire in pre-1945 Japan', *Ethnic and Racial Studies* 18, 3: 433–56.

Yamabe, K. (1978) *Nikkan Heigō Shoshi*, Tokyo: Iwanami Shōten.

Yasuda, H. (1992) 'Kindai Nihon ni okeru "Minzoku Kannen no Keisei"', *Shisō to Gendai* 31: 61–72.

Yoshino, K. (1992) *Cultural Nationalism in Contemporary Japan*, London: Routledge.

Yun, K.C. (1993) 'Minzoku Gensō no Satetsu', *Shisō*, December: 4–37.

Zensei, E. (1930) 'Chōsenjin no Naichi Tokō', *Gaikō Jiho* 607: 173–7.

2 Ainu

Japan's indigenous people

Richard Siddle

The Ainu are the indigenous people of northern Japan. At first glance this may appear a straightforward and uncontroversial statement; after all, the subordination and dispossession of the Ainu under a colonial regime in Hokkaidō has numerous parallels among other Fourth World populations like Native Americans, Australian Aborigines, Inuit, Maori, Sami and others, estimated to number between 200 and 300 million people. Sparked into political activism during the wave of worldwide decolonization following the Second World War, many internally colonized 'native' or 'tribal' populations have redefined themselves as 'indigenous peoples'. In common with these other groups, the Ainu were dispossessed of their ancestral land and resources by the expansion of a vigorous colonial state. Traditional lifeways collapsed as hunting and fishing territories were settled by waves of immigrants and transformed into agricultural land. Government policies of relocation and assimilation aimed at the eventual extinction of the Ainu as a people, aided by a system of 'native education' that actively discouraged Ainu language and customs.

While clearly supported by the historical record, such an interpretation arouses considerable opposition within Japan. Official and popular history views the creation of Hokkaidō as an exercise in 'development' (*kaitaku*), not colonialism. At the level of common-sense understanding a master narrative of seamless national homogeneity denies the existence of the Ainu as an ethnic minority group; the Ainu are regarded as either totally assimilated or biologically extinct.

Nevertheless, a striking 'ethnic revival' is underway among the Ainu. The cultural symbols and rhetoric of Ainuness have become highly visible in recent decades as Ainu leaders press their claim for justice and rights as a separate and indigenous people. Since 'ethnic' identities are not essential static 'primordial' remnants, but are constructed and articulated within specific junctures of material and power relations, this chapter will focus on the creation of a modern ethnicity by Ainu leaders in the context of continued Ainu marginalization within Japanese society.

HISTORICAL OVERVIEW OF AINU–JAPANESE RELATIONS

The origins of the Ainu are the subject of controversy. While human beings have inhabited Hokkaidō since the retreat of the last Ice Age, it is virtually impossible to reconstruct the movements of populations throughout north-east Asia until well into the historical period. What is known is that the indigenous populations of the island were in contact with peoples and cultures to both the north and south. By the ninth century, two distinct cultures flourished in Hokkaidō, named by archaeologists as the Satsumon and Okhotsk. The Okhotsk people lived along the north and north-east coastlines of Hokkaidō while the Satsumon, regarded as the direct ancestors of the Ainu, occupied the rest of the island and perhaps the northernmost tip of Honshū (Utagawa 1988). What is now regarded as Ainu culture made its appearance around the thirteenth century, by which time the inhabitants of southern Hokkaidō were engaged in regular trade with Honshū.

A population of perhaps forty thousand Ainu lived throughout Hokkaidō, the Kuriles and the southern half of Sakhalin. The Ainu occupied an area rich in natural resources, Hokkaidō in particular having abundant deer and salmon. Ainu culture was characterized by hunting, fishing, and the gathering of edible plants, and a complex spiritual relationship with the phenomena of the natural world (personified as *kamuy*, deities) on which the Ainu depended (see Munro 1963, Watanabe 1973). The main religious rite was the *iyomante*, where the spirit of a deity (usually a bear) was 'sent back' to the land of the gods, although when the ceremony developed to its present form is a matter of debate. Economic activities were conducted in clear hunting and fishing territories (*iwor*) based on river systems, and in some communities were not merely for subsistence but also to provide a small surplus for trade. Local groups were incorporated into trade networks that extended both to the south and to the Asian continent through Sakhalin and the Kuriles. Social organization was based on patrilineal and matrilineal kin-groups with clearly demarcated distinctions in status. The communities were ruled by a leader (*kotankorokur*), selected on the basis of both inheritance and ability, who took a leading role in trade and mediated disputes based on customary law. Larger regional groups also developed, speaking different dialects and displaying some cultural variation, especially in Sakhalin and the Kuriles where the Ainu were in close contact with other northern peoples. A rich oral literature evolved, and what has survived hints at a complex and stratified society (Philippi 1979).

For the Japanese (usually known as 'Wajin'), who regarded the inhabitants of the northern regions through the prism of Chinese notions of civilization and barbarism, the inhabitants of Ezogashima (Hokkaidō) were little more than a variety of demon. These barbarians, however, controlled natural resources that the Japanese desired. As time passed and warlords rose and fell in the centres of power to the south, a flourishing trade developed in furs and sea products. By the fifteenth century, Japanese trading settlements were dotted around the southern tip of the Oshima peninsula (for the development of these settlements and subsequent Ainu history, see Takakura 1960, 1972; Kaiho 1979; Matsumae-chō Shi Henshū Shitsu 1984; Emori 1987). In 1456, friction between the indigenes and newcomers flared into open warfare after a Wajin blacksmith killed an Ainu in a quarrel over a blunt knife. The following year, Ainu led by Koshamain destroyed all but two of the settlements and almost drove the Wajin out of Ezogashima altogether, initiating a century of intermittent warfare. In 1514 the Kakizaki family emerged as the leader of the Japanese in Oshima, subject to the Andō clan in Tsugaru. In 1551, Kakizaki Suehiro, convinced that continued warfare was not beneficial for trade, sought an accommodation with the local Ainu. The resulting agreement split the profits of trade between Ainu and Wajin leaders, but it gave Kakizaki monopolistic control over trade and established Japanese territorial control over the land between Kaminokuni and Shiriuchi. While this was only a very small area, it represented the first physical incorporation of part of Ezogashima into the political system of the 'mainland'.

In 1599 the Kakizaki family took the name of Matsumae, and in 1604 their small domain (*han*) was incorporated into the Tokugawa regime as a minor fief. The black seal edict of Tokugawa Ieyasu that legitimized the Matsumae domain, following an earlier edict of Hideyoshi in 1593, limited Matsumae political authority to the narrow confines of the domain. The rest of the island and surrounding areas remained a strictly demarcated foreign land, known as Ezochi (Ainu-land) in contrast to the Matsumae domain which was called Shamochi, Matsumaeryō or (later) Wajinchi. The same edict granted a trade monopoly to the Matsumae. While the Matsumae domain possessed rich fishing grounds there was little agricultural potential and the mainstay of the domain economy was the Ainu trade, so it was imperative for the Matsumae to gain control of this process. Ezochi was therefore vital to Matsumae interests.

To impose control on trade, the Matsumae set up a series of trading posts in Ainu territory known as *akinaiba* and discouraged the Ainu from trading at Matsumae. Products from the *akinaiba* were exchanged with Honshū traders who were limited to certain ports where they were subject to control and taxation. After 1644 Ainu boats were no longer to be seen in Tōhoku ports, an indication of the success of Matsumae attempts to monopolize trade. The *han* was becoming increasingly dependent on traders from Honshū, especially those of Ōmi (modern Shiga Prefecture), who brought in all the necessities of life that could not be produced in Matsumae. The domain, for instance, required some 55,000 bales of rice annually, of which the Matsumae and their retainers took 20 per cent (Matsumae-chō Shi Henshū Shitsu 1984: 580). Ōmi trading houses such as Ryōhamagumi and Yawatagumi began setting up branch offices in Matsumae from the 1630s and lending money to the ruling family. As debts increased the trading houses were able to take over the running of the trade with the Ainu. Motivated by risk and profit, the traders began to exploit the Ainu. The size of the *ezotawara*, the special small rice bales used in the Ezo trade for convenience of transportation, was reduced while rates of exchange were maintained, in effect raising prices for one of the staple Wajin goods on which Ainu around the trading posts had become dependent.

While political alliances in the region were complex and did not split neatly along 'ethnic' lines into Ainu versus Japanese (Howell 1994: 86), in 1669 discontent among some Ainu again flared into open warfare. Led by Shakushain, leader of the regional group centred on Shibechari (modern Shizunai), the Ainu attacked trading posts and vessels over much of Ezochi, killing hundreds of Wajin. The Ainu army, a few hundred strong, then marched west to confront the Matsumae near their domain. Here, however, they were defeated, and a pacification campaign sent after Shakushain later in the year resulted in the Ainu leader's assassination during feigned peace negotiations. As a result, the previously autonomous regional groups in western and central Hokkaidō fell under Matsumae control. Ainu in the outlying areas to the north and east, however, still remained independent or maintained a *uimam* or 'tribute' relationship with Matsumae. But with the rise in Matsumae dominance, the trading posts and trade vessels gradually began to penetrate into their territories as well, reaching Karafuto (Sakhalin) in 1679, and the island of Kunashiri in 1754. In 1774 Kunashiri became the trading territory of the merchant Hidaya Kyūbei, although the establishment of permanent commercial operations in this area was impossible until 1782 due to the intransigence and power of local Ainu leaders.

From the early eighteenth century the trading territories, now numbering around seventy and known as *basho*, began to come under the direct control of mainland traders. *Han* expenses were increasing. The Matsumae had been granted full *daimyō* status in 1716, and, even though obligations to the Bakufu were limited to visiting Edo once every three or five years rather than residing alternate years in the capital (*sankin kōtai*), this put a severe strain on *han* finances. Before long the Matsumae were deeply in debt to mainland merchants. The Matsumae hoped that letting merchant contractors operate the *basho* after paying a fee (*unjōkin*) would increase trade volume and profits, and therefore tax receipts. This arrangement gradually developed over the course of the eighteenth century and has come to be known as the *basho ukeoi* (subcontracted trading post) system. By 1804, clan income from contractors' fees alone stood at 7,000 *ryō*, whereas income in 1739 from all taxes levied on trade had come to 3,200 *ryō* (Takakura 1960: 31). Conversely, to pay these taxes and *unjōkin* (along with forced 'loans' to the Matsumae of which there was little chance of repayment), the traders had to move away from barter trade to a more rationalized system designed to increase the volume of trade. This was aided by the development of mainland agriculture, which led to a subsequent increase in demand for fish fertilizer and an interest in the fisheries of Ezochi. According to one contemporary source, by 1740 over half the rice paddies in western Japan were using fish-meal fertilizer from Ezochi, while goods from the region entered international trade routes via Nagasaki (Kaiho 1979: 121). These developments were made possible by the systematic exploitation of fishing grounds using merchant capital, technology and management, and Ainu labour. This was a gradual process that did not reach full development until the nineteenth century. Contractors introduced advanced fishing methods and equipment, built processing facilities and barracks for the Ainu labourers, and shipped the products directly to markets in the Kansai. But the risks were great. A combination of high fees and forced loans to the Matsumae put pressure on the contractors to make the highest profits possible. One result was cruel treatment of the Ainu.

Emphasis had shifted from obtaining the products of Ainu labour through trade to the direct exploitation of that labour itself. Ainu around the *basho*, dependent on Wajin goods and whose leaders derived authority from their relationship with the *basho*, were coerced into working for rations and goods. Conditions were varied, but in the worst *basho* were often harsh. In 1789, after some years of suffering an exceptionally cruel regime, Ainu attacked and killed seventy-one Wajin on Kunashiri and in the Nemuro area. This final act of armed resistance was eventually suppressed by the Matsumae with the help of local Ainu leaders under their political control. After an investigation thirty-seven Ainu were executed at Nokkamappu.

The appearance of Russians in the north around this time meant that Ezogashima and the Ainu were now a matter of utmost concern in Tokugawa political circles. In 1792 Adam Laxman landed at Nemuro requesting the opening of trade relations with Japan. Permission was refused. In Edo, arguments for the annexation of Ezochi, stimulated primarily by the perceived Russian threat, became increasingly influential. In 1798 the Bakufu sent a large expedition to Ezochi, including Sakhalin and the Kuriles, and in 1799 overrode Matsumae objections by annexing part of the region. By 1807 all of Ezochi had been placed under direct Bakufu control through offices established in Matsumae and Hakodate. In most respects, however, Ezochi retained the nature of a foreign land (*iiki*) since it was too vast and rugged to administer in the same way as other Tokugawa lands. The Bakufu stationed garrisons around the coast and intervened in the Ainu trade to alleviate the worst injustices, but most Wajin still lived in the narrow bounds of the Matsumae domain or at the fishing stations. One change, however, was the introduction of a policy that aimed to 'civilize' the Ainu by converting them (often forcibly) to Japanese customs and lifestyle.

When the Russian threat receded and Ezochi was handed back to the Matsumae in 1821, one of the first acts of the contractors was to scrap the assimilation policy and return to the previous situation in which Ainu had been forbidden to use Japanese language and customs. The gulf that separated the Bakufu's rhetoric of 'civilizing' the Ainu from the actual conditions in Ezochi was reflected in the further economic exploitation and consequent degradation of the Ainu that occurred under the re-established Matsumae in the final decades of Tokugawa rule. Forced labour and resettlement became a feature of Ainu life. Ainu labour was used for roadbuilding, transportation and servicing the fisheries, in addition to direct economic production. Ainu were brought down from the mountains to work on the coast, or were transferred between *basho* run by the same trader. The sexual exploitation of Ainu women also became commonplace. In the Kushiro *basho*, for instance, thirty-six out of the forty-one *dekasegi* (Wajin migrant workers) had forcibly taken Ainu women after sending their husbands to work in the fisheries at Akkeshi (Matsuura [1860] 1969: 786). The recruitment of labour was accomplished by the use of physical coercion if necessary, leaving the elderly and infirm behind. Diseases introduced by the *dekasegi* also contributed to the destruction of Ainu society. While the statistics are unreliable, the Ainu population of West Ezochi appears to have declined sharply from 9,068 in 1798 to 4,384 in 1854 (Emori 1987: 103). As the Ainu ceased to be the main economic producers of Ezochi, the movement of immigrants increased, encouraged by the easing of travel restrictions and tolls. As a result, by the 1850s the strict distinction that had previously been maintained between Wajinchi and Ezochi had begun to break down. In 1855 the Bakufu re-established control over the area and reintroduced Japanization of the Ainu.

With the Meiji Restoration of 1868 and the establishment of the Kaitakushi (Colonization Commission) in 1869, Ezochi was renamed Hokkaidō and transformed into an internal colony of the new Japanese state, a strategic 'empty land' to be settled by immigration and developed along capitalist lines. Both of these policies required the dispossession of the Ainu as a prerequisite. This was initiated with the appropriation of Ainu land as *terra nullius* by the Kaitakushi under the Land Regulation Ordinance (Jisho Kisoku) of 1872. The salmon and deer upon which the Ainu depended were soon depleted by uncontrolled exploitation. Mass immigration, a market economy, and a colonial administration served to create an unequal order within which the indigenous and powerless Ainu were enmeshed. The authorities began to round up and relocate Ainu communities to clear them out of rich lands designated for agricultural settlement, and to make them easier to control. Also relocated were communities from Sakhalin (under Russian control after 1875) and the Kuriles. By the end of the century, the 17,000 Ainu accounted for around 2 per cent of the population of Hokkaidō (Emori 1987: 126).

Modernization was accompanied by new concepts of 'race' and 'nation' that served to interpret and sustain changing economic, social and political relations between Wajin and Ainu. The barbarian was transformed into a member of a 'primitive race', a wandering savage incapable of using the land or progressing to higher levels of civilization, and thus doomed to die out in the 'struggle for survival'. A humanitarian movement to halt the physical extermination of the 'dying race' resulted in the institutionalization of Ainu inferiority with the enactment of a Protection Act in 1899. Under this Act the

Ainu were granted small plots of land in an attempt to turn them into farmers. Assimilation was also encouraged through a special system of native education (Ogawa 1993). By the beginning of the twentieth century, the activities of scholars, educators, colonial officials and journalists ensured that the image of an inferior 'dying race' informed both government policy and public opinion. Against a broader background of sustained ideological efforts to forge a Japanese 'sense of nation' and the colonial expansion of an increasingly powerful and assertive state, 'race' and nation became increasingly synonymous as common-sense categories of understanding for most Japanese since 'blood, as expressed in "racial" homogeneity, provided the essential adhesive which bonded the constituent parts into a uniquely powerful Japanese collectivity' (Weiner 1994: 20). National identity was located within the consanguineous family-state. While legally Japanese citizens, the Ainu were thus excluded from the racialized national community as an internally colonized 'native' population. In the view of the state, the economic and social inequality of the Ainu was due to innate natural difference and justified their continued subordination.

While Ainu responses were limited by their extreme lack of power and resources, especially after the military defeats of 1669 and 1789, traditional ways of life survived into the Meiji period until the resources of land, fish and game upon which this lifestyle depended were appropriated or destroyed by the development of Hokkaidō. By the early twentieth century, most Ainu were sunk in chronic destitution and only barely managing to survive. Hampered by poverty and isolation, lacking in education, money or any other resources, the Ainu response was limited to isolated acts of individual violence or attempts to adapt to the rapid changes taking place in the new colonial milieu. Nevertheless a few Ainu succeeded in overcoming many of the constraints imposed by the colonial order to obtain an education, or even achieve economic prosperity. In the 1920s and 1930s younger Ainu like Iboshi Hokuto, Chiri Yukie and Ega Torazō became the forerunners of a movement to better the condition of those they perceived as Utari (their people). Lacking resources and dependent largely on Wajin allies in positions of authority or Christians associated with the British missionary John Batchelor, they sought assimilation within dominant society by attempting to influence the institutional and ideological structures through which they were controlled. Their movement therefore concentrated on the revision of the Protection Act and the denial of the image of the 'dying race'. The year 1930 saw the formation of the first organization for all Hokkaidō Ainu, the Ainu Kyōkai. Although headed by a Wajin bureaucrat and operated as an extension of the Social Section of the Hokkaidō Government (Dōchō), the Ainu Kyōkai provided an important forum for like-minded young Ainu from previously isolated communities to come together. Despite their ultimate objective of assimilation, these men and women remained proud of their heritage and helped create a new, but fragile, sense of Ainu unity (Siddle 1995; Baba 1980).

The failure of their efforts to assimilate became clear in the decades after the collapse of the Empire in 1945. Narratives of Japanese 'racial' homogeneity and superiority continued to shape Ainu lives and deny those so identified the opportunity to participate in Japan's economic and political renewal. Although the Ainu Kyōkai was resurrected, the momentum and vitality of the pre-war movement was never regained. Torn by division and deprived of resources, the Ainu were unable to challenge relations of domination until the social and political climate of the 1970s contributed to the emergence of a new, and often radical, Ainu politics. Influenced by domestic and international movements for civil and human rights and the struggles of indigenous peoples elsewhere (e.g. Cornell 1988), young radicals challenged the comfortable institutional position of the Utari Kyōkai, the successor of the Ainu Kyōkai, as a distributor of government largesse, and also launched an attack on the assimilation policies of the government itself. In common with other indigenous populations around the world, cultural symbols were activated to encourage a sense of identity around which to mobilize politically. And so the Ainu nation was born. A flag, a history, and a homeland, *Ainu Moshiri* (the quiet earth where humans live) legitimized the existence of the Ainu people and underscored their claims for increased access to wealth and power. The remainder of this chapter explores this process of ethnic mobilization.

'RACE' AND THE AINU IN POST-WAR JAPAN

Although the dominant pre-war ideology of the consanguineous family-state was officially discredited after 1945, it continued, somewhat transformed, in hegemonic narratives of Japanese uniqueness, often reflected in notions of the *tan'itsu minzoku kokka* or homogeneous nation-state. Popular literature on Japaneseness (*Nihonjinron*) began appearing in the late 1940s and 1950s, and had reached boom proportions by the 1970s (Yoshino 1992; Befu 1993). As Yoshino has noted, the common-sense notions of a unique Japanese culture and society that were expressed in the genre were, and are, ultimately dependent upon a racialized understanding of Self, since 'a Japanese expresses the "immutable" or "natural" aspect of Japanese identity through the imagined concept of "Japanese blood"' (Yoshino 1992: 24).

Conversely, Others are categorized on the basis of their non-Japanese blood, regardless of quantity. Irrespective of how Ainu perceived themselves, the determining factor of Ainu identity among Wajin in local society was the possession of Ainu blood (*Ainu no chi o hiku*). Even if an individual was able to conceal his or her ancestry, they might still be marked by physical appearance. As one Ainu expressed it:

> If only half-*shamo*, or even only quarter-*shamo*, even when Ainu blood is only a small proportion of your actual blood, if you have an Ainu face you will surely be treated in general as Ainu. Where can we go, we Ainu who have been left hanging in mid-air?
>
> (Narita 1972: 38)

Such 'racial' categorization ensured that many people of Ainu descent trying to divest themselves of Ainu identity and merge into the mainstream in the post-war period were thus unable to do so unless they physically resembled Wajin and could move away from their home area. Even if they succeeded in passing they often lived in fear of discovery. On the other hand, the master-narrative of the homogeneity of all 'Japanese' denied the existence of the Ainu as a separate group with a right to a separate identity. Since the empire no longer existed, minority groups incorporated during the colonial period were ignored under this common-sense notion of a homogeneous Japan. Ascribed in local society a negative, essentialized 'racial' identity as individual 'Ainu' that overrode socio-economic, occupational or gender roles, but denied under the notion of national homogeneity any possibility of a positive 'Ainu' self-identification as a minority group, most Ainu existed in an identityless void that could only be escaped by passing. As a result, many Ainu themselves had come to believe that the only way to escape prejudice was by the thorough dilution of blood through intermarriage. In the words of an Ainu of Biratori interviewed in 1972:

> There are women who think that as long as a man is from *naichi*, anyone will do if only Ainu blood can be diluted (*Ainu no chi sae usumerarereba*), so they produce illegitimate offspring with the labourers who drift into Hokkaidō. There are also some who

have married for such humiliating reasons and suffered many years of unhappy married life.

(Kaizawa 1972: 145)

'Racial' categorization as an essentialized Other was accompanied by the continuation of the negative images associated with the subordination of the Ainu as colonized and inferior. Negative stereotypes and discrimination were rife in the integrated schools that the Ainu leaders of the pre-war period had fought so hard for, including a continued identification of Ainu with dogs; most children of this period were taunted with the words '*Aaa – inu*' (Ah – a dog). When Ainu children left school and entered into the adult world of employment and marriage, they encountered yet more discrimination (Sugawara 1966: 31–48). In response, many young Ainu turned their backs on their Ainu heritage and attempted to disassociate themselves from anything Ainu, in particular the activities of the tourist Ainu (*kankō* Ainu) or those working with scholars to preserve Ainu culture (Kayano 1994: 98–100; Sugawara 1966: 220; Hilger 1967: 285). As Hatozawa Samio warned with regard to tourism, 'all Ainu will just end up in the image created for them by Wajin' (Hatozawa 1972: 64).

Against this background of poverty and division, the main organization of Ainu, the Ainu Kyōkai, was virtually powerless. Most of its members continued to be drawn from among the elites of both the pre-war and post-war eras. In 1961 the Ainu Kyōkai was renamed the Utari Kyōkai due to a widespread dislike among Ainu of the word 'Ainu', largely because Wajin used it as a pejorative term. This cosmetic improvement did little to attract new members, whose numbers in 1963 stood at about 770 (*Senkusha no Tsudoi* 1: 25). Many poorer Ainu remained suspicious of the motives of the leadership, while others, attempting to divest themselves of any Ainu identity, criticized the Utari Kyōkai for perpetuating the illusion that an Ainu people existed, or simply ignored the organization (Sugawara 1966: 214–19; Peng and Geiser 1977: 276–8). The Utari Kyōkai did manage to persuade the authorities to create a welfare package for the Ainu in 1961, the Furyō Kankyō Chiku Kaizen Shisetsu Seibi Jigyō (Project for the Improvement of Facilities in Areas with Unsatisfactory Environments) that constructed new communal bath houses and ferro-concrete blocks of public housing in Ainu communities (Sugawara 1966: 209–10). The project was administered with the help of the Utari Kyōkai and drew that organization further into a corporatist relationship with the authorities.

In effect, the Association functioned as an arm of the government from which it received both financial and personnel assistance.

The Ainu welfare project illustrates that although Japanese society had undergone many changes, the Ainu were still enmeshed within power structures reminiscent of the pre-war period. The Ainu remained powerless wards of the state under the Protection Act, and were controlled by the Dōchō through channels established in the 1930s. Ainu scholars also made use of their positions within the structures of institutional power. Kodama Sakuzaemon of Hokkaidō University, driven by a sense of scientific mission, resumed his quest for Ainu bones after the war. Enlisting the help of local authorities and police when excavating Ainu cemeteries in the face of local opposition from Ainu, teams under his supervision brought the collection of Ainu remains at Hokkaidō University to a total of 1,004 individuals (Siddle 1993). Scholars worked hard to ensure the separation of Ainu culture from living human beings by labelling it 'traditional', a relic of the past. Even sympathetic scholars believed that 'the happiness of the Ainu lies in complete assimilation to the Wajin', though Ainu culture would of course be 'preserved' in museums (Sakurai 1967: 15).

In general, then, the continuation of colonial structures of domination during this period ensured that the circumstances of most Ainu did little to offset the image of the 'dying race'. Indeed, this characterization of the Ainu continued to be used in various guises by both Japanese and foreigners alike. Ainu communities were deeply divided, and it seemed that the fragile flame of common identity and purpose kindled by the pre-war Ainu movement had been all but extinguished. But when the issues that formed the 'Ainu problem' were brought sharply into focus by events in the late 1960s, younger Ainu were able to respond and initiate a radically different style of Ainu politics.

THE NEW AINU POLITICS AND THE STATE'S RESPONSE

The Ainu resurgence in the late 1960s and early 1970s emerged in the form of groups of young Ainu activists who were sharply critical of the Ainu establishment and its links with the Dōchō, as represented by the Utari Kyōkai. Taking their cue from more radical currents in Japanese society, they bypassed the administrative structure of previous relations and sought instead to confront the social and administrative mechanisms that underlay Ainu marginalization. In a reversal of the flight of Ainu youth from Ainu identity, these young men and women rejected assimilation. Asserting pride in their Ainuness, they actively undertook a search for their roots.

While most Ainu youth rejected their heritage and attempted to pass, a small number had responded to discrimination with anger. During the early post-war decades, many Ainu had moved out of their home communities and migrated to Sapporo or the cities of the mainland where, influenced by student and social activism, some began to form small study or social groups. Younger Ainu who had remained behind in rural Hokkaidō had also occasionally been active. In Akan, young Ainu involved in the production of Ainu crafts began experimenting with contemporary Ainu art, while in Biratori, Hatozawa Samio was active in local literary circles after 1960. Although representing diverse interests and lacking a clear political agenda, when provided with a cause these younger Ainu were able to respond independently of the Utari Kyōkai, drawing inspiration from left-wing, student and Burakumin political movements.

Between 1968 and 1970, various events occurred which highlighted the marginal status of the Ainu and stimulated activity among the emerging Ainu groups. The year 1968 marked the centennial of the Meiji Restoration and was also the hundredth year of Hokkaidō 'history'. Considerable sums were spent on celebrations, including public ceremonies at Maruyama Stadium in Sapporo attended by the emperor on 2 September, and on the first stages of construction of a large memorial park with a tower, Museum of Development (Kaitaku Kinenkan), and 'pioneer village' outside Sapporo. Almost no mention was made of Ainu history or their role in the colonization of Hokkaidō. This was not mere oversight; such historical amnesia was integral to the legitimizing narrative of Hokkaidō *kaitaku* (development) that served to mask the violence of the colonial enterprise by casting it in terms of the application of the beneficial effects of 'progress' to a 'natural' extension of Japanese territory. The Ainu were largely excluded from this narrative, or given marginal roles as guides or coolies for the early explorers, since as a 'dying race' of primitives they had claim to neither land nor civilization.

This denial of their existence aroused much resentment among Ainu of all generations. In a letter to the *Hokkaidō Shinbun*, one young Ainu from Kushiro called for Wajin not to forget that the ground under the commemorative tower was 'soaked with Ainu blood' (*Hokkaidō Shinbun*, 13 May 1968, evening edition). Another issue that provoked discussion among the Ainu was the revision of the Protection Act in June 1968 as part of a government initiative to streamline bureaucracy. On 5 June 1970 the debate over the future

30   Richard Siddle

of the Protection Act was further stimulated by the unanimous acceptance at a conference of the Mayors of Hokkaidō of a motion for the
abolition of the Act. In response, on 17 June the Utari Kyōkai voted
overwhelmingly for its continued existence on the grounds that it
could be used as a convenient umbrella for special welfare policies,
as in the early 1960s. This attitude drew considerable opposition
from other Ainu, especially in Asahikawa, who saw the Protection
Act as the institutional expression of discrimination and inferiority
(see, for instance, *Hokkaidō Shinbun*, 18 June 1970; also readers'
letters in *Hokkaidō Shinbun*, 8 July 1970, evening edition; and
Hokkaidō Shinbun, 4 September 1970, evening edition). Such attitudes were reinforced when, in August 1970, Asahikawa celebrated
eighty years since foundation with the unveiling of a statue, the
Fūsetsu no Gunzō (Wind and Snow Group), depicting four young
Wajin colonizers surrounding an elderly Ainu. Even though the
pose of the lone Ainu had been altered after protest from a kneeling
to a sitting position, Ainu activists handed out leaflets during the
inauguration ceremonies to protest this symbolization of Ainu subordination (Sala 1975: 50–1; Miyoshi 1971: 449–80).

Stimulated by these developments, a proliferation of small groups
began to appear, many with overlapping membership. Ironically, the
growth of the movement was facilitated by the Utari Kyōkai since
the existence of a network of over thirty branches throughout
Hokkaidō enabled ideas to spread rapidly. Many Utari Kyōkai members joined or formed these new groups. Urban Ainu also moved
to find a voice within the Utari Kyōkai, from which they had been
largely excluded. In late 1971, the Ishikari, later Sapporo Branch
(*shibu*) was formed in Sapporo with Ogawa Ryūkichi as first chairman. In February 1972, the Tokyo Utari Kai (Tokyo Ainu Association) was formed. Other activist organizations were formed in the
same year. The Ainu Kaihō Dōmei (Ainu Liberation League) was
the brainchild of a young Director of the Utari Kyōkai, Yūki Shōji,
and took its name and tactics of denunciation (*kyūdan*) from the
struggles of Burakumin. The Yai Yukara Kenkyūkai (Yai Yukara
[By Ourselves] Research Group) was formed by Narita Tokuhei.
In Biratori, young Ainu formed the Ashi no Kai (Reed Society)
(Suga 1976: 195–201). From late 1972 the movement received added
impetus from the fall-out generated by a terrorist campaign by
Wajin radicals in the name of Ainu Liberation, inaugurated by the
detonation of two bombs on 23 October, one of which blew apart
the Asahikawa statue. Three days later, forty Ainu from Asahikawa
met to protest the incident and deny any involvement, and formed

the strongly local Ainu Kyōgikai (Ainu Council). On 21 January 1973, one hundred and fifty Ainu gathered in Sapporo for the Zenkoku Ainu no Kataru Kai (National Ainu Discussion Meeting) organized by younger Ainu but open to all. Conservative leaders and those engaged in tourism were suspicious of the motives of the younger activists, who insisted, for their part, that it was a 'people's meeting' to discuss issues faced by all Ainu (Sala 1976).

During the next few years, the 'Ainu Problem' received considerable national attention as terrorist incidents continued. Besides numerous defacements of monuments with paint and graffiti, more serious incidents included arson attacks and attempted murder. The worst incident was the bombing of the Dōchō on 2 March 1976 in which two people were killed and over ninety injured. With the exception of a single case involving the erasure of the name of the Governor of Hokkaidō from the statue of Shakushain, there is no proof of Ainu involvement in any of these incidents, despite intensive police surveillance and harassment. Instead, the bombings were the work of a small cell of radical Wajin terrorists, the Higashi Ajia Han-nichi Busō Sensen (East Asia Anti-Japan Armed Front). Most were later arrested, convicted, and sentenced to death (Sala 1976; Chikap 1989).

Despite the lack of involvement in terrorism, Ainu throughout Hokkaidō could not ignore events so widely reported in the media. These incidents contributed to the increasing politicization of communities as the issues that underlay continued Ainu marginalization were brought to the surface. Most Ainu were stunned by the violence carried out in their name and felt that they were being used. As Kaibazawa Hiroshi wrote in the July 1975 issue of the Utari Kyōkai newsletter *Senkusha no Tsudoi*:

> Although the attempted murder of the Mayor of Shiraoi and the erasure of Governor Machimura's name from the Shakushain statue have been tied to the Ainu through various arguments, how do they contribute to Ainu liberation? I think not at all. Rather, I wish to say that they are an unwanted interference.

As Kaibazawa implied, the new Ainu groups were quite capable of acting on their own account. Their tactics generally differed radically from previous Ainu activity, which had been welfare-oriented and conducted through institutional channels by the Ainu/Utari Kyōkai. Yūki Shōji's Ainu Kaihō Dōmei, for instance, adopted forceful tactics of confrontation and denunciation, particularly against academics. On 25 August 1972, in the company of Wajin activists, Yūki stormed the podium of the Joint Conference of the Anthropological and Ethnological Societies of Japan at Sapporo Medical University, where he read a list of criticisms to the assembled scholars. Yūki's most effective campaign, however, was his denunciation of Professor Hayashi Yoshishige of Hokkaidō University between July 1977 and January 1978 in which Hayashi was eventually forced to offer a public apology after making allegedly 'racist' remarks about the Ainu in lectures (Siddle 1993: 43–5).

Protests were also made against media companies which conveyed discriminatory stereotypes of the Ainu. In March 1972 Ogawa Ryūkichi of the Sapporo branch of the Utari Kyōkai forced the cancellation of a TV programme put out by the Hokkaidō Broadcasting Company. A protest in May 1973 against an episode of the popular TV series *Mito Kōmon* resulted in the screening of an apology during the broadcast (Suga 1976: 201–2). Another successful denunciation was a campaign by Ainu Kaihō Dōmei and Tokyo Ainu in 1978 against the magazine *Pureiboi* for publishing a discriminatory cartoon, which resulted in the recall of 6,300 copies and a public apology (Sapporo Hōmukyoku, n.d.). In 1981 the denunciation of the Nihon Kōtsu Kōsha (Japan Travel Bureau) was organized by Narita Tokuhei in response to advertisements in the English daily *The Japan Times* inviting foreign residents to visit a 'real Ainu village' to see 'the ancient customs and culture of the famed hairy Ainu' (Narita and Hanazaki 1985).

In contrast to such direct action, other Ainu activists and their allies attempted to pursue the struggle within the institutions of the state, in particular the courts. In March 1973, for instance, the trial of Hashine Naohiko, an Ainu migrant worker in the notorious Tokyo district of Sanya who had killed a fellow worker in a fight, was turned into a showcase of discrimination and publicity for the Ainu cause by Wajin radicals (*Hokkai Taimuzu*, 25 November 1973). In July 1974 the lawyers defending an Ainu accused of murder in Shizunai asserted that the defendant was not Japanese and therefore not subject to Japanese law, an action that drew angry protests from the Utari Kyōkai, the Asahikawa Ainu Kyōgikai, and others (*Hokkaidō Shinbun*, 16 July 1974; *Hokkaidō Shinbun*, 21 July 1974). In October 1974 an elderly Ainu woman from Shizunai and her supporters launched a court action to regain her Protection Act lands which had allegedly been obtained by a Wajin neighbor through illegal means, emerging victorious in October 1979 despite an appeal by the Wajin farmer (Pon Fuchi 1992: 246–7). An unsuccessful attempt to gain national political representation was made in the Upper House elections of July 1977, when Narita Tokuhei stood in Tokyo as an independent in the national constituency, gaining a respectable 53,682 votes (*Hokkaidō Shinbun*, 12 July 1977). The impact of these activities on the Utari Kyōkai was mixed. On the one hand, many of the younger radicals were also members, or even, as in the case of Yūki, officials of the Association. The authority and assimilationist orientation of the more elderly and conservative leaders was therefore threatened by generational divisions within the Association, and by further differences between the Association and other Ainu groups. While it resisted the regular proposals of younger activists to revert back to the former title of Ainu Kyōkai, the Association moved to distance itself from the state and transferred from a desk in the Public Welfare Section of the Dōchō to an 'independent' office in May 1974. It still received an annual subsidy from the Dōchō, however, as well as administrative expertise from Dōchō personnel. On the other hand, the publicity surrounding the 'Ainu problem' (Ainu *mondai*) was instrumental in eliciting a political response from the authorities. This response received added impetus from the interest in the issue among opposition political parties, in particular the Japan Socialist Party and the Japan Communist Party which established Special Committees for Ainu Issues with agendas similar to that of the Utari Kyōkai (Nihon Kyōsantō Chūō Iinkai 1974: 57–8; Nihon Shakaitō Seisaku Shingikai Ainu Minzoku Mondai Tokubetsu Iinkai 1974: 223–6). As a result, the position of the Utari Kyōkai as the established institutional channel for Ainu negotiation with the state was strengthened.

This began to bear fruit with the establishment of another large-scale welfare project for the Ainu in the early 1970s. A survey released in 1972 confirmed that Ainu socio-economic conditions lagged far behind those of Wajin. As a result, in August 1973 the authorities drew up the Hokkaidō Utari Fukushi Taisaku (Hokkaidō Utari Welfare Countermeasures), a package of welfare measures similar to the Dōwa assimilation policies for Burakumin. The first Utari Taisaku policy was implemented from fiscal 1974 and ran for seven years with a budget of almost 12 billion yen, 41 per cent from the national treasury (Teshima 1990: 88–92). Following the corporatist pattern established in the 1960s, the policy was administered largely through the Utari Kyōkai, and the membership and influence of the Association began to revive. By 1976, 2,103 households (8,540 people) belonged to the organization, nearly half of the total identified Hokkaidō Ainu population (*Senkusha no Tsudoi* 13: appendix).

The Utari Taisaku aimed to bring the Ainu problem firmly back within the sphere of social welfare. The government's position was made clear in the Diet by Welfare Minister Saitō Kuniyoshi in March 1973:

> Our basic attitude towards Ainu persons, or Utari, is that we definitely do not take the standpoint that the Ainu are a separate people (*minzoku*) within the citizenry of Japan. We strictly adhere to the view that they are equal Japanese citizens under the law.
>
> (Hokkaidō Utari Kyōkai 1990: 594)

But contrary to government wishes, it was this very consciousness of being a separate people – indeed, a nation – that was gaining strength among Ainu leaders, whether radical or moderate. One of the main motivations for the construction of a counter-narrative of Ainu nationhood was precisely the denial of Ainu existence that historical amnesia and the master-narrative of homogeneity countenanced.

THE EMERGENCE OF AINU NATIONHOOD

Perhaps the most important, and often conscious, development of the new Ainu politics was the mobilization of Ainu identity as the basis for political action. This was not a completely new phenomenon, and had its roots in the genuine pride that many Ainu had retained in their heritage despite Wajin attempts to denigrate it as primitive. This pride can be seen, for instance, in the writings of the leaders of the pre-war Ainu Kyōkai even as they urged assimilation (Siddle 1995). What was new, however, was the manipulation of the symbols of Ainu identity by activists in the service of a new political agenda that aimed to regain both a measure of control over their own lives and a larger share of the resources of society.

This use of 'Ainuness' for political ends operated in a number of ways. Firstly, in an attempt to overcome Ainu powerlessness, it served to create a sense of community that could overcome differing interests and divisions of class, gender or generation, and produce a unified front in negotiations with the state. Secondly, as an assertion of difference, it challenged the assimilation policies that aimed at the eventual extinction of the 'Ainu problem' through complete absorption of all Ainu into majority society. Finally, through identification with indigenous movements in other states, the politics of Ainuness represented an attempt to redefine the relationship of the Ainu to the state in terms of a culturally and historically unique group with distinct rights. The Ainu, as an indigenous people, were not just another disadvantaged social group in need of state welfare but a 'nation' desirous of decolonization.

The fact that little sense of unity existed among Ainu was self-evident to many activists in the early days of the movement. The need 'to create a forum for Ainu to participate and discuss freely' the divisive issues that made up the Ainu problem was the main motivation for the young Ainu, led by Sunazawa Biki, who organized the Zenkoku Ainu no Kataru Kai in January 1973 (*Hokkai Taimuzu*, 18 January 1973). The divisions among Ainu activists were reflected in the variety of political ideologies they espoused. Many of the activists disagreed not only with the elderly rural-based elite of the Utari Kyōkai, but also among themselves. Yūki Shōji, for instance, despite severe criticism from fellow Ainu, drew much early inspiration from his association with the ultra-left Wajin revolutionary Ōta Ryū, who argued that mass revolution would begin with the Ainu (Ota 1973). Most of the leaders of the Utari Kyōkai, on the other hand, were wealthy farmers or businessmen with strong local links to the ruling LDP. The Chairman, Nomura Giichi, writing in *Senkusha no Tsudoi* in January 1974, attempted to downplay political differences in favour of action on the 'three pillars' of Ainu welfare – education, housing and secure livelihood:

> Recently, discussion of the Ainu problem has been rife among the general public, and many Utari have become self-aware as a result. As it is, although I and the Utari Kyōkai have also been subject to criticism from various quarters, for me the Utari problem is not one of ideology or party politics. We must draw back from these and appeal to the Dōchō and the state on the three main issues.

Between the views of Yūki and Nomura there existed a wide spectrum of opinion. One way to bridge the differences between the divergent wings of the movement was to appeal to the common bonds of Ainu identity. While some activists like Narita and Yūki were aware of the power of 'ethnic' identity to promote unity, for others, especially the alienated young, a rapidly growing interest in Ainu history and culture was part of a general movement to rediscover Ainu heritage that accompanied politicization. The young staff of the Ainu newspaper *Anutari Ainu* (published bimonthly between 1973 and 1976), for instance, compared 'racial prejudice' against the Ainu to the situation of the American blacks, and began a similar search for their roots, seeking out elders and publishing lengthy interviews. The cultural manifestations of Ainuness – embroidered traditional costume, prayers in the Ainu language, oral literature, dance – became increasingly evident at community events, for the benefit of Ainu, not tourists. Festivals and ceremonies, such as those enacted each year before the new statue of Shakushain in Shizunai, became occasions to celebrate this heritage and link the present struggle to the feats of past heroes. At a new festival by the Shakushain memorial, Narita Tokuhei was impressed by the Ainu dancing, 'not that seen in tourist areas, but real dancing from the heart', that had enabled him to see 'a splendid Ainu people', and led him to feel that the gathering had 'lit the lamp of the solidarity that the Utari have long lost' (Narita 1972: 38–9).

In 1974, Yūki, advised by Kushiro elder Yamamoto Tasuke, carried this movement further by setting up a committee to organize an *icharpa* (Ainu memorial service) at Nokkamappu for the thirty-seven Ainu executed there in 1789. The first *icharpa*, held in September 1974, was attended by fifty Ainu from around Hokkaidō and this 'invented tradition' thereafter became an annual event. In 1976, Yukara Za, an Akan based group of young Ainu artists led by elder Yamamoto Tasuke, performed modern dramatized versions of Ainu epics as part of a UNESCO cultural festival in Paris. The Yai Yukara group organized various field trips into the countryside, again drawing on the knowledge of Yamamoto, to 'learn the wisdom of life with nature' (*Anutari Ainu* 12: 1; *Senkusha no Tsudoi* 13: 3). The Utari Kyōkai also began to organize local groups among members for the preservation and transmission of Ainu dance and handicrafts, holding annual competitions. While much of the traditional cultural expertise involved in the ceremonies or field trips came from elders in rural or tourist communities, the initiative for these events came from the politically active, younger, urban Ainu. Members of the Sapporo branch of the Utari Kyōkai, for instance, politically left-wing and now a major power base within the organization, began holding the Ashiri Chep Nomi (Ceremony to Welcome the New Salmon) on the banks of the Toyohira river in Sapporo annually from 1982. Not all traditional Ainu, however, agreed with the changes to the old ways initiated by the activists; some expressed grave reservations or anger against what they saw as 'fake' (*detarame*) ceremonies and insults to the gods (Ekashi to Fuchi Henshū Iinkai 1983: 383).

Along with its 'culture', a nation needs a history, a collective memory of a coherent, idealized past that provides a sense of continuity while enabling a group to mediate its experiences of the present. Ainu activists, following the lead of Wajin radicals (e.g. Shinya 1977), emphasized a historical narrative based on heroic Ainu resistance to rapacious Wajin aggression and the 'emperor system' that directly challenged the master-narrative of peaceful and orderly Hokkaidō *kaitaku*. The Ainu version of the past was then objectified by the festivals honouring Shakushain and the victims of Nokkamappu as national heroes. The importance of reviving an Ainu version of the past was keenly felt by Yūki Shōji, who, in common with most Ainu, had never heard of the Nokkamappu incident until the early 1970s (Shinya 1979: 36–8). But this entailed glossing over certain gaps and tensions in the historical record. The Nokkamappu story, for instance, was complicated by the role of Ainu leaders like Tsukinoe who had sided with the Matsumae. While some called Tsukinoe a 'traitor' (*goyō Ainu*), for Yūki he was a national leader engaged in delicate diplomacy while sandwiched between the forces of two expansionist powers, Japan and Russia (Yūki 1980: 125–8).

As with culture, this renewed interest in Ainu history was not just the preserve of radical activists. Since the early 1970s there had also been a movement within the Utari Kyōkai, led by Kaizawa Tadashi, for the production of a 'correct' Ainu history that would challenge the official narratives of Hokkaidō *kaitaku* and the Northern Territories, the islands of Shikotan, Kunashiri, Etorofu and the Habomai group which had been under Soviet control since 1945, and regarded in official circles as inalienable Japanese territory. This coincided with a new movement for 'people's history' among sympathetic young Japanese historians and also in the ranks of the left-wing teachers' unions.

Besides revisiting or reformulating the old, activists created new symbols to reinforce their concept of the Ainu *minzoku*, the Ainu people, as what Anderson calls a 'deep, horizontal comradeship' or an imagined political community – a nation (Anderson 1991: 7). An Ainu flag first appeared at the 1973 May Day parade in Sapporo. The Ainu sculptor Sunazawa Biki had designed the flag to 'symbolize Utari pride, struggle, and passion'. Light-blue and green represented the sea, sky and earth of the homeland, while a stylized arrowhead in white and red symbolized snow and the Ainu god of fire, Abe Kamui (*Anutari Ainu* 1: 2). One of the most potent symbols became that of Ainu Moshiri, the homeland. Ainu Moshiri (usually translated as 'the quiet earth where humans live' – *ningen ga sumu shizuka na daichi*) had connotations in both space and time; besides national territory in a physical sense, it stood also for a golden age in which Ainu lived independent and happy communal lives in harmony with nature until these were destroyed by subsequent invasion and colonization. This vision was articulated by Yūki Shōji, who added:

> Ainu Moshiri was the Mother Earth that formed Ainu culture, and this remains unchanged to this day. The Gods in whom the people believe have not left Ainu Moshiri for ever. The present situation where magnificent ethnic ceremonies are carried out every year in various regions, and prayers are offered respectfully to the Gods of Nature, is confirming Mother Earth, Ainu Moshiri, as the territory, albeit spiritually, of our people.
>
> (Yūki 1980: 43)

As Yūki's adoption of the concept of Mother Earth (*haha naru daichi*) suggests, a further stimulus to the growth of Ainu nationhood was provided by contact with indigenous peoples in other countries. Whereas Ainu activists had first looked to domestic movements for inspiration and tactics, in particular those of the Burakumin and radical left, from the early 1970s they began to turn increasingly to forging links with indigenous and other minority peoples abroad. Knowledge of civil rights movements, and, particularly, indigenous activism in North America, Australia and New Zealand, was obtained through the media and personal contacts. Hiramura Yoshimi, the young founder of the Ainu newspaper *Anutari Ainu*, consciously identified with Native Americans after a trip to the United States in 1972, and the first issue of the paper devoted a page to the confrontation at Wounded Knee between activists of the American Indian Movement and Federal authorities, while subsequent issues referred to the struggles of American blacks in both prose and poetry.

The first delegation of Ainu to travel overseas toured autonomous minority regions in China, the result of an invitation by the Chinese Ambassador to Japan on a tour of Hokkaidō in December 1973. Led by Kaizawa Tadashi, the group of fifteen Ainu arrived in China for a stage-managed three-week tour in February 1974. Nevertheless, the Ainu were impressed by what they saw of Chinese policies towards minority peoples, and made three further visits. But ultimately of more importance in shaping Ainu nationhood were direct contacts with the emerging worldwide indigenous peoples' movement. In December 1977 two Eskimo from Barrow attending a meeting in Japan of the International Whaling Commission visited the Ainu village of Nibutani. This led to an official invitation from the Mayor of Barrow and a visit by an Ainu group led by Nomura Giichi to the North Slope Autonomous Region in July 1978. They returned to Hokkaidō impressed by the degree of autonomy possessed by the indigenous peoples of the American Arctic under the Alaskan Native Claims Settlement Act of 1971, and the fact that it was funded out of tax revenue from the natural resources of the region, oil in particular (*Senkusha no Tsudoi* 19). Contacts increased thereafter. A group led by Narita Tokuhei visited Canadian and American Indian groups in 1978, and in May 1981 Narita became the first Ainu to attend the World Conference of Indigenous Peoples when he travelled to the third conference in Canberra to join a thousand delegates from twenty-one states in discussions on the restoration of indigenous rights, and celebrations of indigenous culture. Not just political strategies were borrowed as a result of such interaction but the symbols of a common underlying 'Aboriginality' based on similar historic lifestyles and experiences of colonization. Yūki Shōji's characterization of Ainu Moshiri as Mother Earth, for instance, was an adaptation of Native American indigenous belief. Speaking to an academic gathering after his return, Narita commented:

> What was interesting was that rather than just watch other groups perform, people got up on the stage together and joined in each other's songs and dances. They just gently joined in without distinction, and it was a really natural feeling to sing and dance together. It's because we all have things in common, on the level of feelings too.
>
> (Egami 1982: 304)

Ainu activists also improved their domestic alliances, seeking common cause with a variety of growing social movements within the framework of the language of universal human rights. Narita Tokuhei laid out the range of Ainu alliances at a Burakumin meeting in 1984.

> [We] are now editing our history, claiming our rights, understanding our identity, beginning to walk for ourselves. As we advance our work, we can gain solidarity with the Buraku Liberation movement, the movement of Koreans in Japan, the physically handicapped, the women's movement, and various citizens' movements. Some people have indicated that the anti-nuclear movement seen from an international viewpoint has close relation to us as a minority's problem.
>
> (Narita 1984: 138)

By their very nature, the narratives of Ainu nationhood and human rights struck at the heart of government attitudes and policies towards the Ainu. From a government perspective, however, the assimilation policies pursued since the 1880s had succeeded to the extent that the 'Ainu people' no longer existed in a Japan conceived of as essentially homogeneous. By the 1970s the discourse of Japanese uniqueness and homogeneity, exemplified by the *Nihonjinron* boom, had achieved near-hegemonic status among officials and mass society alike. The official view of the absence of minority populations in Japan was graphically illustrated by Japan's first report to the Human Rights Committee of the United Nations after ratification of the International Covenant on Civil and Political Rights in 1979. With regard to Article 27 of the Covenant, which concerns the rights of minorities, the Japanese government reported:

> The right of any person to enjoy his own culture, to profess and practise his religion or to use his own language is ensured under Japanese law. However, minorities of the kind mentioned in the Covenant do not exist in Japan.
>
> (Human Rights Committee, 12th Session, Document No. CCPR/C/10/Add.1, 14 November 1980)

This was not how Ainu leaders saw it. On the contrary, the idea of the Ainu nation was gaining strength among both radical and moderate Ainu leaders angered by such official denials of their existence. In the early 1980s this renewed sense of Ainu identity was to be translated into a renewed political agenda.

AINU SHINPŌ: A NEW LAW FOR A NEW NATION

While the strength of the Utari Kyōkai lay in its direct links to government and its role as a channel for the government funds provided by the Utari Taisaku, therein also lay its weakness. Dependent on the state for what power it possessed, and with a vested interest in maintaining the status quo, it could only challenge the established order with great caution. Moreover, a large proportion of its non-activist members were ultimately more interested in the practical benefits of increased welfare provisions than the possibility of Ainu nationhood. The movement for the establishment of the Ainu Minzoku ni kansuru Hōritsu (An), the Draft Legislation for the Ainu People (or *Ainu Shinpō* – New Ainu Law – as it is more commonly known), expressed the realization by the Association that the two aims, if properly balanced, were not necessarily incompatible. In essence, the New Law campaign was one of ethnopolitics – the aim of which was to increase Ainu access to the wealth of society, for the benefit of a constituency defined in terms of a distinct ethnic identity, and not merely by the extent of its relative deprivation. By emphasizing Ainu identity as indigenous, this was to be achieved through the restoration of some measure of rights to the resources once controlled by the Ainu in their ancestral homeland. Thus identity itself became a tactic in the political struggle.

Nevertheless, while expressed in terms of 'ethnic pride' and 'human rights', the New Law had its origins in welfare policy. By 1981, when the disappointing results of the first seven-year phase of the Utari Taisaku were considered, discontent over the policy among Utari Kyōkai members was increasing. Utari Kyōkai leaders felt that the abolition of the Protection Act and the enactment of a New Law would strengthen the welfare policy, but doubts were also being expressed as to whether welfare policies would ever enable the Ainu to catch up with Wajin standards of living (*Senkusha no Tsudoi* 40: 7; Honda 1989: 211–22). Paralleling these developments, the Dōwa Special Measures Law, which the Utari Taisaku closely resembled, was due to expire in 1982 and the debate over its extension had stimulated calls among Burakumin for the enactment of new legislation with a stronger human rights emphasis, the Buraku Kaihō Kihon Hō (Fundamental Law for Buraku Liberation). In May 1981 the Utari Kyōkai instructed its Special Committee to study proposals for new Ainu legislation. The senior Utari Kyōkai leaders, Nomura Giichi and Kaizawa Tadashi, were no longer the conservatives who had argued so strongly for assimilation twenty years previously. Self-perceptions had changed; most Ainu activists identified themselves on the basis of membership in the Ainu *minzoku*, the Ainu people or nation, for whose common good they were working. 'This resulted', said Nomura,

> in a demand for the guarantee of our rights as indigenous people, based on the fact that our ancestors have always inhabited Ainu Moshiri. Unless we made this the first issue the proposal would have no power of persuasion. We had to make clear our historical circumstances up to the present and make them recognize this. Therefore [the New Law] is not merely a demand for a strengthened Utari Taisaku system, but a demand for the guarantee of our rights in Ainu Moshiri from hundreds of generations of our ancestors. It is a basic policy in a completely different dimension.
> (Honda 1989: 213)

A draft proposal for new legislation was aired for comment and discussion at six regional meetings of branches of the Association. On 27 May 1984 the proposal was adopted unanimously by the General Assembly of the Utari Kyōkai.

Although 'indigenous rights' had not at this time been established, and indeed, are still not established, in international law (see Stavenhagen 1990: 93–119), such concepts had begun to be articulated by indigenous activists around the world. The most crucial of these rights, that in a sense encompasses all the others, is the right to self-determination, as stated in the United Nations Charter and other instruments such as the International Covenant on Civil and Political Rights, ratified by Japan in 1979. The Ainu New Law, however, stopped far short of calling for complete political independence. Instead, the draft concentrated on 'ethnic' and 'economic self-reliance' (*jiritsu*), basic human rights and the elimination of 'racial discrimination' (section 1), guaranteed political participation (section 2), and rights pertaining to education, language and culture (section 3). The welfare pedigree of the New Law was evident in sections on agriculture, forestry, commercial activities and employment; instead of demanding native title to land, the New Law was framed in terms of increased grants and assistance (section 4). The demand for a Self-Reliance Fund, moreover, has clear antecedents in Utari Kyōkai policy of the early 1970s. While clearly a law for a group conceived of in terms of a distinct language, culture and common history, no definition of who was or was not Ainu was offered.

Nevertheless, the adoption of the New Law by the General Assembly of the Utari Kyōkai marked the clear emergence of Ainu ethnopolitics. Despite differences of class, generation, gender, or political opinion, many Ainu had come to imagine themselves as linked by history and culture as an indigenous nation. And it was for the benefit of those who identified with this nation that Ainu leaders campaigned. With the continued campaign for the New Law and a strengthening in the understanding of indigenous rights, the symbols and rhetoric of Ainuness have become evermore prominent in Ainu politics since 1984. In their own eyes, and those of an increasing number of Wajin, the 'dying race' have become an 'indigenous people'.

THE AINU IN THE 1990s

Since the adoption of the Ainu Shinpō by the Utari Kyōkai in 1984, it has become the main item on the Ainu political agenda. Although a handful of Ainu leaders are against the Shinpō, most radicals and moderates alike can find something of value in its proposals. The response of the authorities, however, has been mixed. The Hokkaidō government reacted quickly to set up a deliberative body, including Ainu representatives, in October 1984. Known as the Utari Mondai Konwakai (Utari Affairs Council), this body concluded that the Protection Act had lost all validity. In March 1988 the Utari Mondai Konwakai sent a qualified recommendation of acceptance of the New Law to the Dōchō, expressing reservations over the constitutional legality of guaranteed Ainu political representation. The Hokkaidō Prefectural Assembly unanimously accepted the proposal in July, passing it to central government the following month. After taking well over a year to respond, Tokyo also set up a committee but progress was excruciatingly slow.

Ainu activism, however, received a major boost in 1986 when the widely reported remarks of then Prime Minister Nakasone Yasuhiro on the absence of 'racial' minorities and his own possible Ainu ancestry aroused much resentment. Since 1987, stimulated by the increasing involvement of Japanese civil rights groups in the human rights activities of the United Nations, Ainu leaders have also participated in international forums and converged with the worldwide indigenous peoples' movement and its language of indigenous rights. As a result, the cultural symbols of Ainu identity are increasingly visible whenever Ainu campaign to be recognized as a separate and indigenous people in their homeland, Ainu Moshiri. In this, the Ainu leadership have achieved partial success; internationally, at least, the Ainu are regarded as the indigenous people of Japan and were invited to participate in the opening ceremonies for the United Nations International Year of the World's Indigenous People in December 1992. At home, on the other hand, the Utari Kyōkai continues to maintain a close corporatist relationship with the government similar to a *gaikaku dantai* (George 1988) that both limits its power and contributes to severe internal divisions. Nevertheless, the domestic scene does show signs of change. With the political realignment of the early 1990s some progress has been made on the New Law, and in 1994 Kayano Shigeru entered the Upper House as the first Ainu elected to the Diet. But within Japan at large, the dominant narratives of national homogeneity and peaceful development in Hokkaidō remain secure enough to ensure that, despite growing Wajin support, the majority of the population still know little, and care even less, about Ainu demands.

But not all those people socially and officially categorized as Ainu are themselves convinced by the politics of Ainuness. It is clear that the articulation of Ainu identity at the individual level of everyday experience varies widely. For some it may be largely instrumental and related to the pursuit of individual goals like welfare payments, while for others it is mainly affective and an integral component of his or her sense of Self. Many undergo deeply felt experiences in which they 'discover' an Ainu identity that introduces new meaning into their lives. This chapter has concentrated on the activities of the leaders and activists who have most shaped Ainu politics, but there remains a largely silent majority in whose name they claim to act. While it would seem that many people of Ainu ancestry share the aims of the activists to a greater or lesser degree, particularly with regard to increased access to wealth, there are also many who do not belong to the Utari Kyōkai, continue to conceal their Ainu ancestry, and express no interest in Ainu culture as they aim to live out their lives as Japanese. There are also many in an intermediate position who have achieved real gains in economic terms, in many cases as a result of the general prosperity of the 1980s rather than Ainu activism or government policy. They are wary of the continued efforts of Ainu activists to stress 'racial' discrimination, marginalization and indigenous rights, or see welfare policies as perpetuating a 'beggar mentality' (*kojiki konjō*). Most of those who identify as Ainu are married to Wajin, and as their children increasingly leave the rural enclaves, and Hokkaido itself, to merge into a mainstream society which knows very little about the Ainu, how they will react to pressures to conform to social norms is at present an unanswered, and largely ignored, question. While for the foreseeable future at least, it would seem that Ainu ethnopolitics is here to stay, Ainu leaders have achieved real material and political gains, and Ainu culture is more vibrant than at any time since the early decades of the century, the health of the Ainu nation remains fragile.

APPENDIX: AINU POST-WAR POPULATION AND SOCIO-ECONOMIC INDICATORS

Table A2.1 Ainu population in Hokkaidō

Year	Population
1972	18,298
1979	24,160
1986	24,381
1993	23,830

Sources: Hokkaidō Minseibu, *Hokkaidō Utari Jittai Chōsa Hōkoku*, Sapporo: Hokkaidō Minseibu, 1972, p. 5 (hereafter *UJC*); Hokkaidō Minseibu, *Hokkaidō Utari Seikatsu Jittai Chōsa Hōkokusho*, Sapporo: Hokkaidō Minseibu, 1979 (p. 2), 1986 (p. 3), 1993 (p. 2), (hereafter *USJC*).

Table A2.2 Employment (over 15) by industrial sector (%)

	Primary		Secondary		Tertiary	
	Ainu	*All Hokkaidō*	*Ainu*	*All Hokkaidō*	*Ainu*	*All Hokkaidō*
1972	63.2	21.0	20.0	25.5	15.4	53.4
1979	43.0	9.4	30.3	26.1	26.6	64.3
1986	42.3	8.6	29.6	25.0	27.7	66.3
1993	34.6	6.9	32.4	22.8	32.0	69.9

Sources: UJC, p. 7; *USJC* 1979, p. 4; 1986, p. 6; 1993, p. 5.

Table A2.3 Households above minimum income threshold for local tax (%)

	1972	*1979*	*1986*	*1993*
Ainu	24.6	44.2	47.1	53.1
All Hokkaidō	65.7	76.4	71.5	–

Sources: UJC, p. 7; *USJC* 1979, p. 5; 1986, p. 7; 1993, p. 7.

Table A2.4 Numbers receiving welfare (per '000)

	1972	*1979*	*1986*	*1993*
Ainu	115.7	68.6	60.9	38.8
All Hokkaidō	17.5	19.6	21.9	16.4

Sources: UJC, p. 7; *USJC* 1979, p. 5; 1986, p. 8; 1993, p. 7.

Table A2.5 Educational advancement (%)

| | J. High to High School | | High School to College | |
	Ainu	All Hokkaidō	Ainu	All Hokkaidō
1972	41.6	78.2	–	–
1979	69.3	90.2	8.8	31.1
1986	78.4	94.0	8.1	27.4
1993	87.4	96.3	11.8	27.5

Sources: UJC, p. 15; *USJC* 1979, p. 7; 1986, p. 9; 1993, p. 9.

BIBLIOGRAPHY

Anderson, B. (1991) *Imagined Communities: Reflections on the Origin and Spread of Nationalism* (Revised edn), London: Verso.

Baba, Y. (1980) 'A study of minority–majority relations: the Ainu and Japanese in Hokkaidō', *Japan Interpreter* 13, 1: 60–92.

Befu, H. (1993) 'Nationalism and *Nihonjinron*', in H. Befu (ed.) *Cultural Nationalism in East Asia: Representation and Identity*, Berkeley: Institute of East Asian Studies, University of California.

Chikap, M. (1989) 'Long, cold winter: an Ainu childhood recalled', *AMPO* 20, 4 and 21, 1: 32–9.

Cornell, S. (1988) *The Return of the Native: American Indian Political Resurgence*, New York and Oxford: Oxford University Press.

Egami, N. (ed.) (1982) *Shimupojiumu: Ainu to Kodai Nihon* (Symposium: The Ainu and Ancient Japan), Tokyo: Shōgakkan.

Ekashi to Fuchi Henshū Iinkai (ed.) (1983) *Ekashi to Fuchi: Kita no Shima ni Ikita Hitobito no Kiroku* (The Ainu Elders: A Record of the People who Lived on the Northern Island), Sapporo: Sapporo Terebi Hōsō.

Emori, S. (1987) *Ainu no Rekishi: Hokkaidō no Hitobito (2)* (A History of the Ainu: the People of Hokkaidō [2]), Tokyo: Sanseidō.

George, A. (1988) 'Japanese interest group behavior: an institutional approach', in J.A.A. Stockwin (ed.) *Dynamic and Immobilist Politics in Japan*, London: Macmillan.

Hagiwara, T. (1965) 'Ainu Mondai Kenkyūkai ni tsuite' (On the Ainu Mondai Kenkyūkai), *Peure Utari* 3: 91–2.

Hatozawa, S. (1972) *Wakaki Ainu no Tamashii* (The Soul of a Young Ainu), Tokyo: Shinjinbutsu Ōraisha.

Hilger, I. (1967) 'Japan's "sky people": the vanishing Ainu', *National Geographic* 131, 2: 268–96.

Hokkaidō Minseibu (1972) *Shōwa 47-nen Hokkaidō Utari Jittai Chōsa Hōkoku* (Report of the 1972 Survey of Socio-economic Conditions of the Hokkaidō Ainu), Sapporo: Hokkaidō Minseibu.

—— (1979) *Shōwa 54-nen Hokkaidō Utari Seikatsu Jittai Chōsa Hōkokusho* (Report of the 1979 Survey of Socio-economic Conditions of the Hokkaidō Ainu), Sapporo: Hokkaidō Minseibu.

—— (1986) *Shōwa 61-nen Hokkaidō Utari Seikatsu Jittai Chōsa Hōkokusho* (Report of the 1986 Survey of Socio-economic Conditions of the Hokkaidō Ainu), Sapporo: Hokkaidō Minseibu.

—— (1993) *Heisei 5-nen Hokkaidō Utari Seikatsu Jittai Chōsa Hōkokusho* (Report on the 1993 Survey of Socio-economic Conditions of the Hokkaidō Ainu), Sapporo: Hokkaidō Minseibu.

Hokkaidō Utari Kyōkai (ed.) (1990) *Ainu Shi Shiryō Hen 3: Kingendai Shiryō 1* (Materials on Ainu History 3: Modern and Contemporary Materials 1), Sapporo: Hokkaidō Utari Kyōkai.

Honda, K. (1989) *Hinkon naru Seishin: B Shū* (The Impoverished Spirit: Collection B), Tokyo: Asahi Shinbunsha.

Howell, D. (1994) 'Ainu ethnicity and the boundaries of the early modern Japanese state', *Past and Present* 142: 69–93.

Kaiho, M. (1979) *Kinsei no Hokkaidō* (Early Modern Hokkaidō), Tokyo: Kyōikusha.

Kaizawa, M. (1972) 'Ainu no Chi sae Usumereba' (If We Only Dilute Ainu Blood), in 'Nihonjin ni yoru Jinshu Sabetsu Higaisha Hyakunin no Shōgen' (The Statements of One Hundred Victims of Racial Discrimination by Japanese), Special Feature, *Ushio* 150: 144–5.

Kayano, S. (1994) *Our Land was a Forest: An Ainu Memoir*, Boulder: Westview Press.

Matsumae-chō Shi Henshū Shitsu (ed.) (1984) *Matsumae-chō Shi* (History of Matsumae Town), vol. 1, Matsumae: Matsumae-chō.

Matsuura, T. [1860] (1969) 'Kinsei Ezo Jinbutsu Shi' (Stories of Recent Ezo Personalities), in S. Takakura (ed.) *Nihon Shomin Seikatsu Shiryō Shūsei. Vol. 4: Hoppō Hen* (Collected Materials on the Life of the Common People of Japan. Vol. 4: The Northern Regions), Tokyo: Sanichi Shobō.

Miyoshi, F. (1971) 'Ainu ga Horobiru to Iu no ka' (Can you say the Ainu are dying?), in Asahikawa Jinken Yōgo Iin Rengōkai (ed.) *Kotan no Konseki* (Remains of the Kotan), Asahikawa: Asahikawa Jinken Yōgo Iin Rengōkai.

Munro, N.G. (1963) *Ainu: Creed and Cult*, London: Routledge and Kegan Paul.

Narita, T. (1972) 'Ainu Mondai ni Omou' (Thoughts on the Ainu Problem), *Hoppō Bungei* 5, 2: 34–42.

—— (1984) 'Discrimination against Ainus and the International Covenant on the Elimination of All Forms of Racial Discrimination', in Buraku Kaihō Kenkyūsho (ed.) *The United Nations, Japan and Human Rights: To Commemorate the 35th Anniversary of the Universal Declaration of Human Rights*, Osaka: Kaihō Shuppansha.

Narita, T. and Hanazaki, K. (ed.) (1985) *Kindaika no naka no Ainu Sabetsu no Kōzō* (The Structure of Ainu Discrimination within Modernization), Tokyo: Akaishi Shoten.

Nihon Kyōsantō Chūō Iinkai (1974) 'Ainu-kei Jūmin no Kenri no Hoshō to Sabetsu no Issō' (Securing the Rights of Residents of Ainu Descent and the Elimination of Discrimination), in 'Sangiin Senkyo de no Sōten to Nihon Kyōsantō no Yon Dai Kihon Seisaku' (Issues in the Upper House Election and the Four Main Basic Policies of the JCP), *Zenei*, Special Extra Edition, August 1974, pp. 57–8.

Nihon Shakaitō Seisaku Shingikai Ainu Minzoku Mondai Tokubetsu Iinkai (1974) 'Ainu Minzoku Seisaku' (Policy on the Ainu People), *Gekkan Shakaitō* 207: 223–6.

Nogami, F. (Pon Fuchi) (1992) *Ureshipa Moshiri e no Michi* (The Road to Ureshipa Moshiri), Revised edn, Tokyo: Shinsensha.

Ogawa, M. (1993) 'The Hokkaidō Former Aborigines Protection Act and Assimilatory Education', in N. Loos and T. Osanai (eds) *Indigenous Minorities and Education: Australian and Japanese Perspectives of their Indigenous Peoples, the Ainu, Aborigines and Torres Straits Islanders*, Tokyo: Sanyūsha.

Ōta, R. (1973) *Ainu Kakumei Ron: Yukara no Sekai e no 'Taikyaku'* (On Ainu Revolution: 'Retreat' to the World of Yukara), Tokyo: Ainu Moshiri Jōhōbu [Shinsensha].

Peng, F.C.C., and Geiser, P. (1977) *The Ainu: The Past in the Present*, Hiroshima: Hiroshima Bunka Hyōron.

Philippi, D.L. (1979) *Songs of Gods, Songs of Humans: The Epic Tradition of the Ainu*. Tokyo: Tokyo University Press.

Pon Fuchi (see Nogami, F.).

Sakurai, K. (1967) *Ainu Hishi* (Secret History of the Ainu), Tokyo: Kadokawa Shoten.

Sala, G.C. (1975) 'Protest and the Ainu of Hokkaido', *Japan Interpreter* 10, 1: 44–65.

—— (1976) 'Terrorism and Ainu people of Hokkaido', *Mainichi Daily News*, 8 May 1976.

Sapporo Hōmukyoku (n.d.) Log of Ainu-related Incidents, Unpublished report.

Shinya, G. (1977) *Ainu Minzoku Teikō Shi* (A History of Ainu Resistance), Revised edn, Tokyo: Sanichi Shobō.

—— (1979) *Kotan ni Ikiru Hitobito* (People Who Live in the Kotan), Tokyo: Sanichi Shobō.

Siddle, R. (1993) 'Academic exploitation and indigenous resistance: the case of the Ainu', in N. Loos and T. Osanai (eds) *Indigenous Minorities and Education: Australian and Japanese Perspectives of their Indigenous Peoples, the Ainu, Aborigines and Torres Straits Islanders*, Tokyo: Sanyūsha.

—— (1995) 'With shining eyes: Ainu social and political movements 1918–1937', *Asian Cultural Studies* 21: 1–20.

Stavenhagen R. (1990) *The Ethnic Question: Conflicts, Developments, and Human Rights*, Tokyo: United Nations University Press.

Suga, K. (1976) *Kono Tamashii Utari ni: Hatozawa Samio no Sekai* (Pass this Spirit to the Ainu: The World of Hatozawa Samio), Tokyo: Eikō Shuppansha.

Sugawara, K. (1966) *Gendai no Ainu: Minzoku Idō no Roman* (The Modern Ainu: Drama of a People in Motion), Tokyo: Genbunsha.

Takakura, S. (1960) 'The Ainu of northern Japan: a study in conquest and acculturation' (trans. J. Harrison), *Transactions of the American Philosophical Society* 50, 4.

—— (1972) *Ainu Seisaku Shi: Shinpan* (A History of Ainu Policy: New Edition), Tokyo: Sanichi Shobō.

Teshima, T. (1990) 'Utari Taisaku o meguru Jakkan no Yobiteki Kōsatsu' (Some Preliminary Considerations on the Utari Countermeasures), *Buraku Kaihō Kenkyū* 73: 87–109.

Utagawa, H. (1988) *Ainu Bunka Seiritsu Shi* (History of the Formation of Ainu Culture), Sapporo: Hokkaidō Shuppan Kikaku Sentā.

Watanabe, H. (1973) *The Ainu Ecosystem*, Seattle and London: University of Washington Press.

Weiner, M. (1994) *Race and Migration in Imperial Japan*, London and New York: Routledge.

Yoshino, K. (1992) *Cultural Nationalism in Contemporary Japan: A Sociological Enquiry*, London and New York: Routledge.

Yūki, S. (1980) *Ainu Sengen* (The Ainu Manifesto), Tokyo: Sanichi Shobō.

3 Burakumin in contemporary Japan

Ian Neary

INTRODUCTION

One man who married a Burakumin woman about twelve years ago describes his experience as follows,

> My parents said I could not have any relationship with them. I have two sons aged eleven and nine. My father met the first one once when he was a baby and the second time a few months ago by accident at the hospital when we were visiting my grandmother.
>
> (*Daily Telegraph*, 24 May 1994)

The two families have lived eight miles apart from each other for more than a decade with virtually no contact. His father refuses to relent even though his Burakumin daughter-in-law died of cancer two years ago. The shame of untouchable grandchildren appears too much for him.

That discrimination exists against Burakumin in contemporary Japan cannot be denied. Some Japanese may genuinely be unaware of its extent, especially those who live in the Kantō area or places to the north.[1] There is also some disagreement about the significance of the prejudice and discrimination that remains. Even the most radical Buraku activists would accept that over the last thirty years their situation has improved. Discrimination is no longer as blatant; living conditions in the Buraku communities are no longer as obviously impoverished as hitherto. Such improvements lead some to argue that the 'problem' has been solved although others would suggest that discrimination is simply taking on new, less obvious, forms and that research methodology needs to be refined to enable it to pick up the reality of the contemporary situation.

The end of the Cold War removed the threat of massive nuclear destruction but created a new set of uncertainties. These tectonic shifts at the international level rocked the foundations of politics within Japan. One manifestation of this was the Liberal-Democratic Party's loss of its monopoly of political power in 1993, creating the possibility of rapid change for the first time in several decades. This has not only affected the formal political structures; many other institutions are being influenced by the fall-out from change within the central political institutions and the Buraku liberation movement is no exception to this. In the early 1990s the Buraku Liberation League (BLL) announced some fundamental changes in its approach and launched a debate on the movement's 'Third Era'. In common with many social and political institutions in Japan in the mid-1990s, the BLL is seeking new definitions for its role with society and its relationships with the outside world.

With this rather fluid contemporary setting in mind, this chapter will provide an overview of the position of Burakumin in twentieth-century Japan. However, we will need to start with a brief account of the origins of this status discrimination and its evolution up to the mid-nineteenth century. The bulk of the article addresses how, in the twentieth century, Buraku communities have developed within capitalist society and how they have organized themselves to oppose the discrimination they have encountered. Many of the problems which have taxed the movement's post-war leadership were first encountered by their pre-war counterparts in the Suiheisha. The re-emergence of the movement in the freer post-war atmosphere and the early debates over theory and strategy took place at the same time as the mainstream politicians were jostling for positions in the emerging political structure that was to last until the 1990s. It is no coincidence that the Buraku Liberation League was formed in 1955, the year of the re-unification of the Japan Socialist Party (JSP) and the formation of the Liberal-Democratic Party (LDP). And, just as there has been considerable debate and uncertainty beneath the apparently stable pattern of party politics, so within the BLL too there has been acrimonious argument. In the third section (pp. 59–63) we will trace some elements of this discussion.

During the 1960s Japan became committed to a set of policies which ostensibly aimed to 'solve' the Buraku 'problem' once and for all. The Ten-year Plan, made possible by the Special Measures Legislation (SML) of 1969, encouraged and enabled central and local government to allocate substantial resources to the elimination of the worst aspects of disadvantaged status and prejudice. After more than ten years of rapid economic growth the gap between the living standards in the Buraku and mainstream society was becoming

more obvious, but, at the same time, rapid economic growth generated revenue for central and local government enabling them to
afford quite ambitious improvement programmes. The fourth section
(pp. 64–9) will consider the content of these programmes and describe
the impact they had on Buraku communities and the liberation
movement. But the SML did not make discrimination itself illegal
and there is evidence that, particularly in the areas of marriage and
employment, prejudice remains active. The campaigns of the 1980s
for an unequivocal statutory prohibition of discrimination took
place against a background of increasingly bitter disputes among
movement activists about the appropriate way forward. In the fifth
and final section (pp. 69–77) I will review the situation as of the
mid-1990s. At the same time as the LDP lost power the BLL too
announced that it was seeking an end to the 1955 system and that
the second half of the 1990s would see the start of a new era. I will
consider some of these proposals to guide the movement into the
twenty-first century in the context of recent data about Buraku conditions. But first to explain the background to the Buraku Mondai
in the twentieth century.

ORIGINS

The amount of scholarly work on pre-modern Buraku history is overwhelming. Many prefectures have associations of amateur and professional historians which regularly produce journals and
monographs. One commonly finds in these writings discussion of
development of Buraku communities in their region from the time
of their formation until the nineteenth century outlining the prejudice
and formalized discrimination they faced. Few Japanese academics
have tried to summarize this research and for the outsider the task is
fraught with difficulty. One thing that is abundantly clear is that
there was great variation between different parts of the country.
Despite the fact that the strict social distinction between the four
main classes of samurai, peasant, artisan and merchant was laid
down in decrees issued by the central government, how local regimes
dealt with the marginal groups which fell outside these four categories was largely left to their discretion. Even the names used to
describe these groups varied greatly from one area to another with
eta, hinin, kawata and *chasen* being only the most common. (This
and subsequent paragraphs are based on Neary 1989: Chapter 1.)
    One approach to the problem of Buraku origins is to begin with
what they are not. Early this century there was the common belief

that Burakumin were racially distinct from mainstream Japanese; that they were the descendants of slaves from the ancient period, descendants of Koreans, or even descendants of the lost tribes of Israel that somehow ended up in Japan. There is no historical foundation for these ideas and they were publicly repudiated in the 1965 Deliberative Council Report (see pp. 62–3).

During the 1970s a great deal of emphasis was placed on the policies adopted in the Tokugawa era and how they had virtually created Buraku communities where none or few had existed before. This stress on their relatively recent formation served a number of purposes. Firstly, it reinforced the idea that Burakumin were unequivocally Japanese. Secondly, it suggested that, as a relatively recent social formation, the possibility of eliminating prejudice and discrimination – and indeed the communities themselves – in the near future was not a utopian ideal. Thirdly, it provided a clear target for Burakumin protest. Ultimate responsibility for discrimination could be allocated to the Tokugawa regime and the inability or unwillingness of its successors in government to deal with the problem.

Serious academic interest in Buraku history really only dates from the 1970s and the evidence generated at this time went a long way towards supporting the above interpretation. It was discovered, for example, that many Buraku communities could only be traced back to the mid-seventeenth century. Moreover, in contrast to the rather simplistic picture of class boundaries being rigidly drawn at the start of the seventeenth century only to be dismantled in the 1870s, it became clear that the status hierarchy was gradually built up in the seventeenth century and that the boundaries of control over the outcast groups were being almost continually re-drawn over the 250 years of Tokugawa control. This was a dynamic and decentralized system of control that responded to the demands, protests and evasions of its subjects. The outcome of the process was that whereas in the seventeenth century outcast communities were relatively small, subject to only social discrimination and relatively few in number, by the nineteenth they were often large, numerous, at least in western Japan, and subject to formally sanctioned discrimination and prejudice.

Several social processes contributed to this. Firstly, in the period 1710–30 a series of edicts were issued by the central government in Edo that rigidified many aspects of the status system including the definitions of outcast status. Whereas previously some escape from marginal status was possible, now it became impossible to be absorbed into the mainstream. The stricter regulations enforced in the areas directly under Tokugawa control were emulated by many of the local regimes. Soon after this, in the 1730s, there was a major famine in the west of Japan that reduced the size of the peasantry by as much as one third. A typical outcast occupation had been leather-making which was strategically important at a time when much of a soldier's armour was based on leather. Each castle town had its tanners and leather-making community, but its members were considered impure because of their contact with dead animals and they were avoided by the majority. Under the conditions of peace provided by the Tokugawa government, demand for these leather goods dropped and this resulted in an underemployed urban community. However, following the decimation of the peasantry in the 1730s famine, many of the rulers of western Japan urgently sought out labour so that their land could be farmed as productively as possible and their revenue restored. Moreover, as taxes were paid by the village as a unit rather than by individuals or families, many village leaders too were eager to recruit outsiders to farm the now untilled land. So it was that soon after their outcast status had been clearly defined many outcasts moved into rural areas to take up farming, often on the least productive land.

As outcasts were not considered fully human, they were not included in the periodic censuses that took place from 1720 onwards. These demonstrate that, overall, the population of Japan increased hardly at all in the period 1720–1850. Meanwhile, it is estimated that the outcast population may have increased by as much as three times and there are examples of communities which grew more than sixfold. In part this was because bad luck or bad behaviour would force people to leave their homes and they would end up living in the outcast areas. Even those who moved to work the land in the seventeenth century, becoming in many ways indistinguishable from peasants, often maintained their connection with leather-making or some handicraft trade which made them less vulnerable to periodic crop failures. Their access to meat also made them better able to sustain themselves following poor harvests. Finally, it is suggested that they were less likely than the majority to restrict the size of their families by selective neo-natal infanticide.

Whatever the reason, the outcast population which had been scattered – fairly small and not looming large in the public mind – had by the mid-nineteenth century become large, visible communities tightly regulated to segregate them from the majority and regarded with contempt by most of them. From the 1720s increasingly detailed sets of regulations were imposed on most aspects of their lives. Their content varied from place to place but usually Burakumin were only permitted certain types of clothing to ensure they were clearly visible; they were often not allowed to enter towns at night and banned from entering religious sites. There were even rules controlling the size of their houses and which forbade their windows from facing the road. Efforts by members of these communities to ignore or evade regulation were rewarded by evermore detailed sets of rules. The result was that segregation and discrimination was at its peak shortly before the start of the Meiji era.

None of the evidence which supports this overall picture has been discredited, but there have recently been some suggestions that there should be a change in emphasis. For example, it is clear that there are some Buraku communities whose history can be traced back well before the foundation of the Tokugawa regime to the fourteenth or fifteenth centuries, suggesting that the 'regulation origin thesis' does not completely explain the origins of all the Buraku communities. Then there is the need to clarify how the discrimination of the pre-Tokugawa period against those in leather (*kawata*) and handicrafts trades was translated into the seventeenth and eighteenth centuries: not all of the *kawata* of the earlier period became outcasts in the Edo era. Whereas before 1600 the emphasis was on occupation afterwards it was on bloodline, but why this should be has not been clearly explained. Moreover, many have pointed out that it is too simplistic to blame an individual or even a set of individuals for developments in a social system that were the results of a complex set of political and social forces. Alongside the debate about the future of the BLL there have grown demands that the communities' history also needs re-evaluation (Watanabe 1993: 4).

LIBERATION AND ORGANIZATION

The process of dismantling the Tokugawa state included the abolition of all the regulations that had restricted the *eta, hinin*. However, whereas in Japanese society at large consciousness of one's former feudal status quickly became irrelevant, prejudice and discrimination against the former outcasts continued. They remained on the margins of society and were largely excluded from the development of the capitalist economy. Their attempts to take advantage of the new possibilities, for example by establishing modern shoe factories, usually failed. Where they did become involved in the process of industrialization, as in the development of the coal industry in northern

Kyushu, they were to be found doing the dirtiest jobs usually in small mines with poor capital investment.

Until recently it was the continuity between the Edo and Meiji periods which was emphasized and the lack of positive effort by the Meiji regime to help Burakumin to slough off the disadvantage accumulated over the previous centuries which was the object of criticism. Now it is argued that the Liberation Edict of August 1871 should be regarded as the start of a new phase in Buraku history, much as the start of the Tokugawa era had been. While Burakumin did not benefit from the Meiji reforms, it is difficult to argue that they were impoverished by feudal restriction *and* that the ending of these restrictions also made them poor. Rather the 'revisionists' are pointing out that the Buraku communities which grew in the second half of the nineteenth century were in urban areas such as Osaka or Tokyo or newly developing regions such as the north of Kyushu, not the Buraku which had grown in the Edo era. This suggests that there were different social processes now at work. There is a clear change from institutionalized discrimination of the Tokugawa period to social discrimination of the Meiji era, although this is not to deny that there were also some common features. Discrimination in marriage, education and employment which the young Burakumin encountered in the later nineteenth century simply had not been possible in the highly regulated feudal period. They should be regarded as new phenomena. In this connection we should note a document of 1918 which describes Buraku discrimination as being based not on custom but because they are unhygienic, unschooled and poor. In other words unable to fulfil the duties of the citizen of the Japanese empire: to serve in the army, to be educated and to pay taxes; indicating a new rationalization for discrimination had developed within the discourse of modernization and the creation of the Imperial state structure (Watanabe 1993: 10–12).

Burakumin were not passive participants in this process and, freed from the feudal regulation, they took part in the resistance to the creation of the emperor-centred Meiji state. Thus, for example, we find that as the liberal ideas of the Jiyūminken Undō percolated down to the educated peasantry in the 1870s, there were discussion groups formed in Buraku communities to study these ideas. After a brief blossoming in the 1870s these groups fade away only to revive as an active force in the 1890s when they begin to consider ways in which discrimination could be overcome. One imagines that this was in part a response to a realization of the discrepancy between the notions of the equality of the citizen's obligation to the emperor as expressed in the Meiji Constitution and the reality of the special disadvantages faced by younger, educated Burakumin. Groups were formed in areas across the west of Japan and there developed a realization that there was a set of problems that were being faced by similar groups across the country. This was the necessary precursor to a desire to create a national movement. Indeed in 1903 the first national conference of Burakumin, the DaiNippon Dōhō Yūwakai (Greater Japan Fraternal Conciliation Society) was held in Osaka and was attended by 300 Burakumin from all over Japan, but it failed to develop into a sustained organization. One characteristic feature, one weakness perhaps, of these early groups was that they accepted the dominant idea that there was something wrong with them that had to be put right before they would be accepted by society at large.

Political activity independent of the organs of state became difficult after 1905 as the Meiji oligarchs created a network of government machinery which aimed at restricting the influence of 'dangerous' liberal and socialist ideas. One aspect of this which affected the Buraku communities was a set of initiatives which were launched in many prefectures to encourage the formation of 'Yūwa' (conciliation) discussion groups within the Buraku which were always under the watchful eye of a trusted member of the community such as a schoolteacher. There were even some places where local government bodies provided small amounts of money to relieve Buraku poverty. As measures designed to inhibit Buraku activism they were partially successful. Surveys taken after the Rice Riots of 1918 found that the Buraku communities where such a supervised group existed had not become involved in violent activity. On the other hand, in the medium term the existence of these groups enabled the relatively rapid growth of the Suiheisha when it was launched in 1922. They did so in two ways. Firstly, they encouraged younger Burakumin to consider ways in which their situation could be improved such that when the Suiheisha declaration was launched there was a ready audience for its ideas. Secondly, at an organizational level, many of the discussion groups were in communication with others in their area forming a network along which the Suiheisha's ideas could quickly flow. In some areas these groups changed, virtually overnight, from being Yūwa to Suiheisha groups.

The Suiheisha was formed in the social context of the rapid increase in activity of tenants' groups and labour unions and the related ideological context of the rapid spread of socialist ideas which followed the revolution in Russia. Intellectuals were taking a

serious interest in social problems, including those of the Burakumin.
For example, in 1922 Sano Manabu, soon to take a leading role in
the creation of Japan's Communist Party, wrote *Tokushū Buraku
Kaihōron* (On the Liberation of Burakumin). This was a great encouragement to the young Burakumin of the Kyoto region to push ahead
with their plans to create their own independent movement for
Buraku emancipation. The Declaration of the Suiheisha is worth
quoting in full as it is still a point of reference for Burakumin
activists.

> Burakumin throughout the country, unite!
> Long suffering brothers:
> In the past half century, reform undertakings on our behalf by so
> many people and in such various ways have failed to yield any
> favourable results. This failure was a divine punishment we
> incurred for permitting others as well as ourselves to debase our
> own human dignity. Previous movements, though seemingly moti-
> vated by compassion, actually corrupted many of our brothers. In
> the light of this it is necessary for us to organize a new collective
> movement through which we shall emancipate ourselves by our
> own effort and self-respect.
>
> Brothers – our ancestors sought after and practised liberty and
> equality. But they became the victims of a base, contemptible
> system developed by the ruling class. They became the manly mar-
> tyrs of industry. As a reward for their work in skinning animals,
> they were flayed alive. As a recompense for tearing out the hearts
> of animals, their own warm, human hearts were ripped out. They
> were spat on with the spittle of ridicule. Yet all through these
> cursed nightmares, their blood still proud to be human, did not
> dry up. Yes! Now we have come to the age when man pulsing
> with this blood, is trying to become divine. The time has come
> for the victims of discrimination to hurl back labels of derision.
> The time has come when the martyr's crown of thorns shall be
> blessed. The time has come when we can be proud of being *eta*.
>
> We must never again insult our ancestors and profane our
> humanity by slavish words and cowardly acts. Knowing well the
> coldness and contempt of ordinary human society, we seek and
> will be profoundly thankful for the warmth and light of true
> humanity.
>
> From this, the Suiheisha is born. Let there now be warmth and
> light among men.

(DeVos and Wagatsuma 1973: 44)

As is the case with most mass movements, after the first few years of enthusiastic activity there was a lull and debates erupted about the most appropriate theory and tactics to guide the movement forward. And, like most social movements of the time, there were three main factions – the anarchists, the Bolsheviks and the social democrats – each of which had a different diagnosis of the movement's ills and a different solution for its problems. Moreover the government attempted to regain control over the Buraku communities by creating a rival, the Yūwa movement, which offered an alternative national leadership structure and a solution to the Buraku problem which lay within the perfection of the emperor-centred state system.

Despite the often fierce internal debate and external pressure, the Suiheisha outlived all of its contemporary social movement organizations. It remained active until 1937/8 and only finally capitulated to demands that it dissolve in 1942. Two factors enabled it to stand out so long against the pressure to conform. Firstly, Buraku leaders were determined to 'emancipate ourselves by our own efforts and self-respect'. Experience showed that they could not rely on the efforts of others whether they be communists or government officials. They had rejected the idea that the problem was something to do with their inadequacy and instead argued that it was social attitudes that needed changing not Burakumin. Secondly, the development of the *kyūdan tōsō* – denunciation struggle – became for the Suiheisha what the strike was to the labour union and the rent-strike was for the tenants' union; their weapon in the class struggle or at least in the battle against discrimination. At one level the aim was simply to encourage Burakumin to protest about discrimination when they encountered it rather than accepting it as an inevitable part of their lives. In the first few years of the movement's existence the tactic was adopted enthusiastically, if indiscriminately, and activists attacked in word and deed all who were regarded as discriminators. Fights broke out which sometimes developed into more extensive violence. However, as the movement developed, the leadership was able to be more selective about which campaigns to pursue and they tried to use the denunciation process so it had an educative impact both on the discriminator and the wider society.

POST-WAR RECREATION OF THE MOVEMENT

Matsumoto Jiichiro emerged as leader of the Suiheisha in the late 1920s, and in the 1936 General Election he was elected to the Diet as a member of the Social Masses Party. Though the Suiheisha ceased to exist during the Pacific War, Matsumoto remained in the Diet and was a central figure in the events which led to the recreation of the movement after defeat. Only days after the surrender was announced, former Suiheisha leaders met to consider how the Suiheisha might be reformed (Asada 1969: 171). In 1946 the National Committee for Buraku Liberation (NCBL) was launched as a successor to the Suiheisha with the support of most of the left-of-centre parties. Both the Communist and Socialist parties included support for Buraku liberation in their first post-war manifestos and nine Burakumin were elected to the Diet in the first election under the new constitution, seven of them as members of the JSP, one of whom was Matsumoto. However, it proved difficult during the occupation to arouse much enthusiasm for the project of Buraku liberation. This can be explained at one level by the fact that most people needed to spend so much time and effort in maintaining a bare existence that they had little time for political activity. Moreover the reform of Japan instigated by Supreme Command Allied Powers (SCAP), which included guarantees of human rights in the constitution, land reform and education reform, suggested that the prospects for a thorough democratization of Japan were good and that this would include the elimination of Buraku discrimination. Indeed the Communist Party endorsed this view. Even before the war they had argued that the Buraku communities were a remnant of the feudal era that had persisted because of the incomplete nature of the bourgeois revolution of the nineteenth century. It seemed to them that the US occupation with its dismantling of the aristocracy, dispossession of the large landowners and similar reforms was completing that process so that Buraku discrimination would naturally disappear.

In 1951, just before the occupation ended, an incident occurred which demonstrated that segregation was being recreated in postwar Japan and that there was an important role for the new Buraku movement. In October of that year a pulp magazine, *All Romance*, published a story entitled *Tokushū Buraku* set in a Buraku community in Kyoto. It portrayed a 'hell on earth full of black marketeers, illegal sake brewing, crime, violence, and sex' (Wagatsuma 1976: 352–8). It turned out that the author of the story was employed in the Kyoto city offices and, as the word spread, a campaign was mounted which criticized not only the publisher of the story but also the Kyoto authorities. The incident became a hook on which the

NCBL could hang a campaign about the continuing poverty and deprivation of Buraku in the city. They demanded that:

> officials in charge of various administrative districts mark on a map all sections of the city lacking public water supplies, sewage disposal, fire hydrants and all areas with inadequate housing, high rates of TB, trachoma and other public health problems, high absenteeism in the schools and high concentrations of families on relief. The result was a vivid demonstration of Burakumin problems since the marked areas fell entirely within the eighteen Buraku of Kyoto and its environs.
>
> (DeVos and Wagatsuma 1973: 76)

Embarrassed by these findings the Kyoto city government began a programme of improvements to the environment ensuring an adequate water supply and sewage system and starting rehousing schemes and building nursery schools. During the 1950s NCBL groups, particularly in the larger cities, launched similar 'administrative struggles' against local government in which instances of discrimination were used as the basis for campaigns which came to include demands for the provision of improved local facilities. Possibly because the movement was seen to be able to deliver real improvements, it attracted more support and in 1955 it was relaunched as the Buraku Kaihō Dōmei (Buraku Liberation League – BLL) a name which was thought to have more mass appeal than the 'vanguardist' national committee (Asada 1969: 269).

The movement's growing significance prompted the political parties to take the issue more seriously. In 1957 a nineteen-man JSP committee deliberated for over eight months before producing a document which argued that, although complete Buraku liberation was only possible through the creation of a socialist society, even within the capitalist structure it was possible and necessary to improve the Burakumin living environment and their life chances. They called for the creation of a special commission within the Prime Minister's office with a remit to devise a comprehensive policy (Neary 1986: 560–1; Morooka 1981–2, Vol. 2: 383–7, 446–50). Shortly after this the JCP produced its own Buraku policy which linked the issue more closely to the reactionary rule of US imperialism and Japanese monopoly capitalism. They rejected the view that there was anything special about the problems faced by Burakumin workers. Their poverty was just one product of the contradictions within capitalist society and therefore the main target of the Buraku struggle should be the overthrow of the class system rather than making special demands on that system which would weaken their solidarity with the rest of the working-class movement (Morooka 1981–2, Vol. 2: 392–5).

Around this time there was an unusually wide interest in the problem. Over the winter of 1957/8 the topic was discussed in newspapers and magazines, on radio and television. The BLL began to argue that the fragmented improvements funded by local government would never be sufficient to have a significant impact on attitudes or living conditions; a national strategy was required to co-ordinate policies and to provide new resources. The JSP and its labour union supporters backed these proposals. Even the then Prime Minister, Kishi Nobusuke, expressed his view that the continued existence of discrimination against Burakumin was 'regrettable' and he undertook to introduce appropriate policies (Morooka 1981–2, Vol. 3: 297–8; speech made on 11 March 1958). Nothing came directly from this promise, but in October of that year the LDP set up a committee – the Dōwa Policy Committee – to consider the problem and in May 1959 it suggested that 'model' Buraku be provided with central government funds.[2] This was strongly criticized by the opposition as 'tokenism' but the late 1950s did witness an increase in the provision of central government funds (see Table 3.1).

The LDP had always resisted demands from the JSP for a special commission, but in March 1960, at the height of the Ampo struggles in which a broad front of left-wing groups were campaigning against the renewal of the Security Treaty with the USA, the chairman of the LDP Dōwa Policy Committee proposed to the Cabinet that such a commission of inquiry be established. The bill was passed in August 1960. It is tempting to be sceptical about the LDP's motives. The government was in the middle of the most serious political crisis since the occupation, it had been forced to drop several key pieces of legislation over the previous five years because of mass protest

Table 3.1 Central government spending on Dōwa projects, 1958–61

Year	¥ (m)	Year	¥ (m)
1958	52	1960	580
1959	140	1961	1,260

Source: Asada 1969: 314

and it was only just able to get Diet approval for the revised security treaty with the USA. Moreover, two months after the announcement of the plan to create a special commission, the Nihon Dōwakai was created with Yamamoto Masao, formerly an administrator of the Yūwa programme, as its head. In 1961 the government announced its decision to cease to work with the BLL and to co-operate with the Dōwakai henceforth. Moreover, despite the rapid passage of the Act in 1960, it was not until November 1961, not long before the time limit specified in the Act, that a commission of inquiry was actually appointed. All of this suggests a strategy designed to split and weaken the BLL rather than a determination to eliminate Buraku discrimination.

Nevertheless the report that the Commission of Inquiry on Dōwa Policy published in August 1965 came very close to what the BLL was asking for. It divides into two parts. The first section gives a brief history of the problem in which it made three very important points. Firstly, that there is no substance to the widely held view that Burakumin are in some way racially or ethnically different from mainstream Japanese. This is something that was particularly important, given the tidal wave of literature emphasizing Japan's uniqueness that was to sweep across the country over the next thirty years. Secondly, it did not accept that the problem was a remnant of feudalism that would disappear with the development of advanced capitalism. And, thirdly, it also rejects the view that the best solution is to ignore the Buraku issue since discussion or special action only serve to perpetuate a problem which, if ignored, would disappear. A solution to the problem, it argued, must be based on knowledge not ignorance. The second section is a survey of the current state of Buraku communities which used both existing data and some especially commissioned research. The report portrays ghetto-like communities located on land liable to flooding where the quality of the housing stock was poor and often totally lacking in such public services as sewers, tap water, streetlights and fire protection. Standards of educational achievement were well below the national average, few Burakumin were employed in major firms or had 'lifetime' employment and there was a very high degree of dependence on unemployment benefit. The report concluded that it was the duty of the state to take steps to eliminate some of these problems beginning with the introduction of legislation which would enable government to address the social deprivation described in the report (Harada and Uesugi 1981: 252–9; Neary 1986: 563–4; Upham 1987: 84–6).

IMPLEMENTATION OF THE SPECIAL MEASURES
LEGISLATION: 1965–1993

In 1969 the main recommendations of the report were written into the Dōwa Taisaku Tokubetsu Sochihō (Law on Special Measures for Dōwa Projects – SML). The special measures were initially devised in the form of a Ten-year Plan which can be divided into seven categories of Dōwa policies: for the physical environment; social welfare and public health; promotion of agriculture forestry and fisheries; promotion of small and medium-sized enterprises; employment protection and social security; education; human rights protection. However the Act was vague about who was to receive these benefits. It talks of the residents of 'target areas', 'where the security and improvement of living environment has been obstructed for historical and social reasons' (Upham 1980: 46). However, by the late 1960s many Buraku communities also had residents who were poor Japanese whose ancestors had not been outcasts or, especially in the Osaka area, who were Koreans. Should these non-Burakumin benefit from the programmes? The JCP view was that they should, but the BLL argued strongly that they should not. Moreover the BLL was anxious that the various programmes might be used by central or local government to pacify Buraku radicalism and put them under some kind of administrative control. There was also a fear that if the Dōwa administration adopted a method to identify 'genuine' Burakumin this would create a set of records that at a later stage could be used for the purpose of discrimination. So, in many areas applicants for benefits from the programmes were screened by a committee which was composed of members of the BLL and local officials. Rather than being co-option of the BLL into the state structure, it was regarded as the only way of guaranteeing that Burakumin were not co-opted.

There was some regional variation, but broadly speaking there were three main types of programmes. Firstly, there were the projects which targeted the physical environment – improving streets, schools, clinics and community centres and constructing high-rise housing to replace the old housing stock. Secondly, there was a system of grants that were paid directly to Buraku families. Upham describes the situation in the 1970s where a family in Osaka with two children could receive over ¥400,000 annually from a combination of grants rewarding school attendance, twice-yearly grants given to all families, not to mention the one-off payments on marriage or the birth of a child (Upham 1980: 49). The third type of programmes related to education: both programmes within the school classroom and enlightenment programmes which aimed to change public attitudes. In 1978 the programmes were extended for three years and since then, mainly due to successful lobbying by the BLL, they have been renewed several times with the current programme set to expire in 1997.

Between 1969 and 1993 the total amount spent on SML projects was ¥13,880 billion. Most projects were carried out at the level of the municipal authorities (city, town, village), where the cost was split 20:10:70 between the state, prefecture and local authority. Others, to a value of ¥3,562 billion, were implemented by the prefectural authorities and the costs shared 20:80 by the state and prefecture. Each time the programmes have been extended their scope has been redefined and narrowed. First to go were the generous grants, later the scale of the construction programmes was also curtailed. At the start of the programmes most expenditure was on capital projects, mainly related to housing schemes. To take the municipal schemes as an example, the balance between spending on material projects to that on non-material schemes during the first phase of the SML was 67:33; this had changed to 42:54 by the 1990s (Sōmuchō 1995: 7).

When the first family records (*koseki*) of the Meiji era were produced, many local officials made sure that former outcasts would continue to be identifiable by marking the new registration form in some way. In some areas they even insisted that all 'new commoners' adopt the same surname so that it would be easy to distinguish between them and the rest of the population. These and subsequent family registration forms were open to public inspection, making it easy for a potential employer or parent-in-law to check out an individual's family background. In the late 1960s the BLL led a campaign to restrict access to these records. Local governments placed their own restrictions on access and it became national policy in 1976 with the revision of article 10 of the Koseki Law. At the end of 1975 Buraku activists were anonymously informed that *Chimei Sōkan* (comprehensive guide to place-names) were being offered for sale to major companies. The one and only use that can be made of these is to ascertain from an individual's family address whether or not he or she might be from a Buraku community. Purchase of the first edition was condemned by the Osaka office of the Ministry of Justice as 'an exceedingly pernicious violation of human rights', and firms purchasing it were urged to achieve a 'fuller understanding of Dōwa problems'. However this did not deter the production of at least seven more such lists or their purchase by several hundred firms and at least one university (Tomonaga 1995; Upham 1980: 65). Faced with this evidence of pervasive discrimination among major employers the Ministry of Labour, in 1987, issued an order encouraging the creation of 'Dōwa Problem' study groups within companies. Simultaneously, companies in Osaka, Tokyo and other cities created local organizations which put on series of lectures, seminars and similar events to be attended by personnel officers within the company. In Fukuoka the Kigyō Dōwa Mondai Suishin Kyōgikai now has 469 company members involved in one or more Dōwa meetings each month and produces pamphlets for use in training programmes.

The JCP and its supporters within the BLL had long held a different view of the fundamental causes of Buraku discrimination from the movement's mainstream. Not surprisingly then, in contrast to the cautious welcome the JSP and BLL gave the report of the Commission of Enquiry, the JCP was highly critical both of the report and the subsequent Ten-year Plan. They argued that it would separate Burakumin from the wider working-class movement, thus weakening opposition to the LDP domination of politics and the capitalist structure (Morooka 1981–2, Vol. 3: 352–3). The tension between the two rival wings of the BLL was formalized with the creation in 1970 of a separate group within it which aimed to change the movement's policy to make it closer to the JCP line. Over the next few years JCP policy changed its emphasis from one which talked of the need to confront US imperialism/Japanese monopoly capitalism to one which was more sensitive to the historical background of the Burakumin. Prejudice and discrimination were remnants from the feudal period which had continued to exist with the landlord–tenant relationship or the management relations of small and medium-sized enterprises. In the post-war period monopoly capitalism had ignored human rights and used discrimination to divide the working class but Buraku discrimination itself, they argued, is no longer a necessary part of the system. There is therefore no structural foundation for discrimination and no reason why it should continue to exist into the twenty-first century. Parallel to the development of this new policy there was violent disagreement between the two groups within the BLL that precipitated the creation of a completely separate organization, the Zenkoku Buraku Kaihō Rengōkai – Zenkairen (National Buraku Liberation Alliance) in 1979.

This split manifested itself in a number of ways. Not only did the JCP oppose the SML, they were also very critical of the way the benefits of the improvement programmes were partially administered by, and allegedly channelled to, supporters of the BLL. The JCP was unhappy about the principle of providing benefits only to those with an outcast ancestry, arguing that all residents of the 'target areas' were entitled to improvements in their living standards. Moreover as the division between the two factions hardened, JCP supporters complained that BLL control of the 'administrative window' was unfair. The BLL argued that their involvement in the programmes' administration was essential to ensure that Dōwa policy was not 'a means of conciliationism but one of liberation' (Buraku Kaihō Undō Suishi Iinkai 1973). In practice, however, JCP supporters claimed that if an applicant were an active member of the BLL he or she would have no difficulty in getting whatever was applied for, but, if the applicant was not an activist, or worse, was a member of a JCP group, it would be difficult to receive the benefit (Upham 1987: 91–3).

The post-war movement had continued to use the *kyūdan tōsō* tactic, and we have seen how it was used in the 1950s to demand local government fund local improvements. The denunciation tactic was justified by post-war activists on the grounds that, although human rights were guaranteed by the post-war constitution, there was no legislation or system of redress that could be used by Burakumin when they found their rights to equality of opportunity in marriage, education or employment infringed. Denunciation, they argue, is a way in which Burakumin can assert their rights and is founded on constitutional provisions. Denunciation is thus a means used to regain human dignity by those who have been deprived of it (Upham 1987: 105–10).

However, on two occasions what ostensibly were denunciation campaigns against discrimination in schools developed into violent confrontations between the BLL and JCP supporters. Following the Yata incident of April 1969, two BLL officials were tried for unlawful imprisonment of three junior high school teachers (Upham 1987: 87–103). The Yōka incident involved more people and greater violence: fifty-two teachers were confined to school premises by supporters of the BLL in order to persuade them to sign statements of self-criticism and promise future co-operation with the League. The teachers were detained for twelve hours and subjected to harassment which resulted in forty-three of them being hospitalized, thirteen for as long as six weeks (Rohlen 1976: 682–99). The mainstream newspapers were unsure how to deal with these events and gave them little coverage, though *Akahata*, journal of the JCP, devoted many column inches to pictures and reports.

Each of these cases is complex but the crux was the resistance of JCP supporters to demands that they adopt the BLL approach to the treatment of Buraku issues in their schools. In the aftermath of both events the JCP criticism highlighted the violence which, they claimed, often accompanied BLL-led denunciation struggles. Not only was this bad in itself, 'a violent assault on the individual's human rights' (Rohlen 1976: 692), but it alienated many who might otherwise be sympathetic to the Buraku situation. Any hope of reconciliation between the two parts of the movement disappeared with the Yōka incident. Appeals to the higher courts following convictions of the three involved in the Yata affair confirmed the verdict but did give qualified approval of the denunciation tactic itself. Only in this case the activists had gone beyond 'the socially reasonable bounds as set by the legal order' (Upham 1987: 100). The Yōka case has yet, at the time of writing (June 1995), to be fully resolved. The initial verdicts of conviction of the thirteen accused were sustained on appeal to the Osaka High Court. This once again affirmed the right to denunciation but argued that the methods used had gone beyond the socially sanctioned limits (*Gendai Yōgo Chishiki* 1995: 864). There is no indication when the case will finally be settled.

There has been further dispute between the two groups about another issue which has been central to the BLL activities in recent years: its demands for a 'Basic Law on the Buraku Issue'. Basic laws have a special place in the Japanese legal framework midway between the generalities of the Constitution and the nitty-gritty of ordinary legislation. In the words of one American legal scholar, 'they are symbols of permanent national commitment to certain goals . . . [and] . . . establish a framework for government policy making in a particular area' (Upham 1993: 330).

The BLL seeks the introduction of a law with three aims:

- to institutionalize national commitment to the goals of the 1965 report and to establish a legal framework for a comprehensive approach to the Buraku problem;
- to oblige government to take action in a broad range of areas beyond urban renewal;
- to prohibit a wide range of discriminatory acts and provide the statutory basis for direct legal attacks on discrimination by individuals and groups.

Government would be expected to submit an annual report to the Diet and conduct a survey on Buraku conditions every five years. Moreover, it is proposed that a Buraku Deliberative Council be created to investigate Buraku discrimination-related problems (BLRI 1994: 27). This would ensure that the issue remained prominent within the public domain.

The LDP and the JCP were opposed to this proposal. The JCP argues that there is now no obstacle to a complete solution to the problem. Some elements of prejudice and discrimination may remain but new legislation will do nothing to improve matters. In this their attitude is very similar to that of the government which considers that:

> To root out discrimination it is necessary to reform the psychology that gives birth to it. This can only be done by enlightenment. Not only can it not be done by punishment . . . punishment will drive discriminatory consciousness underground and harden it.
>
> (Quoted by Upham 1993: 331)

The campaign for the Basic Law has not had wholehearted support from within the BLL either. The justification for the denunciation tactic has been that it is appropriate and constitutional because private and public legal redress are not available when individuals find their rights are infringed. If a law were introduced to create just that kind of legal machinery, there would be no legal or theoretical justification for the denunciation tactics; the decision of whether and how to deal with a specific instance of discrimination would pass out of the hands of the BLL and into those of the state. Not only would the movement lose one of its central functions but it would also give the state the kind of influence that it has sought since the time of the Yūwa movement. Discussion of the Basic Law thus touches on issues which are fundamental to the movement's future, and we will address this topic in the final section.

THE 1990s AND BEYOND

After forty years of BLL activity and over twenty-five years of special improvement programmes the question quite naturally arises of what remains to be done and who should be doing it? As we have already seen there are those on both left and right of the political spectrum who argue there is no longer any need to give the Buraku communities any special treatment.

This prompts the question: what evidence is there that the improvement process is incomplete? One can begin by pointing to the existence of 'non-designated areas'. For the purposes of SML administration, local governments had to formally designate certain areas as 'target areas'. But, for a variety of reasons, some local authorities declined to do so or missed some out. Some 4,603 'target areas' were designated but it is estimated there are between 800–1,000 which were not and which therefore have not benefited from the SML policies. What is to be done about them?

There is, however, copious evidence about the current state of designated Buraku communities following the publication of a 2,000-page report which is based on surveys carried out in 1993 of all 4,603 designated Buraku, nearly 60,000 Buraku households and of the attitudes of 60,000 Burakumin and over 24,000 non-Burakumin. This is the most extensive and sophisticated survey of conditions and attitudes ever undertaken and its very extent defies summarization. All one can do in the space available is to mention some of the features relevant to the argument presented here.

Firstly, it is quite striking that the proportion of Burakumin making up the population of the Buraku areas has fallen from a national average of 71.9 per cent in 1971 to 41.4 per cent in 1993. It is tempting to conjecture that the loans and grants of the SML programmes have enabled social and geographic mobility out of Buraku communities. However, these average figures hide wide local variation. At the extremes only 2.7 per cent of Miyazaki Prefecture's (tiny) Buraku communities are made up of Burakumin compared to a figure of 97.9 per cent in Fukui Prefecture. There is even considerable difference between the figures for Osaka (87.3 per cent) and Fukuoka (36.6 per cent) which might suggest why BLL groups in different regions favour different tactics (Sōmuchō 1995: 2).

Secondly there is some evidence of improved income levels: only 52 per cent of Buraku households received 'livelihood security support' in 1993 compared to 76 per cent in 1975. However, this is almost twice as high as the non-Buraku households in the same areas (28.2 per cent) and well above the national average of 7.1 per cent (Sōmuchō 1995: 4). At the same time, while a substantial proportion of the Buraku population own their own homes (62.7 per cent compared to a national average of 59.8 per cent), around a third live in local government-owned apartments. As such they pay very low rents, on average ¥8,138 compared to a national average of ¥33,762 (Sōmuchō 1995: 21–2).

The evidence pertaining to educational performance shows a similar pattern, suggesting both improvement and unresolved problems. Overall the entry of Burakumin children into senior high school is close to that of the mainstream, 91.8 per cent compared to over 96 per cent for the non-Buraku samples. However, the rate of persistent, long-term absenteeism among Burakumin children from primary and junior high schools is almost twice the mainstream averages: 1.6 per cent and 4.5 per cent compared to 0.8 per cent and 2.4 per cent respectively. Access to higher education has improved; less than 2 per cent of Burakumin over fifty-five had any experience of higher education whereas over 20 per cent of today's Buraku teenagers can expect to continue their education past high school (Sōmuchō: 10–11, 15). This is a considerable improvement but still lags behind the figure of nearly 40 per cent for the population as a whole. Probably linked to this difference in educational achievement is the fact that only 10.6 per cent of Burakumin were reported to be employed in enterprises of over 300 employees, well below the national average of 23.3 per cent (Sōmuchō 1995: 20). Since it is only the larger enterprises that can provide stable employment, higher salaries and fringe benefits, these figures suggest that Burakumin remain marginal to Japanese society.

Such differences in employment might also be explained as the result of continuing discrimination in the employment practices of the larger companies. The discovery in 1975 that lists of Buraku communities had been sold to many Japanese companies showed that many firms did seek to avoid employing Burakumin. It is hard to be certain that this no longer exists. When asked about their experience of discrimination, only one-third of the Buraku respondents reported feeling their rights had been violated at some time. Most frequently this was in incidents which took place at work, at school or involving marriage (Sōmuchō 1995: 25). Few of them did anything about it; the largest single group, 46 per cent of the sample, kept quiet and put up with the treatment.

If marriage outside the Buraku community can be regarded as showing the decreasing power of discrimination there is some encouraging evidence. Around 80 per cent of those over the age of eighty married fellow Burakumin but this had dropped to less than 25 per cent of those under twenty-five years of age. When asked a hypothetical question about marriage of one of their children to a Burakumin 45 per cent of the non-Buraku sample said they would respect their wishes, 41 per cent said if they felt strongly enough there was nothing they could do about it; only 5 per cent said they would completely oppose the marriage. This latter figure is down from 7.6 per cent in 1985 (Sōmuchō 1995: 31). However, despite the categorical rejection in the 1965 report of the different racial origins of Burakumin which has been repeated widely, there were still about 10 per cent of the population which reported subscribing to this explanation of the background to the Buraku problem (Sōmuchō 1995: 29).

This brief review of some of the findings in the report suggests that although there has been substantial change in conditions in the Buraku communities there remains more that needs to be achieved before it is realistic to speak of the end of discrimination against Burakumin. But, as we have seen, even if we accept that more should be done there is serious disagreement about what, if anything, government should do and what the movement can now achieve.

Since the 1950s it was a major BLL aim to persuade central government to fund an improvement programme and having succeeded in this to have the various programmes extended. In September 1992, however, Uesugi Saichiro announced that the movement would not demand any further extension to the SML when its present lease of life expires in 1997. This came as something of a shock to many of the movement's activists and it marks the start of an ongoing debate on how the movement should prepare for its 'third era'. The first era was that of the Suiheisha which came to an end in the late 1940s. The 'second era' really began with the formation of the BLL in 1955, but for most of its latter half it has been characterized by its involvement in and the support it has received from the various improvement programmes. Preparing for the 'third era' the BLL must devise new tactics.

In the early 1990s the movement seemed to have lost its sense of purpose. This is in part related to the general ideological confusion that followed the collapse of Cold War certainties, but it may also reflect the fact that the improvements of the previous twenty-five years had succeeded in resolving many of the problems faced by Burakumin. The movement could no longer attract the support of the bright young people of the Buraku communities. Indeed, many of them were moving out altogether. In 1993 the central committee followed up the decision not to work for the further extension of the SML with a call for a re-examination of the movement's situation. Three areas were identified for consideration:

- what would amount to a 'solution' to the Buraku problem?
- what is the link between Buraku discrimination and poverty?
- what international dimensions to the problem exist? For example, to what extent do Japanese companies practise discrimination abroad?

Proposals for each of these areas were presented to the BLL conference in May 1995 to allow for wide debate within the movement over the following twelve months so that the new policy can be adopted by the movement at its conference in March 1996, well before the expiration of the SML. The proposed set of aims and principles has set aside the 'class history' perspective in favour of one founded on democracy and human rights. It outlines what a society without Buraku discrimination would amount to and links this to a vision of creating a 'Suiheisha for the whole world' (*Kaihō Shinbun*, 8 May 1995: 9–10).

The BLL has been closely associated with the JSP since its formation in 1955, their overall political approach has been similar and the League's central and local bodies have usually given the JSP support in election campaigns. However, in 1992 the Okayama branch of the BLL decided to support the LDP candidate in the next election on the grounds that he would best represent their interests in the Diet. Following the LDP's loss of political power and the adoption of an electoral system based on single member constituencies, the BLL 52nd Conference held in 1994 resolved not to have direct links to any political party. At the time the split from the JSP was a dramatic move causing internal division, including the resignation of the movement's secretary Komori Ryuho. It was also perhaps one which the BLL regretted when the JSP joined the LDP in a coalition government led by Murayama Tomiichi since this gave it the best chance it is likely to get to press for the introduction of the Basic Law.

Since the formation of the LDP/JSP coalition government the BLL has tried hard to have its proposal for a Basic Law accepted by the Diet. Its representatives met with Murayama and senior members of the Cabinet and bureaucracy, project teams were formed by both government and opposition parties and the BLL had its hopes set on passage during the 131st session of the Diet which ended in June 1995. Even if they had been successful this would only have been the first stage in the process. A Basic Law does little more than establish a set of principles, and at least two more specific pieces of legislation would be needed to make discrimination illegal and to create the framework for the regular provision of reports about Buraku conditions. The campaign for Buraku legislation will continue to be an important part of the BLL's activities for some time to come.

In the longer term, though – as the parties re-group and re-align following Lower House elections under the new system, which seems likely to result in the decimation of the JSP – the BLL decision to free itself from the automatic support of any party may not turn out to be particularly important. It may even free the movement to pursue its best interests however the political system finally settles down.

The debate about the movement's next steps has been a lively and wide-ranging one. As we have already seen, it has prompted some to argue the case for a reconsideration of the orthodoxies of Buraku history. At a more mundane level, one commentator has pointed out that over half of those attending the BLL conferences and study sessions have their expenses paid in some form by the Dōwa programme. Will the movement get such enthusiastic support when people have to pay all their own expenses (Ohga 1993: 34–5)? For others the start of a new era suggests the need to redefine the movement's aims; it is not enough simply to seek an end to discrimination. Just as peace is more than the absence of war, so the aim of the BLL should not be the mere abolition of prejudice but the creation of a society in which there is a positive respect for human rights. As a part of this, the movement should move beyond demands for 'reparations' in recompense for the damage cumulatively inflicted by discrimination in the past and begin to formulate demands for the creation of a rights-based society. 'From fighting the results of discrimination, to combating its causes.' None of the problems facing Burakumin are exclusive to them. The movement must distinguish between the universal and specific elements in each issue area, then the movement can work with other social movement groups to create a comprehensive solution to that particular problem. In this way the BLL's demands could act as a catalyst for rapid social change in Japan in the 'window of opportunity' provided by the breakdown of the '1955 system' (Okuda 1994: 95–107).

Others are a little more sanguine. Discrimination is no longer as severe a problem as it was, but it may be that it is not disappearing but changing its form. For example, crude statistics suggest that Buraku exogamy is increasing. In Osaka the number of marriages to non-Burakumin has increased from 23.5 per cent in the late 1950s to 55.4 per cent in the late 1980s. However a more careful analysis of the statistics reveals that few of these marriages were with people from the neighbouring communities – what one might regard as the 'normal marriage area'. Usually they were to people who came from outside the town or village or prefecture. Research methods have hitherto merely sought to demonstrate the existence of poverty and deprivation. What is needed now are more sophisticated research methods (Ishimoto 1994: 85–7).

The Buraku liberation movement has been as influenced as any other sector of Japanese society by the perceived need to become 'internationalized'. At first sight this might seem strange given the peculiarly domestic nature of the problem. But, given the growing significance of the international human rights movement, it was almost inevitable that the movement would move in this direction. Matsumoto Jiichiro was an internationalist, reportedly having visited twenty-seven countries during his lifetime, and having argued that however far the BLL might develop Burakumin would not be completely free from discrimination as long as there was discrimination in the world (Uesugi 1995: 4).

The movement has recently emphasized the 'human rights' dimension to the Buraku issue, a feature that it shares with minorities and groups in many countries. Since the early 1980s it has organized conferences and symposia which have included representatives of such groups as the Romanies of Europe, the *harijan* of India and minorities of North America. The BLL has also been a prominent supporter of the campaign to persuade the Japanese government to ratify the International Convention on the Elimination of All Forms of Discrimination. Partly in pursuit of this aim, in the summer of 1983 the BLL and the Zenkairen sent representatives to attend meetings of the UN Commission of Human Rights where they spoke under the auspices of the London-based Minority Rights Group. This made government officials more alert to the work of the United Nations human rights apparatus but did little to advance the cause. Prime Minister Nakasone, speaking in 1984, announced that, 'I am basically for the International Convention. However at this minute, I am making efforts to adjust domestic laws' (*Buraku Liberation News*, 23 January 1985: 5). Eleven years later it remains unratified, Prime Minister Murayama, following the advice of the Ministry of Justice, arguing that its ratification would conflict with the constitutionally guaranteed freedoms of speech and publication (Uesugi 1995: 6).

In 1988 the International Movement Against All Forms of Discrimination and Racism (IMADR) was organized under the leadership of the BLL to support groups in Japan and throughout the world which are campaigning for equality and against discrimination. This group was granted formal non-government organization (NGO) status by the United Nations in 1993 which entitles it to address UN organizations in its own right. It has tried to create a network of groups active in defending the interests of minorities and indigenous peoples which will enable them to exchange ideas and co-operate, especially in relation to United Nations' policies. One area where the IMADR has been asked to assist recently is where NGOs in Asia have been engaged in protest against Japan's ODA policies or activities funded by Japanese ODA (Interview with Ms Mieko Suzuki, 16 May 1995). Although the most important single support group is the BLL, IMADR also receives funding from a number of labour unions and other social movement groups.

The most recent development has been the creation of the Asia Pacific Human Rights Information Centre (APHRIC) which started operations in December 1994. It aims to provide information about human rights activities in the Asia Pacific region, promote research in Japan and in the region as a whole and provide human rights education both locally and regionally. Finally, it aspires to be the precursor of some kind of formal human rights organization that will operate within Asia Pacific to promote and protect human rights (Hurights Osaka 1995: 9). Most of the funding has come from the Osaka prefectural and city authorities but again, though other local NGOs have also been involved, the BLL has been the most important single support organization which has fought for the creation of this new body.

CONCLUSION

Although there has been opposition to its activities both from the Dōwa groups to the right and the JCP on the left, it has been the BLL that has set the pace for Buraku change since 1955. These next few years will be crucial for the movement and for the Buraku communities. The BLL has for some years now claimed 200,000 members in 2,200 branches spread over thirty-nine prefectures. The movement's leadership though is clear that the number of active members is declining. Young people face less severe discrimination and are less likely to involve the BLL when they do encounter it. As it becomes easier to find housing outside the Buraku, many move out and, even if they have previously been active, they are likely to cease involvement with the movement when they leave. The movement is losing the support of the younger able people who hitherto have been its driving force.

The decision not to press for an extension of the SML beyond 1997 is probably correct given the fairly common perception that Burakumin these days are privileged compared to other Japanese. The low rents paid by many Burakumin seem to be a sore point with many people. But the end of the SML is a threat to the movement. If all subsidies cease then both its publications and series of meetings and conferences may have to be curtailed as it may not be possible to fund them from the BLL's own resources or those of its members.

Secondly, it will have no influence over the flow of tangible benefits and therefore there will be no material benefit to be gained from BLL membership. Moreover, were the Basic Law campaign to be successful it would lose its role as the instigator and co-ordinator of denunciation campaigns, and the Buraku Deliberation Council would take over some of the functions of the BLL leadership.

On the other hand, the international human rights regime is likely to become even more important and the BLL is uniquely placed to play a significant role in the developments which will link changes to human rights practices in Japan with those in the surrounding Asia Pacific region. At the moment there is no human rights framework for any part of Asia – no regional conventions, no commissions. If the BLL can co-operate with other groups inside and outside Japan to create a broad-based alliance it could make a valuable contribution to integrate human rights standards into the Asian tradition. But can it command support at an international level if it becomes weak at home?

NOTES

1 A recent national survey of the attitudes of more than 24,000 people found that only 41.4 per cent of those living in Hokkaidō and Tōhoku and 73.1 per cent of those living in the Kantō area were aware of the problem. This compares to 95.3 per cent of those in the Kinki region (Sōmuchō 1995: 29).

2 The pre-war government referred to the Yūwa – conciliation – policy until in 1940 the name was changed to Dōwa, an abbreviation of Dōhō Ichiwa – all citizens should assimilate – a phrase devised for the wartime environment. Dōwa thus translates as assimilation, but it was and is disliked both as a euphemism and because of its wartime overtones.

BIBLIOGRAPHY

Asada, Z. (1969) *Sabetsu to Tatakai Tsuzukete* (The Struggle Against Discrimination Continues), Tokyo: Asahi Shimbunsha.

BLRI (1994) *Suggestions for Human Rights Policies in Japan*, Osaka: Buraku Liberation Research Institute.

Buraku Kaihō Undō Suishi Iinkai (1973) *Madoguchi Ipponku* (The Single Window Policy), Osaka.

Buraku Liberation News (1985) Osaka: Buraku Liberation Research Institute, January.

Daily Telegraph, 24 May 1994.

DeVos, G. and Wagatsuma, H. (1973) *Japan's Invisible Race* (2nd edn), Berkeley: University of California Press.

Gendai Yōgo Chishiki (1995), Tokyo: Kokuminsha.

Harada, T. and Uesugi, S. (1981) *Long Suffering Brothers and Sisters Unite!*, Osaka: Buraku Liberation Research Institute.

Hurights Osaka (1995) 'What will Hurights Osaka do?', Osaka: Hurights Osaka Newsletter, 1.

Ishimoto, K. (1994) 'Buraku no Henka to Gendai Kenkyū no Kadai' (Changes in the Buraku and Topics of Recent Research), *Buraku Kaihō Kenkyū* 97, 77–94.

Kaihō Shinbun, 8 May 1995, No. 1718, Osaka: Kaihō Shimbunsha.

Morooka, S. (1981–2) *Sengo Buraku Kaihō Ronsōshi* (A History of the Post-war Buraku Liberation Theory Debate), 3 vols, Tokyo: Tsuge Shobō.

Neary, I.J. (1986) 'Socialist and Communist Party attitudes towards discrimination against Japan's Burakumin, *Political Studies* 34, 556–74.

—— (1989) *Political Protest and Social Control in Pre-war Japan: The Origins of Buraku Liberation*, Manchester: Manchester University Press.

Ohga, M. (1993) 'Daisanki no Buraku Kaihō Undō ni tsuite' (On the Third Era of the Buraku Liberation Movement), *Buraku Kaihō Kenkyū* 94, 31–40.

Okuda, H. (1994) 'Daisanki no Buraku Kaihō Undō e no Mondai Teiki', *Buraku Kaihō Kenkyū* 95, 95–107.

Rohlen, T.P. (1976) 'Violence at Yoka High School: the implications for Japanese coalition politics of the confrontation between the Communist Party and the Buraku Liberation League', *Asian Survey* 16, 7, 682–99.

Sōmuchō (1995) *Heisei Gonendo Dōwachiku Jittai Haakutō Chōsakekka no Gaiyō* (Outline of the Results of the 1993 Surveys to Assess Conditions in the Dōwa Areas), Tokyo: Sōmuchōkan Kanbō Chiiki Kaizen Taisa-kushitsu.

Tomonaga, K. (1995) 'Buraku Chimei Sōkan Jiken Nijū nen' (Twenty Years After the First Publication of the Chimei Sōkan), *Human Rights* 84 (March), 2–21.

Uesugi, S. (1995) '"Dōtaishin" Tōshin Sanjūnen to Buraku Kaihō' (Thirty Years After the Deliberative Council Report and Buraku Liberation), *Human Rights* 85 (April), 2–7.

Upham, F. (1980) 'Ten years of affirmative action for Japanese Burakumin: a preliminary report on the Law on Special Measures for Dowa Projects', *Law in Japan: An Annual* 20, 39–87.

—— (1987) *Law and Social Change in Postwar Japan*, Cambridge, Mass.: Harvard University Press.

—— (1993) 'Unplaced persons', in A. Gordon (ed.) *Postwar Japan as History*, Berkeley: University of California Press.

Wagatsuma, H. (1976) 'Political problems of a minority group in Japan: recent conflicts in the Buraku Liberation Movement', in W.A. Veenhoven and W. Crum-Ewing (eds) *Case Studies on Human Rights and Fundamental Freedoms*, The Hague: Martinus Nijhoff.

Watanabe, T. (1993) 'Ima "Buraku Rekishi" o toinaosu' (Time to review 'Buraku History'), *Buraku Kaihō Kenkyū* 94, 1–28.

4 The representation of absence and the absence of representation

Korean victims of the atomic bomb[1]

Michael Weiner

INTRODUCTION

Unlike the other contributions to this volume, which are primarily concerned with contemporary minority issues, the focus of this chapter is historical memory; its commemoration or suppression. This should not, however, be taken to mean that contemporary issues are ignored. The appropriation or nationalization of historical memory in Japan, of which the Hiroshima and Nagasaki narratives are but two examples, has not only obscured historical memory of past participation in the subjugation of parts of Asia, but more importantly denies current exclusions within Japan itself. This chapter begins by locating the issue of compensation for former colonial subjects within a broader and comparative framework.

HISTORY CONTESTED

Francis Fukuyama's *The End of History* is one of a number of post-Cold War publications which have catalogued the ideological uncertainty, moral and political pessimism, and fear about the future within the capitalist world. Current levels of anxiety over immigration, multi-culturalism, and multi-racialism can also be seen as further manifestations of an inability to offer a credible vision of the future. This malaise has most often been described in terms of the crisis of modernity and progress, or, in Fukuyama's case, of history itself. Yet, in adjusting to the post-Cold War environment, national elites have increasingly turned to history in an attempt both to reinvigorate national unity and cohesion and to stake a claim in the 'new world order'. These often contradictory demands have also generated a crisis of historiography, which reflects not only educational, but ideological and political concerns as well. The question of whose history and for what purposes histories are written is, arguably, more relevant today than at any time in the past.

As in the United States and Britain, the articulation of common roots, traditions, and values has been perceived by conservatives in Japan as providing the means for the reproduction of national consensus. It is a narrative designed to affirm a sense of historical continuity, defining which experiences should be remembered, and when and how they should be invoked (Furedi 1993: 27.) This appropriation or rehabilitation of history for political purposes is neither novel nor restricted to politicians or academics of a particular hue (Breuilly 1993: 54–70). In a landscape populated by competing histories, moreover, it is also increasingly difficult to quantify the successes which these attempts to normalize the past have achieved. / What such revisionism undoubtedly does reflect in the Japanese context is an attempt to resist change, defined here as occurring within both the composition of the national community and the international arena. In reaffirming the preservation of an exclusive and absolute national identity, for example, the conservative project suppresses diversity within Japan, while resisting incorporation within a larger, more diverse regional identity in Asia, and this resistance has been buttressed by an ideology of uniqueness – cultural, political and 'racial'. /

Although the appropriation of history for political purposes is common to all nation-states, the way in which each nation interprets the problem of history has been and will continue to be informed by a particular experience of the past and present. In Japan, this agenda has been driven, at least in part, by the apparent need to prevent what has been perceived as the social fragmentation characteristic of other capitalist states. Efforts in Japan to normalize the past need also to be understood as a reaction against the imposition of 'victor's' history (Holloway 1989: 29). Unlike establishment historians in, for example, Britain and the United States, who have a vested interest in sustaining Second World War memories, their counterparts in Japan have often characterized pre-war imperialism as an aberration, or portrayed it as a noble experiment gone wrong (Gluck 1993: 71–3; *Sankei Shinbun*, 11 August 1993). But while each master-narrative is constructed within a clearly defined national framework, there exist areas of intersection and potential conflict. The not always successful attempts (dating back to the mid-1960s) to establish a set of new relationships with its neighbours have also brought Japan's historical ambivalence toward Asia into sharper focus. In articulating a new relationship with its neighbours Japan

has been urged to acknowledge its pre-1945 role as an aggressive colonial power in Asia, rather than representing itself solely as a victim of Western imperialism and the atomic bombings of Hiroshima and Nagasaki (Nakahara 1990: 129–30).
/ Throughout much of the post-1945 period, public education institutions in Japan have represented the Pacific War as a natural disaster which swept all the nations of East Asia. In fact, due to its unique experience of the horrors of atomic warfare, Japan had been depicted by intellectuals of both left and right as having suffered proportionately greater damage and loss than its neighbours (Dower 1993: 19). Externally, however, this retrospective defence of Japanese imperialism has served to reinforce the perception that Japanese regrets for the war extend only to their own sufferings (Yamamoto 1991: 322). Although not to be confused with serious conservative scholarship covering the period 1931–45, the current popularity of 'war simulation novels' in Japan can also be included within a broad genre of historical revisionism which has enjoyed at least the tacit approval of the Ministry of Education. It is as if a moral symmetry exists in which the experience of colonial exploitation in Korea, or atrocities committed by the Japanese military in Nanjing, Singapore and elsewhere in Asia, have somehow been erased by the bombings of Hiroshima and Nagasaki. /
/ The relative ease with which the Japanese state has nurtured what has been termed *higaisha ishiki* (victim consciousness), while successfully excluding dissonant histories, has also been contrasted with the intensity of the historical debate in post-war Germany. This apparent distinction between a recalcitrant Japan, committed to the deletion of embarrassing episodes from textbooks, and a penitent Germany, which has been relentless in its examination of the Nazi past, has been commented on by numerous observers. Of course, comparisons of this sort exaggerate polarities and ignore the growing influence of German historical revisionism, but it is difficult to ignore the narrowness of the Japanese debate. While the Japanese state has consistently refused to consider the payment of compensation to the victims of imperial aggression, Germany, under legislation introduced in 1953 and revised in 1956, has paid out in excess of $50 billion in pensions and indemnities to Holocaust survivors and other victims of Nazi aggression. This figure is twenty-eight times the total amount of war reparations paid out by Japan. As recently as October 1990, the German government established a $300 million fund to compensate Polish citizens for hardships endured as forced labourers between 1939 and 1945 (Shimizu 1994: 137–9). In addition to compensation

provided by the state, private corporations like Daimler-Benz, Siemens, and I.G. Farben, which made extensive use of forced labour, have also paid compensation to the survivors and their families (*Asahi Shinbun*, 25 September 1991; Shimizu 1994: 137–9). Similarly, where Germany has erected monuments to the victims of the genocidal policies of the Nazi Reich, Japan has built monuments only to its own war dead. Despite the precedent established by West Germany after 1945, and more recently by united Germany, the Japanese government has consistently rejected claims for compensation made by individuals who lived under Japanese control during the Pacific War (Tanaka 1994: 123–9). The oft-repeated position of the Japanese government remains unchanged: that all obligations to provide compensation were settled by the San Francisco Peace Treaty of 1951, the 1965 Treaty of Basic Relations which normalized ties with Seoul, and the 1972 Japan–China joint communiqué which re-established diplomatic relations with Beijing. /

Attempts in Japan to normalize the past have inevitably come into conflict with other, dissonant and potentially disruptive narratives (*Mainichi Shinbun*, 24 February 1989; Johnson 1986: 402–28). Recent disclosures regarding the operation of Units 1644 and 731, which conducted germ-warfare experiments on Chinese civilian populations and allied prisoners of war, and the tens of thousands of Asian (mainly Korean) girls and women who were forcibly conscripted for service as 'comfort women' in military brothels are but two of the *kakusareta rekishi* (hidden histories) of the pre-1945 period which post-war governments have sought to suppress (*Mainichi Shinbun*, 15 August 1990). /A third such history which has largely been ignored by all but a handful of Korean researchers is that of the Korean *hibakusha* (Ryu 1991: 256–7). Although the term *hibakusha* is normally reserved for Japanese victims of the atom bombings of Hiroshima and Nagasaki, it applies equally to the tens of thousands of other sufferers, predominantly Koreans. In 1974, the Korean Association for Assistance to Victims of the Atomic Bomb estimated that the number of Koreans affected by the bombings of Hiroshima and Nagasaki were 70,000 and 30,000 respectively, of whom 50,000 had died immediately after the bomb (So 1989: 23–4). /

/ Due in no small measure to the effects of censorship, initially under American aegis and thereafter by the Japanese state, the voices of the thousands of Koreans resident in Hiroshima and Nagasaki in August 1945 have remained largely silent (Ryu 1991: 256–7). Indeed, it was only in 1991 that the Japanese government allocated the sum of $25 million to assist Korean survivors of the atomic bombings, the majority of whom had been transported to Japan as conscripted labour during the Pacific War. This sum is hardly generous compared to the $1.2 billion awarded by the United States government to citizens of Japanese descent who were incarcerated during the war (*Asahi Shinbun*, 29 November 1991). It also came too late for thousands of *hibakusha* repatriated to Korea after the war, and who received few of the benefits provided to their Japanese counterparts (*Mainichi Shinbun*, 18 February 1992; Won 1986: 144–5).

Within the present-day Korean community, which numbers in excess of 700,000, this is but another chapter in an eighty-five-year history which has been characterized by marginalization and exclusion. With the exception of Burakumin and Okinawans, Koreans constitute the largest minority population in Japan. Though the majority were born in Japan, speak Japanese as their first, or indeed only, language, and may identify themselves as Korean-Japanese, their social, economic and political rights are constrained by their status as resident aliens (Harajiri 1989: 67–75). Moreover, while the laws governing the legal status of long-term resident aliens have undergone significant change, particularly during the past decade, there is substantial evidence of the persistence of officially sanctioned practices which discriminate against Koreans and other long-term Asian residents. Irrespective of their status under current immigration and nationality law, Koreans are only rarely employed as unionized, permanent workers in Japanese firms (Won 1986: 86–95).

Public and government service constitute further areas where employment opportunities are extremely limited, though there has been some regional variation – particularly in areas of high Korean population density as in parts of the Kansai and in Kanagawa Prefecture (Harajiri 1989: 74–5). But, even in the most liberal local authorities, Koreans are rarely employed above clerical level. The result of these exclusions is that unemployment rates for Koreans are substantially higher than for the general population. Koreans are also disproportionately represented in poorly paid service and entertainment industries, in small (often Korean-operated) non-unionized, subcontracting companies, and in the construction industry where they comprise a significant proportion of the unskilled and semi-skilled labour force (Harajiri 1989: 120–1). Coupled with a general inability to accumulate wealth, the children of Korean residents have been consistently denied access to opportunities in state sector higher education, either through overt discrimination on the part of the government, or by covert institutional practices. Being less skilled and under-educated, in a society where the possession of these attributes is highly valued, has not only ensured the continued marginalization of Koreans but has reproduced a range of anti-Korean stereotypes whose origins date from the colonial period.

TWICE VICTIMS: THE KOREAN MIGRATION TO HIROSHIMA AND NAGASAKI

The recruitment and mobilization of colonial labour was a practice which all colonial powers have employed at one time or another. For workers from the Korean periphery who entered Japan between 1910 and 1945, economic function and social status were determined by their identity as colonial subjects. Although the Act of Annexation in 1910 conferred the right to travel and take up employment within the empire, Koreans were not guaranteed the rights of full citizenship. On the contrary, as expressed through the economic, social and educational policies of the colonial administration, Koreans were expected to assume their 'proper place' within the empire: to accept a subordinate identity and serve the interests of metropolitan Japan. Economic deprivation and political suppression in Korea figured in the decision to migrate, but the more compelling and decisive incentive was the 'pull' factor. Once underway, the demand for flexible, low-cost industrial labour remained constant, and the migration of workers from colonial Korea a self-perpetuating response to labour market conditions in Japan.

Active recruitment of colonial labour was initially stimulated by the rapid industrial expansion which accompanied Japan's entry in the First World War and continued more or less uninterrupted until 1945. Although wages in Japan were substantially higher than those available in Korea, migrant workers seldom enjoyed the same rates of pay as their Japanese counterparts. Wage rates and conditions of employment varied considerably by industry, but in all cases were determined both by a lack of marketable skills and by 'racially' informed employment practices. On average, Koreans were paid a third less than indigenous workers, and were regarded as inherently suited for tasks involving physical strength but little else (Osaka-shi 1924: 17–21). Concentration in small subcontracting firms, where health and safety standards were poorly enforced or ignored entirely, reduced social costs but resulted in a disproportionately high rate of work-related injury and sickness among Korean workers. Despite an acceptance of inferior wages, undesirable working conditions, unsocial hours and low status, their concentration in unskilled or semi-skilled occupations also ensured that Koreans were particularly vulnerable to lay-offs, dismissal and unemployment (Kim 1977: 26). Their role as migratory, replacement labour, moreover, reduced the likelihood of trade-union affiliation. When they did participate in or organize industrial action against employers it only reinforced the more generalized perception of Koreans as cultural and political antagonists (Osaka-shi 1924: 3).

By virtue of its class position as replacement labour, the migrant worker community was characterized by little of the continuity or regularity associated with modern industrial life. Very few Koreans were employed as permanent factory operatives, while those who were tended to be excluded from large to medium-sized firms – the exception to this being the coal-mining and construction industries, where larger firms relied extensively on migrant labour, particularly during the closing years of the Pacific War. In general, however, Koreans were over-represented in industrial sectors offering the lowest wages, poorest working conditions, and where housing and other benefits were either minimal or non-existent. Exclusion from the general housing market also reduced Koreans to living in tenements and flop houses adjacent to factory sites, or, in the case of day labourers, to work camps operated by labour contractors. As a result, sanitation and basic health care were a constant problem in areas of Korean residence, and this in turn meant that migrant workers were particularly susceptible to dysentery and other infectious diseases. Contemporary accounts, however, attributed the prevalence of poverty, violence and disease within Korean communities to culturally or 'racially' embedded characteristics (Sakai 1931: 133–5). Although Koreans were perceived as an adequate source of low grade manpower, it was assumed that their standard of living took for granted a decadent cultural heritage (Osaka-shi 1933: 32–3). Received by a society concerned only with their labour power, the survival of the migrant worker was dependent upon an ability to adapt to an environment vastly different to that which existed in rural Korea where most originated. But for the individual migrant, whose previous horizons had rarely extended beyond the village of his birth, and whose skills did not easily translate into the industrial marketplace, life in Tokyo or Osaka was one of unfamiliarity and isolation. Likewise, the basic alienness of the Korean worker, his disadvantaged position within the labour market and the almost visceral contempt in which he was held as a member of a subordinate 'race', perpetuated and 'naturalized' further exploitation (Osaka-shi 1933: 32–3).

Throughout the colonial period, Korean labour exhibited characteristics common to other contemporary migrations. Newly arrived workers, be they permanent immigrants or sojourners, formed the most exploited and least protected segment of the working class. By comparison, the benefits of employing migrant labour were considerable. In the labour-intensive industries where Korean labour was concentrated, their employment facilitated expanded production without investment in mechanization (Sakai 1931: 118). Reliance on migrant labour also consolidated and perpetuated pre-existing social and economic inequalities. The presence of large numbers of Koreans in the mining and construction industries, for example, decreased the likelihood that indigenous workers would seek employment in these dirty, dangerous and low status occupations, thereby reducing the possibility of improved wages and working conditions. Large-scale employment of migrant labour also had a deflationary impact on the level of wage increases in certain industries, though 'racially' determined wage structures ensured that direct competition with Japanese workers was the exception rather than the rule. Although initially perceived as disposable replacement labour, the migrant worker was highly visible and formed a more or less permanent feature of the industrial landscape.

As marginal and relatively disadvantaged workers, Koreans enjoyed far less security of employment and were regarded by employers as a disposable source of inexpensive labour. At times of economic expansion their presence was of benefit to employer and indigenous worker alike, since it resolved labour shortages and facilitated economic growth, thus creating further employment opportunities for Japanese workers. Likewise, during recessionary periods, indigenous labour continued to benefit since it was the Korean who was most vulnerable to lay-offs or dismissal (Akiyama 1929: 112). This was not, however, recognized by the majority of Japanese workers, who were encouraged by employers, the media and the state itself to regard Koreans as competitors. Undoubtedly, the response of Japanese workers was not conditioned solely or even primarily by a rational estimate of the economic consequences of immigration. It also owed a great deal to the prevalence of 'racially' informed stereotypes which contrasted the enduring purity and superiority of the Japanese 'race' with the cultural degeneracy and 'racial' inferiority of subordinate populations. The high visibility of Koreans, clustered in shanty towns or abandoned work sites, also confirmed Japanese perceptions of the immigrant as an unwelcome intruder. As a result of these subjective and objective factors, Koreans came to be regarded not only as distinct and disadvantaged, but as a threat to the physical and moral well-being of the working classes (Sakai 1931: 133–5).

/ In common with other Korean communities which dotted the industrial landscape of pre-1945 Japan, those in Hiroshima and Nagasaki had developed as a consequence of both colonial economic policies and the demand for temporary, low-cost industrial labour in metropolitan Japan (Weiner 1994: 112–53, 187–208). As set out in Table 4.1, in comparison with Osaka (general manufacturing and construction) and Fukuoka (coal-mining and construction) Prefectures, neither Hiroshima nor Nagasaki became primary immigrant destinations until economic recovery, stimulated by increased military expenditure, began in the 1930s. Although the development of Hiroshima as a centre for naval construction, armaments manufacturing, and military education at the Naval Academy at Edajima, dated from the early part of the century, relatively few Koreans migrated to the region before 1930. Aside from security considerations, the demand for unskilled labour in construction, for example, had previously been met through local supplies of seasonal workers drawn from rural areas around Hiroshima. At the same time, the relatively higher level of skills required in military procurements will have excluded all but a very small minority of Korean labourers.

Table 4.1 Resident Korean population, 1910–45: Osaka, Hiroshima, Nagasaki, Fukuoka prefectural totals

	Osaka	Hiroshima	Nagasaki	Fukuoka
1910	206	24	173	335
1913	338	39	283	549
1916	762	68	381	894
1919	4,502	808	1,844	6,704
1922	13,337	1,681	2,008	8,304
1925	31,860	4,025	2,407	13,357
1928	55,209	5,827	4,324	21,042
1931	85,567	8,156	4,320	25,126
1934	171,160	18,311	8,934	36,115
1937	234,188	19,525	7,625	50,565
1940	312,269	38,221	18,144	116,864
1943	395,380	68,274	47,415	172,199
1945	333,354	84,886	61,773	205,452

Source: Harada, T. and J. Kang (eds) (1985) *Sabetsu to Jinken (4) Minzoku*, Tokyo: Yūzankaku, pp. 46–7.

Compared with the astonishing growth in the size of the Korean community in Osaka in particular, the size of the Hiroshima population only increased by about 11,000 between 1930 and 1937. None the less, this represented a more than twofold increase in the size of the local Korean community. Migrant labour from the peninsula poured into Hiroshima following the Manchurian Incident in 1931 when naval facilities at Ujina were expanded, and again after the Shanghai Incident in 1935, which coincided with the expansion of the various naval and military installations in and around Hiroshima. The outbreak of the Pacific War and the subsequent mobilization of colonial labour to offset domestic labour shortages stimulated further expansion of local communities in Hiroshima and Nagasaki, both of which more than doubled in size between 1940 and 1945. Although precise figures are not available, an estimated 52–53,000 Koreans were living in the city of Hiroshima in August 1945, with smaller communities spread throughout the prefecture (Yi 1979: 251–2). Estimates for Nagasaki are even less reliable, but it is likely that about half (30,000) of the prefectural population of 61,773 could be found within the city proper.

As elsewhere, Korean ghettos in Hiroshima and Nagasaki were located in both the poorer downtown districts and the so-called *basue-machi* (fringe towns) which served as halfway zones connecting rural sources of seasonal labour with urban industrial centres (Yi 1979: 254). In both cities the great majority of Koreans were accommodated in *nagaya* tenements, low-cost wooden structures, covered in corrugated iron or in some instances straw. Tenements were normally constructed in clusters, at some distance from ordinary housing, but providing easy access to the factories which employed the residents. In Hiroshima, the largest *Chōsenjin Buraku* (Korean ghettos) were concentrated within 4 or 4.5 km of the hypocentre. These included areas along the Fukushima River between Yodogawa Bridge and Dobashi Bridge, Fukushima-cho (now Miyako-cho and Ogawauchi-cho), between Minami Kannon and Higashi Kannon-cho, and in Funairi. Approximately 3,000 conscripted Koreans employed by Mitsubishi at its Shipyard and Engine Manufacturing facilities at Koi and Eba respectively (both of which were located 3 km from the hypocentre) were housed in a single dormitory (Yi 1979: 252). Further immigrant clusters could be found in Hirose-machi, Yokogawa, Tenma and Kusunoki-cho located in the western part of the city.

Many of the residents of these areas were employed in general construction or demolition work in the city centre. Others were employed as manual labour in factories operated by Mitsubishi Heavy Industries and Toyo Kogyo, while large numbers of Korean women were working in small and medium-size factories in Nakahiro and Kusunoki-cho, or at the Military Clothing Depot located in Ujina. The nearby Kure Naval Dockyard, whose extensive facilities had accounted for the construction of some fifty-five warships including the battleship *Yamato*, and employed approximately 10,000 workers at its peak in 1944, was also thought to have employed considerable numbers of conscripted Korean labourers. It was not, however, until 1990 that this was confirmed by documentary evidence. Of the more than 6,000 Koreans identified in these records about 1,400 were employed at the Naval Arsenal and the remainder at other military installations in the Kure area (*Kobe Shinbun*, 7 July 1990). Similar conditions existed in Nagasaki, where large numbers of Koreans were employed in general construction, the Kawanami Shipyard, and at the Mitsubishi Shipyard and Ironworks (*Kobe Shinbun*, 8 July 1990; Harada and Kang 1985: 23; *Chōsenjin no Hibakusha* 1989: 78–82).

Though fewer in number than their counterparts in Hiroshima, the proportion of Koreans residing within 1.5 km of the hypocentre in Nagasaki was greater (*Chōsenjin no Hibakushu* 1989: 87). Reconstructing an accurate picture of Korean settlement in either city, however, remains difficult for several reasons: (1) the destruction of contemporary documentary evidence by the atomic explosions and the subsequent firestorms which swept both cities; (2) very high labour turnover rates and general mobility among Korean workers made identification impossible in many cases, particularly during the closing stages of the war; and (3) the fact that survivors were often unable to provide addresses or otherwise identify the precise locality in which they lived in August 1945 (Kosho 1991: 113).

/ At the time, the decision to use the atomic bomb against Japan was viewed by most within the American political and military establishment as little more than a continuation of the policy of strategic bombing (Lifton and Markusen 1990: 23). The distinction between a military target and a city had already been largely erased by the bombings of Dresden, Hamburg and Tokyo, where the incendiary raids of March 1945 resulted in the deaths of more than 100,000 people. None the less, the consequences for the victims of the atomic bombings of August 1945 were unprecedented. The Hiroshima bomb of 6 August exploded with the force of 20,000 tons of TNT near the centre of a flat city constructed mainly of wood. All buildings within a two-mile radius were completely destroyed, and flash burns occurred at a distance of up to 2.5 miles from the hypo-centre. The number of fatalities, both immediate and as an indirect consequence of the bombings, may never be known. The figure most commonly cited is 78,000, but previous estimates have ranged as high as 240,000, while the city of Hiroshima's estimate of 200,000 is equivalent to between 25 and 50 per cent of the daytime population in 1945. /

/ Three days later a further 70,000 inhabitants of Nagasaki suffered a similar fate. Of approximately 50,000 Koreans residing in Hiro-shima, an estimated 30,000 died, either as a direct result of the blast, or soon thereafter. The surviving 20,000 Koreans constituted between 15 and 20 per cent of the total Hiroshima *hibakusha* population. The corresponding figure for Korean *hibakusha* in Nagasaki has been esti-mated at 20,000, including 10,000 fatalities (*Chōsenjin no Hibakusha* 1989: 87; Sato and Yamada 1986: 111). The wide disparity in esti-mates is at least in part accounted for by the fact that systematic health surveys of *hibakusha* were not introduced until 1950, five years after the bombings had taken place./During the American Occupation, the Atomic Bomb Casualty Commission was charged with examining survivors of the Hiroshima bomb, but the resulting data was dispatched to the Pentagon for analysis and little was done to alleviate the condition of those suffering the effects of radiation. In its attempts to downplay the after-effects of nuclear warfare, the Occupation authorities initially denied the existence of residual radia-tion. The Japanese government was equally slow to provide aid to those suffering from what had become known as 'atomic bomb dis-ease'. It was not, in fact, until 1956 that the Atomic Bomb Hospital was opened, and not until 1957 that the government enacted the Law for Health Protection and Medical Treatment for Atomic Bomb Sufferers. Since then the *hibakusha* have been entitled to subsidized and, in certain instances, free medical treatment.

In 1988, Shigematsu Itsuzo, Director of the Japan–US Radiation Effects Research Foundation in Hiroshima, originally established by the US in 1947 as the Atomic Bomb Casualty Commission, provided estimates which, though not as high as those contained in municipal surveys, exceeded the official figures by a considerable margin. His estimates, published by the *Mainichi Shinbun* to mark the forty-third anniversary of the bombing, were that 90–120,000 people in Hiro-shima, comprising 33 per cent of the population, had died within five months of the atomic bombing of 6 August. By comparison, Nagasaki lost an estimated 28 per cent (60–80,000 people) of its population (*Mainichi Shinbun*, 6 August 1988). According to the most recent national survey conducted by the Health and Welfare Ministry, a total of 295,956 people had died between 1945 and 1988 as a direct or indirect consequence of atomic bombings. These findings exceed the estimates of independent surveys carried out in Hiroshima and Nagasaki by about 12,000. The national figures also support the contention that many of the people mobilized to help clear the cities after the attacks had been fatally affected by the long-term effects of exposure to radiation (*Mainichi Shinbun*, 5 August 1990). Many thousands more, who survived the initial devastation, were left burned and mutilated, and the totality of their experience has never left the minds of the victims. The lingering and debilitating effects of radiation sickness, mainly in the form of cancers and leukaemia, continue to claim the lives of survivors and their children, fuelling fears of hereditary transmission (Lifton and Markusen 1990: 24).

Hibakusha have a 17 per cent greater chance than the average population of developing stomach cancer, the most common form of cancer in Japan, and are four times more likely to develop leukaemia (*Mainichi Shinbun*, 6 August 1988). The higher than average incidence of still births and microcephalic babies among *hibakusha* has also lent credence to fears of genetic scarring, and this stigma weighs heavily in a society which places great store on family lineage. Quite apart from the health-related problems associated with physical disability and the effects of radiation, the *hibakusha* have also endured various forms of discrimination, ranging from social exclusion to avoidance (it is still common for visitors to ask whether there are restricted areas in the two cities). Paradoxically, the *hibakusha*, as a group, have also been constructed as tragic heroes, sanctified on the left as an unimpeachable argument against rearmament, and on the right as victims of American racism.

HIBAKUSHA HEALTH AND LIVELIHOOD

In November 1967, the Ministry of Welfare released the results of the first national survey of *hibakusha* health and living conditions. In its final submission, covering some forty-six pages, the Ministry concluded that there was insufficient evidence to substantiate claims that significant differences existed between ordinary citizens and *hibakusha* in areas of health and general livelihood. *Hibakusha* support groups were critical of both the conclusions reached and the methods employed by the Ministry. These criticisms fell into four areas: (1) the Ministry had ignored the results of local surveys which indicated wide differences in health between general public and *hibakusha*; (2) the survey results were inconsistent with other evidence collected over a twenty-year period; (3) all surveys had been conducted at health clinics, thereby excluding those individuals who were either well at the time, or too ill to attend the clinic; and (4) the survey had relied entirely on blood samples and blood-pressure readings – cancer and liver-related disease had been deleted from the survey, despite evidence of higher-than-average incidence of both among *hibakusha* (*Chōsenjin no Hibakusha* 1989: 249–50).

In general, *hibakusha* receive wages which are lower than those available to an able-bodied worker. This suggests that *hibakusha* families will also commit a higher proportion of their income in health-related expenditures than the national average. The Ministry of Health carried out three surveys over a twenty-year period (1965, 1975, 1985) designed to assess income and expenditure levels among *hibakusha* (Ito 1988: 42). The results of the first of these surveys, conducted in 1965, confirmed that, while average income levels among *hibakusha* were lower than the national average, expenditures were, on the whole, higher. Ten years later it was found that, although the gap between income and expenditure had narrowed, the income of *hibakusha* families remained significantly lower than the national average, while expenditures remained stubbornly high. The most recent survey, conducted in 1985, concluded that despite a continuing decrease in some differentials, *hibakusha* expenditures were actually higher than in previous years. One conclusion to be drawn from these national surveys is that, throughout the post-war period, the standard of living among *hibakusha* has remained below the national average. While physical disability may, to a certain extent, account for the persistence of relatively low wage levels, this situation has been aggravated by the fact that *hibakusha* spend a disproportionate share of their income on medical care (Ito 1988: 43). Relative poverty has also given rise to a range of related problems, including underachievement in school, unemployment and underemployment, difficulty in finding marriage partners and the ability to maintain normal patterns of family life. Although no corresponding national survey of resident Korean *hibakusha* has been carried out, the results of an independent inquiry conducted in Hiroshima in 1978 indicate similar levels of deprivation and ill health (Yi 1979: 261–6).

LEGAL RESPONSIBILITY FOR THE TREATMENT OF *HIBAKUSHA*

By virtue of Article 19 of the San Francisco Peace Treaty, the United States was released from any responsibility for the care and treatment of *hibakusha* (*Chōsenjin no Hibakusha* 1989: 244). Thereafter, the matter of compensation was left entirely to the Japanese state, as was the negotiation of appropriate levels of subsidized medical treatment for victims. At national level, two pieces of legislation determine the extent of care provided for *hibakusha*: the 1957 Genshi Bakudan Hibakusha no Iryō nado ni kansuru Hōritsu (Law for the Treatment of Hibakusha) and the 1968 Genshi Bakudan Hibakusha ni taisuru Tokubetsu Sochi ni Kansuru Hōritsu (Special Measures Law for Hibakusha) (Won 1986: 145). In fact, it was not until the introduction of the 1957 law that subsidized medical treatment for disabilities arising from radiation sickness was provided by the state. Likewise, an official allowance, in lieu of accepting responsibility and paying compensation to victims, was not made available until the passage of the Special Measures Law. Under the 1968 legislation, *hibakusha* entitlements covered five areas, all of which were dependent upon possession of a valid *techō* (*hibakusha* allowance book), issued by the appropriate prefectural authorities. These included:

1 Specific allowance.
2 Health-care allowance.
3 Nursing allowance.
4 Medical treatment allowance.
5 Allowance limiting tax liability.
(*Chōsenjin no Hibakusha* 1989: 245)

The same legislation enumerates the criteria which must be met before *techō* are issued. In all cases claimants are required to provide either documentary evidence of their status as *hibakusha*, or depositions from at least two witnesses confirming the individual's presence in Hiroshima or Nagasaki in August 1945. Possession of a *techō* entitles the holder to subsidized medical treatment (both in-patient and out-patient) through a national network of registered clinics. In addition to those identified as direct victims of the bombings, *techō* are also awarded to those who passed within 2 kilometres of the hypocentre before 20 August 1945, as well as those employed in hospitals or morgues who came into contact with irradiated corpses. From 1980, limited access to state benefits has also been extended to the children of *hibakusha*. Since the introduction of the 1957 Law for the Treatment of Hibakusha, more than US$7 billion has been allocated for the creation and maintenance of a nationwide network of *hibakusha* health-care facilities. In common with affirmative legislation directed at other disadvantaged groups in Japan, the creation of this system owes much to the efforts of sub-national organizations. In fact, it was only after a lengthy and vigorous campaign to raise public awareness, mounted by both prefectural and municipal governments in Hiroshima and Nagasaki and various *hibakusha* support organizations, that the state reluctantly drafted the relevant legislation./

KOREAN *HIBAKUSHA*

Overall responsibility for the provision of health and welfare assistance has been determined not only by Japanese domestic law but by international treaties, and latterly through bi-lateral agreements between Japan and the Republic of Korea. The stance taken by national governments, particularly in the Japanese case, has also established a model which private sector firms have largely adhered to. The best-known example of this involves claims for outstanding wages and compensation for injuries sustained as a result of the bombings instituted against Mitsubishi Heavy Industries by former Korean employees. Two Hiroshima-based support organizations, the Kankoku no Mitsubishi Chōyō Hibakusha Dōshikai/(Association of Koreans Conscripted by Mitsubishi) and the Kankokujin Hibakusha Chimbotsu Izokukai (Association of Bereaved Families of Korean A-Bomb Victims Lost at Sea), have been involved in legal action against Mitsubishi since 1975. Korean claims have focused on four issues: (1) the payment of outstanding wages; (2) the payment of condolence money to bereaved families; (3) the payment of compensation to surviving *hibakusha* employees; and (4) an investigation of the circumstances surrounding the deaths of several hundred Korean *hibakusha* during the return crossing to Korea in 1945, and the construction of a memorial for the victims in Korea. Mitsubishi has rejected these claims on the grounds that the matter of compensation had been settled by the 1965 Treaty of Normalization. The corporation did accept that moral issues were involved, and offered assistance to Korean *hibakusha*, conditional on the involvement of both national and prefectural governments. After years of negotiations, involving Mitsubishi and the Ministries of Welfare, Justice and Foreign Affairs, an Assistance Association was created in November

1981. To date, however, no compensation has been awarded, nor an investigation carried out (*Chōsenjin no Hibakusha* 1989: 271–4).

The 1957 and 1968 Hibakusha Laws were clearly designed to alleviate the distress of patients and their families by facilitating access to state and municipal aid under the *techō* system. Neither law contains a *kokuseki jōkō* (nationality requirement) which might otherwise restrict their application to holders of Japanese nationality (Won 1986: 145–6). Moreover, although financial responsibility largely rests with the national government, the *techō* system is administered by the municipal authorities in Hiroshima and Nagasaki respectively (Harada and Kang 1985: 108). In theory this should have ensured equal treatment for non-Japanese *hibakusha*, since both municipalities have declared their intent to provide treatment for Korean *hibakusha* under the *techō* system. For many Korean claimants, however, the acquisition of this essential document requires a lengthy and often fruitless journey through the Japanese bureaucracy.

A literal interpretation of the law suggests that the issuance of a *techō* would immediately follow the submission of written testimony or a contemporary record attesting to the applicant's whereabouts in August 1945. This in itself presents particular difficulties for Koreans who may well have been unaware of where they actually were, or whose identity cards and other forms of identification were destroyed at the time. In many cases this has also prevented Koreans from collecting back-pay owed by their Japanese employers since 1945. The cross-referencing of claims has been further complicated by the fact that many Koreans were known only by the Japanese names they used during the colonial period, coupled with the failure of the Japanese government to undertake a systematic survey of resident Korean *hibakusha* at any time since 1945 (Kosho 1991: 108-15; *Nagasaki Shinbun*, 9 May 1991; Yi 1979: 262). The recently amended policy which required that at least one witness be Japanese also disenfranchised many potential Korean claimants (Won 1986: 146).

Of the estimated 70,000 Koreans who were exposed to the atomic bombings, approximately 40,000 died immediately or within the following year. Most of the survivors (23,000) returned to Korea within a year of the surrender, while some 7,000 remained in Japan (*Yomiuri Shinbun*, 2 August 1986). Although the decision to return to Korea will have been affected by numerous factors, Korean *hibakusha* were also targeted by SCAP (Supreme Command Allied Powers) for early repatriation. Concerned with the slow pace at which repatriation of 'non-Japanese' nationals was taking place, SCAP issued a series of enabling directives in November 1945.

Financial responsibility for the operation was shifted to the Japanese government, and the Ministry of Welfare was assigned the task of providing transportation via the ports of Hakata, Senzaki, Sasebo and Maizuru. Priority transportation was to be made available to Korean members of the Japanese armed forces, conscripted labourers, and atomic bomb casualties (Kōseishō 1950: 53–5). The right of Korean claimants, whether resident in Japan or Korea, to seek redress or compensation was further eroded by the post-war loss of Japanese nationality.

Despite vigorous campaigns mounted by *hibakusha* support organizations in both countries, the Japanese position, which has since been repeated in the case of comfort women and Korean war veterans, has been that Japan had been relieved of any responsibility for the payment of compensation to Korean nationals by the 1965 Treaty of Normalization. This is particularly relevant in the case of *hibakusha* resident in Korea where, until recently, little effort had been made either to identify or to provide treatment for sufferers. During the immediate post-war period of repatriation, 23,000 Korean *hibakusha* would have been lost among the nearly 2 million Koreans who returned to their country of birth. Similarly, there is no way of knowing how many *hibakusha* were numbered among the nearly 3 million Koreans who died during the Korean War, or how many have died of radiation-related illnesses since that time. These factors, coupled with the absence of specialist medical facilities in rural parts of South Korea, where the largest concentrations of *hibakusha* can be found, have made identification extremely difficult. The most reliable figures available are those provided by the South Korean-based Association of Korean Atomic Bomb Victims (Kankoku Genbaku Higaisha Kyūgokai) (*Chōsenjin no Hibakusha* 1989: 253; *Yomiuri Shinbun*, 2 August 1986). In 1979 there were 1,878 foreign holders of *techō* certification residing in Hiroshima, almost all of whom were Korean nationals. The corresponding figure for Nagasaki was 126. These, of course, represented only a fraction of the total number of Korean *hibakusha*. An estimated 15,000 *hibakusha* were thought to be living in South Korea, and a further 2,000 in North Korea (Sato and Yamada 1986: 111). Of the approximately 10,000 *hibakusha* currently (1994) resident in Korea, more than one-third (3,570) live in the township of Hapchon in Kyōngsang Province. In 1973, with financial assistance provided by the Japanese Conference for the Abolition of Atomic Weapons, a specialist clinic was constructed in Hapchon. It remains the only centre for the treatment of radiation-related illnesses to be found in South Korea.

/ In 1971, under pressure from local government officers in Oka City, the Mayor of Nagasaki conceded that the existing system discriminated against Korean claimants, and undertook to ensure greater flexibility in the issuance of *techō* in future. It was not, however, until 1983 that Koreans began to enjoy the results of this commitment to greater flexibility (*Chōsenjin no Hibakusha* 1989: 248). In 1972 there were an estimated 2,000 Korean *hibakusha* living in Nagasaki, yet as late as 1978 only 110 had been issued with an allowance book (So 1989: 24; Ito 1987: 228). /

/ The lack of adequate resources, coupled with a fear of social discrimination, and the low level of public awareness in Korea concerning the effects of nuclear warfare, also encouraged Korean *hibakusha* to enter Japan illegally in search of medical treatment. Included within this category were Koreans like Son Jin-doo who, though born in Japan and a Hiroshima resident in 1945, had returned to Korea when deprived of Japanese nationality in 1951. Son was arrested and held by the police in Fukuoka for nearly a year after he re-entered Japan in 1970. In fact, Son had been apprehended on two earlier occasions (1951, 1964), when he had sought medical treatment in Japan. His application to the Fukuoka Court for *techō* status was also initially rejected on the grounds of nationality, but an appeal to the Fukuoka District Court was successful. After further appeals lodged against this decision by the Fukuoka municipal authorities, Son's case was argued before the Japanese Supreme Court. In a landmark decision handed down in the spring of 1978, the Supreme Court ruled in favour of Son's application for *techō* status on both humanitarian grounds and because the Japanese state, as party to the war, was liable for compensation (*Chōsenjin no Hibakusha* 1989: 253; Harada and Kang 1985: 109). This decision did not, however, legalize Son's status in Japan, and he was subsequently deported by order of the Ministry of Justice (Tanaka 1993: 50–1). Son's experience was not an isolated one, and many other such 'illegals', regardless of their length of residence in Japan or their state of health, have been summarily deported to Korea. /

/ The Son case, which received considerable attention in the national press, highlighted the ambiguous position in which thousands of Korean *hibakusha* in Korea found themselves: guaranteed medical treatment by the Japanese Supreme Court, but prevented from entering Japan by the Immigration Control Law. / Due largely to the adverse publicity generated by the Son case, a joint Japan–Korean committee, comprised of Liberal Democratic Party and Democratic Socialist Party Diet members and their opposite numbers in the ruling Democratic Republic Party in Seoul, produced an intergovernmental aid scheme for the treatment of Korean *hibakusha.* The programme outlined three areas of bilateral co-operation:

1 The training of Korean doctors in Japan.
2 The despatch of Japanese doctors and facilities to Korea.
3 Treatment in Japan for *hibakusha* resident in Korea.
(*Chōsenjin no Hibakusha* 1989: 253)

In November 1980, a pilot scheme was introduced under which ten Korean *hibakusha* were admitted for treatment at special hospitals in Japan. This was followed in December 1981 by a five-year agreement on Japan-based treatment for Korean *hibakusha* under which Japan agreed to provide free treatment for approximately seventy Korean *hibakusha* annually, provided that the South Korean government would accept responsibility for the selection of *hibakusha* as well as for all necessary transportation costs between the two countries. The agreement also stipulated that the initial period of treatment would be two months, with extensions of up to six months if medically necessary (*Chōsenjin no Hibakusha* 1989: 254; Harada and Kang 1985: 110). As a result of this agreement, 322 Korean *hibakusha* received treatment in Japan between December 1981 and July 1986. In the majority of cases arrangements were made through state agencies, while in others treatment was sponsored by action groups in Hiroshima and Nagasaki (*Mainichi Shinbun*, 25 October 1986). Although this went some way towards alleviating the distress of some Korean *hibakusha* and their families in Korea, the programme encountered a number of unanticipated difficulties. In some cases aged Koreans were reluctant to abandon their families for lengthy periods, or to return to the source of their illness. Others feared the discrimination which might follow their exposure as *hibakusha*, or were distrustful of Japanese intentions, and some were too ill to make the journey. Further difficulties arose in November 1986 when the South Korean authorities announced that they would not support an extension of the programme. As later explained to Hageta Shingo, a representative of the Ministry of Welfare Planning Section, the Korean withdrawal of support was prompted by two considerations: (1) the steady improvement in medical provision available through the Korean health system had rendered the programme redundant; and (2) those Koreans most in need of treatment had either been treated in Japan or had died during the previous five years (*Chōsenjin no Hibakusha* 1989: 254).

The Korean decision to discontinue the bi-lateral treatment programme also needs to be seen within the broader political context of the mid-1980s. First, despite the benefits to be gained through support of a well-publicized programme of humanitarian assistance, for some Korean officials there was an element of humiliation inherent in accepting aid of this type from the former colonial power, particularly when it also highlighted the inadequacy of health provision in Korea. Other Korean officials argued that, since the Korean presence in Hiroshima in 1945 was a direct consequence of colonial policies, the Japanese government should bear full financial responsibility, including the transportation of patients between Korea and Japan. / But any suggestion that it should accept sole responsibility for the *hibakusha*, either political or financial, conflicted with Japanese determination to avoid the creation of precedents which would encourage demands for compensation from other categories of war victim. Second, the treatment of *hibakusha* risked being subsumed or at least overshadowed by other more contentious issues during this period. The years 1985 and 1986 marked the first occasion on which the political and legal status of Korean residents in Japan had been incorporated in the agenda for bi-lateral negotiations between Japan and the Republic of Korea since 1965. It was during this same period that a campaign of civil disobedience directed at laws which required the fingerprinting of foreign residents in Japan had reached a critical stage. There were also suspicions that an extension of the *hibakusha* programme would be seized upon by the Japanese in an attempt to deflect criticism of its policies towards foreign residents, most of whom were Korean nationals. /

Despite the insistence of Korean officials that the programme had successfully run its course, hundreds of Korean *hibakusha* were either deprived of specialist medical attention altogether, or suffered relapses due to early termination of vital treatment. The official Korean position was subject to considerable criticism, particularly from among those groups which had vigorously lobbied for the introduction of the treatment programme./But the most scathing condemnation was reserved for the Japanese government, which continued to deny responsibility for compensation, and which had required a South Korean financial commitment as a precondition for treating Korean *hibakusha*./ With neither government prepared to accept responsibility, local organizations, mainly in Japan, campaigned for reinstatement of the *hibakusha* treatment programmes. The (Nagasaki Zainichi Chōsenjin no Jinken wo Mamorukai) Association for the Protection of Korean Rights in Nagasaki took a leading role in petitioning the Ministry of Welfare for assistance, while the (Hiroshima Tonichi Chiryō Iinkai) Hiroshima Committee for the Transport and Treatment of Koreans funded follow-up treatment at a private clinic in August 1986 for fifty-one Koreans whose hospitalization under the bilateral programme had been interrupted (*Chōsenjin no Hibakusha* 1989: 254–5).

Even before the discontinuation of the treatment programme, the South Korean-based association of Korean Atomic Bomb Victims had sought assistance from the Human Rights Committee of the Japan Federation of Bar Associations in establishing a legal basis for compensation. The issue of a state indemnity is one which unites both Japanese and Korean *hibakusha* (Harada and Kang 1985: 108–9). Indeed, Japanese support groups have argued unsuccessfully since 1962 for the introduction of legislation guaranteeing compensation to complement the subsidized medical care available under the 1957 Law for the Treatment of Hibakusha.

/ Following an investigation carried out in southern Korea during the previous summer, the Japanese Federation of Bar Associations submitted an interim report in October 1986 which urged the Japanese government to negotiate an extension of the original treatment programme. This initial report was supplemented by a 1987 survey of the health and welfare requirements of Korean *hibakusha* resident in Japan. Once again, the Bar Federation was unsuccessful in persuading the government that it was legally responsible for compensation and the provision of adequate livelihood assistance (*Chōsenjin no Hibakusha* 1989: 270–1). /Undeterred, the Korean Association for Atomic Bomb Victims submitted a claim for compensation totalling US$2.3 billion in 1987 (Takasaki 1994: 146). This sum was arrived at through a formula which took into account the annual allowances paid to Japanese *hibakusha*, and the number of years which had elapsed since the bombings.

The emergence of new governments in both Seoul and Tokyo in 1988 stimulated a far more positive response, particularly from the Japanese side. Foreign Minister Uno's expression of support for the resumption of a treatment programme was followed by the despatch of an investigatory team to South Korea in May (*Asahi Shinbun*, 18 May 1988). The Foreign Ministry team confirmed the severity of the situation in Korea and identified three areas requiring immediate attention: (1) resumption of the previous bi-lateral system of care, but with Japan bearing full responsibility for the transportation of patients; (2) establishment of an exchange and training system for medical staff; and (3) funding for a mobile clinic in Korea for *hibakusha* whose health did not permit travel to Japan. These recommendations were, however, largely ignored./Instead, in 1989 the government contributed ¥42 million ($300,000) to the South Korean Red Cross for the care of *hibakusha*, with a similar amount committed for 1990. In May that year, during an official visit to Japan by President Roh and marked by an official apology from Prime Minister Kaifu for past injustices committed against the Korean people, the Japanese acceded to Korean demands for increased levels of support and assistance.│An initial sum of US$25 million was allocated to implement the recommendations of the 1988 Foreign Ministry team, and this was followed in 1991 by the appropriation of $12.6 million to fund assistance programmes for Korean *hibakusha*. At a conference sponsored by the Korean Association of Atomic Bomb Victims in Seoul during August 1992, however, the Japanese government was strongly criticized for having failed to fulfil this commitment (*Asahi Shinbun*, 6 and 13 August 1992)./

/In the absence of any details as to how these figures had been arrived at, or how the fund would be distributed, it was clear that future assistance programmes would be administered locally. Since 1990, the municipal authorities in Nagasaki and Hiroshima appear to have adopted a positive approach to addressing the needs of Korean *hibakusha*. In August of that year, at a commemorative ceremony marking the forty-fifth anniversary of the Nagasaki bombing, the obligation to compensate Korean *hibakusha* was publicly acknowledged for the first time (*Asahi Shinbun*, 9 August 1990; *Yomiuri Shinbun*, 9 August 1990). An official apology to Korean *hibakusha* was included in the annual peace declaration, and Korean women were invited to appear at the ceremony in traditional (*chima chogori*) dress. Prime Minister Kaifu also became the first national leader in more than a decade to attend memorial services in both Nagasaki and Hiroshima. Although no specific reference to Korean *hibakusha* was contained in his address, Kaifu committed the government to improving relief measures for all atom bomb victims. /

/In October 1992, the socialist Mayor of Nagasaki, Motoshima Hitoshi, became the first mayor of either city to visit South Korea for the purpose of meeting atom bomb survivors. This was followed by an announcement that the Nagasaki municipal government would allocate part of its budget to assist Korean survivors of the atomic bombings. The sum of ¥2 million for the fiscal year 1993 was set aside to fund projects designed to facilitate access to Japanese-government-sponsored programmes./Under the project, Nagasaki city officials would visit South Korea to provide information about medical treatment available in Japan, and explain to survivors the process by which *techō* could be obtained (*Mainichi Shinbun*, 24 February 1993). In August 1993, a peace conference in Hiroshima issued an appeal for a revision of *hibakusha* assistance legislation to ease access for Korean survivors (*Asahi Shinbun*, 3 August 1993). A similar appeal to delete all nationality requirements from existing legislation was made by the mayor of Hiroshima during the annual commemorative ceremony (*Asahi Shinbun*, 3 August 1993). In a related decision taken by the Ministry of Welfare, it was announced that the nationality restrictions governing war pensions for former members of the Imperial Army would be relaxed (*Asahi Shinbun*, 20 August 1993). Despite this and more recent undertakings given by former Prime Minister Hosokawa to reconsider the matter of compensation, the same ministry is currently contesting the right of Korean residents of Yokohama to claim compensation for injuries sustained during the war (*Asahi Shinbun*, 5 February 1994).

CONCLUSION

Between 1945 and 1990, numerous factors accounted for the failure of Korean *hibakusha*, whether resident in Korea or Japan, to obtain adequate and consistent treatment. The governments of the United States, South Korea and Japan were undoubtedly responsible for the suppression of information concerning Korean *hibakusha*. But this in itself does not account for the virtual disappearance of Korean *hibakusha* from post-war history. Neither can the deletion of Korean *hibakusha* from the Hiroshima/Nagasaki narratives simply be regarded as a manifestation of discrimination or prejudice directed at a particular minority population. As with many other events in the eighty-five-year history of the Korean presence in Japan, the marginalization of the Korean atom bomb experience within a dominant image of the past is but one aspect of a broader revisionist historical project. In contesting the official narratives of Hiroshima and Nagasaki, Korean *hibakusha* have sought not only to restore this episode in the history of their community, but to challenge the ways in which minority issues are presented to the public.

In marked contrast to the almost celebrity status accorded their Japanese counterparts, there has been little public awareness, domestically or internationally, of the existence of Korean *hibakusha*. While the visceral horror of atomic warfare has been captured in print and on film, there are no Korean equivalents of *The Hiroshima Maidens*, Lifton's *Death in Life*, Minear's *Hiroshima: Three Victims*, Seldon's *The Atomic Bomb: Voices from Hiroshima and Nagasaki*, the film version of Ibuse's *Black Rain*, or the works of Kurihara Sadako, Hayashi Kyoko, and others. To date, there have been only three films which provide an account of the Korean *hibakusha*: *To the People of the World* (1981); *To the Friends of the World* (1985); and *The Song of Arirang: One More Hiroshima* (1987) – none of which received financial support, publicity, or international screenings. /

For much of the post-1945 period the attention of human rights and other Korean organizations in Japan has focused upon broader concerns with civil liberties, particularly those pertaining to alien registration, immigration and nationality, employment and education, and welfare provision. /The struggle for *hibakusha* recognition has therefore been but one aspect of a multi-layered agenda, which has been affected not only by political and institutional processes within Japan but also by the continued division of the Korean peninsula and the political fragmentation of the Korean community in Japan. This is not, however, to suggest that Koreans can or should be held accountable for this lack of progress, but to highlight the extent to which external factors, in the form of competition between Seoul and Pyŏngyang, have also helped to shape the contours of the civil rights struggle within Japan. /Even the Hiroshima Peace Park has not been entirely free of controversy, as competing interest groups have attempted to mobilize this most potent symbol of anti-nuclearism for parochial interests.

While the Peace Park and cenotaph, around which the park was constructed, reflect a long-standing commitment to the three anti-nuclear principles, the appeal of this shrine also extends to spokesmen for the pro-nuclear lobby. The multi-dimensional politicization of *hibakusha* iconography has also been apparent in the decades-long battle to commemorate Korean victims of the Hiroshima bomb. It is a conflict which also illustrates the continued marginalization of a dissonant Korean history within the master narrative of post-war Hiroshima.

/ To circumvent city ordinances which prohibited the construction of additional cenotaphs within the borders of the Peace Park, the Hiroshima branch of Mindan (Korean Residents Union in Japan – the principal South Korean-affiliated Korean support group in Japan) erected a separate memorial to Korean victims on the opposite bank of the Ota River in 1970. While the positioning of the

Kankokujin Genbaku Giseisha Irei Hi (Memorial for the South/ Korean Victims of the Atomic Bomb) outside the Park's boundary is itself suggestive to many Koreans of their continued alienation, the use of the term 'Kankokujin', which usually denotes citizens of the Republic of Korea, has been regarded as an affront by members of the North Korean-affiliated Chōngnyon (General Federation of Korean Residents in Japan). As a result, the latter has unsuccessfully petitioned the city government for permission to construct a further memorial since the mid' 1970s. /

Two decades later, and forty-five years after the bombing, the Foreign Ministry and the Hiroshima city authorities finally sanctioned the construction of a memorial representing all Korean victims within the Peace Park (*Asahi Shinbun*, 18 May 1990). Although publicized as a purely humanitarian gesture, several factors were evident in the city government's decision to belatedly address this issue. Firstly, in contrast to previous statements made by the Showa emperor, Emperor Akihito's expression of *tsuseki* (painful remorse) to the people of Korea in May 1990 was accompanied by a public commitment to improve the status of Korean residents in Japan and to move towards a resolution of Korean claims for compensation dating from the Pacific War. Secondly, mounting criticism of the municipal authority's position contradicted Hiroshima's carefully constructed post-war image as an international centre of peace and prosperity.

While the Hiroshima announcement of May 1990 certainly reflected a new spirit of co-operation, the issue of the cenotaph remains unresolved. To a certain extent this has been due to the inability of the various Korean parties to reach an agreed wording for the inscription on a joint memorial (*Asahi Shinbun*, 16 July 1990). At the same time, however, by publicly distancing itself from the negotiations, the city government has not only obscured its own neglect of the issue of Korean remembrance for forty-five years, but has reinforced dominant perceptions of Koreans as marginal, unruly, and incapable of organizing their lives; images which have their origins in the pre-1945 period. Through its silence on this and other minority-related issues, the city authorities have effectively delegated responsibility for the resolution of this issue to members of the minority community. This, in turn, has created the impression that a Japanese problem originates within the minority community.

NOTE

1 This chapter is a revised and expanded version of an article which first appeared in *Immigrants and Minorities*, vol. 2, no. 1, 1995.

BIBLIOGRAPHY

Akiyama, O. (1929) 'Senjin Rōdōsha to Shitsugyō Mondai', *Shakai Seisaku Jihō* 111: 96–120.
Breuilly, J. (1993) *Nationalism and the State* (2nd edn), Manchester: Manchester University Press.
Chōsenjin no Hibakusha (1989) see Nagasaki Zainichi . . . (ed.).
Dower, J. (1993) 'Peace and democracy in two systems: external policy and internal conflict', in A. Gordon (ed.) *Postwar Japan as History*, Berkeley and Los Angeles: University of California Press.
Furedi, S. (1993) *Mythical Past Elusive Future, History and Society in an Anxious Age*, London: Pluto Press.
Gluck, C. (1993) 'The past in the present', in A. Gordon (ed.) *Postwar Japan as History*, Berkeley and Los Angeles: University of California Press.
Harada, T. and Kang, J. (eds) (1985) *Sabetsu to Jinken [4] Minzoku*, Tokyo: Yūzankaku.
Harajiri, H. (1989) *Zainichi Chōsenjin no Seikatsu Sekai*, Tokyo: Kōbundo.
Holloway, N. (1989) 'Curriculum conflict', *Far Eastern Economic Review*, 23 March: 29.
Ikutaro, S. (1980) 'The nuclear option: Japan be a state', *Japan Echo* 7, 3: 33–45.
Ito, T. (1987) *Genbaku Kimin: Kankoku, Chōsenjin no Shōgen*, Tokyo: Harubu Shuppan.
—— (1988) *Genbaku Hibakusha no Hanseiki*, Iwanami Bukkuretto 116, Tokyo: Iwanami Shōten.
Johnson, C. (1986) 'The patterns of Japanese relations with China 1952–1982', *Pacific Affairs* 59, 3: 402–28.
Kim, C.J. (1977) *Kaze no Dōkoku, Zainichi Chōsenjin Jokō no Seikatsu to Rekishi*, Tokyo: Tahata Shōten.
Kōseishō (1950) *Hikiage Engo no Kiroku* Tokyo: Ministry of Welfare.
Kosho, T. (1991) 'Chosenjin Kyōsei Renkō Meibo Chōsa wa Naze Susumanaika', *Sekai*, September: 108–15.
Lifton, R.J. and Markusen, E. (1990) *The Genocidal Mentality*, New York: Basic Books.
Nagasaki Zainichi Chōsenjin no Jinken wo Mamorukai (ed.) (1989) *Chōsenjin no Hibakusha: Nagasaki kara no Shōgen*, Tokyo: Shakai Hyōronsha (cited as *Chōsenjin no Hibakusha* 1989).
Nakahara, M. (1990) 'Tonan Ajia no me ni haetta Nihon', *Sekai* 544: 125–39.
Osaka-shi Shakai-bu, Chōsa-ka (1924) *Chōsenjin Rōdōsha Mondai*, Osaka.
Osaka-shi Shakai-bu, Rōdō-ka (1933) Shakai-bu Hōkoku Dai 177, *Chōsenjin Rōdōsha no Kinkyō*, Osaka.
Ryu, D.O. (1991) 'Zainichi Chōsenjin no Shogu Kaizen to wa dono yō na koto ka', *Sekai*, January: 248–60.

Sakai, T. (1931) 'Chōsenjin Rōdōsha Mondai' (2) *Shakai Jigyō Kenkyū*, July: 115–36.

Sato, A. and Yamada, T. (1986) *Zainichi Chōsenjin – Rekishi to Genjō*, Tokyo: Akashi, Shōten.

Shimizu, M. (1994) 'Sengo Hoshō no Kokusai Hikaku', *Sekai*, February: 133–43 .

So, K.S. (1989) *Kominka Seisaku kara Shimon Onatsu made*, Iwanami Bukkuretto, 128, Tokyo: Iwanami Shōten.

Takasaki, S. (1994) 'Nihon wa nani wo shita ka, nani wo utaerarete iru ka: Kankoku, Kita Chōsen', *Sekai*, February: 144–9.

Tanaka, H. (1993) *Zainichi Gaikokujin*, Tokyo: Iwanami Shinsho.

—— (1994) 'Nihon wa Sensō Sekinin ni: dō taishite kita ka', *Sekai*, February: 122–32.

Weiner, M. (1994) *Race and Migration in Imperial Japan*, London and New York: Routledge.

Won, J.G. (1986) *Zainichi Chōsenjin no Seikatsu to Jinken*, Tokyo: Dōseisha.

Yamamoto, T. (1991) 'Shokuminchi Shihai wa Seitō datta no ka', *Sekai*, November: 315–23.

Yi, S.K. (1979) *Hibaku Chōsenjin Mondai to (Chōhikyō)*, Tokyo: Rōdō Junposha.

FURTHER READING

The following notes refer only to additional books and articles in the English language. This should not be taken to mean that they are necessarily the best available, or that the listing is comprehensive. In fact, the bibliography of Japanese language materials relating to the history and current status of Korean residents is so extensive that no attempt is made here to provide even a selective list. The books and articles listed below do, however, contain bibliographical references to sources in the Japanese language.

Among general works of historical reference, E. Wagner's *The Korean Minority in Japan 1904–1950* (1950) was the first to appear. Written during the Allied Occupation of Japan, it reflects Japanese concerns with Koreans as a security problem. R.H. Mitchell's *The Korean Minority in Japan* (1967) provides a largely descriptive account of the political and economic contours of the Korean community. More detailed accounts of the pre- and post-war contexts can be found in M. Weiner, *The Origins of the Korean Community in Japan 1910–1923* (1990) and *Race and Migration in Imperial Japan* (1994), and in C.S. Lee and G. DeVos, *Koreans in Japan, Ethnic Accommodation and Conflict* (1981) respectively. Issues of human rights are addressed specifically in two articles by C.I. Chee: 'Japan's Post-war Denationalization of the Korean Minority in International

Law', *Korea and World Affairs* (1983) and 'Alien Registration Law of Japan and the International Covenant for Civil and Political Rights', *Korea and World Affairs* (1986). More extensive coverage of contemporary social, political, economic and cultural issues can be found in Y. Iwasawa, 'Legal Treatment of Koreans in Japan – The Impact of International Human-Rights Law on Japanese Law', *Japan Human Rights Quarterly* (1986); H. Hardacre, *The Religion of Japan's Korean Minority; The Preservation of Ethnic Identity* (1984); T. Umakoshi, 'The Education of Korean Children in Japan', in D. Rothermund and J. Simon, *Education and the Integration of Minorities* (1987); S. Ryang (2) 'Why Koreans Oppose the Fingerprint Law', *Japan Quarterly* (1985); 'Ethno-Political Community of North Koreans in Japan', *International Migration* (1990); K. Oguri, 'Resident Koreans are Native Speakers too', *Japan Quarterly* (1990); and D.M. Hoffman, 'Changing Faces, Changing Places – The New Koreans in Japan', *Japan Quarterly* (1992).

5 A model minority

The Chinese community in Japan

Andrea Vasishth

INTRODUCTION

Although Chinese emigration to Japan was far smaller than that to South-east Asia or the Americas, there is a lengthy history of Chinese settlement in Japan. From the Chinese viewpoint, trade with Japan reflected the latter's incorporation within the traditional Sinocentric East Asian order. Considered the source of a superior culture and a model of civilized political and social behaviour, China was highly regarded by traditional elites in Japan. In times of political disorder, Chinese scholars and intellectuals found refuge in Japan, while Sino-Japanese commercial links persisted despite intermittent attempts by both countries to restrict trade. Further emigration from China occurred in the half century after the 'opening of Japan' in 1853, and as late as 1915 Chinese labourers and merchants comprised the largest foreign population in Japan.

In contrast to other minority populations in contemporary Japan, the Chinese are distinguished by their affluence. But, the conceptualization of the Chinese as a 'model minority', in contrast to the Korean community, for example, obscures a history of exclusion and exploitation, while the lack of scholarly interest in the Chinese community can be taken as a further manifestation of this marginalization. This chapter offers a preliminary analysis of the historical formation of the Chinese community within the broader context of Chinese emigration.

THE OVERSEAS CHINESE

Emigration from China during the pre-war period was the continuation of a long tradition of internal and external Chinese sojourning and migration. By the Southern Song dynasty (1127–1280), internal migration linked to trade had resulted in significant communities of traders and entrepreneurs residing in major Chinese commercial centres (Skinner 1976: 335). In addition, despite Ming (1368–1644) and Qing (1644–1911) prohibitions on foreign travel which were not formally revoked until 1893, a tradition of external migration was established in many coastal areas. From the sixteenth century, certain counties of coastal Fujian had developed patterns of overseas sojourning and reliance on remittances, and by the eighteenth century a similar pattern had been established in many coastal regions of Guangdong, Zhejiang and Jiangsu. Numerous Chinese trading communities, whose membership was replenished by chain migration, were scattered throughout South-east Asia (Wickberg 1994: 14).

After 1850, external migration increased rapidly and over 2 million people left China between 1848 and 1888 alone. This was a consequence of both the encounter with European imperialism and China's increased incorporation within the world capitalist system, although internal changes within China also led to new economic opportunities and demographic pressures which encouraged migration. 'Push' factors within China included the dislocations caused by the Opium War and the Taiping Rebellion, as well as widespread natural disasters. By 1850 the population of China had reached 430 million, with 28 million in Guangdong alone. These problems were compounded by the intrusion of the world economic system into coastal China. The shift in Western demand, for example, for Indian rather than China tea led to widespread poverty and emigration from the tea-producing regions of Fujian. 'Pull' factors included labour demands in South-east Asia and the Americas which, with the demise of the African slave trade, was largely filled by the Chinese 'coolie' trade between 1845 and 1874. Paralleling this there arose a system of indentured labour in which new immigrants, sponsored by Chinese already in the new country, repaid the cost of their ticket before being allowed to work on their own account. Although most who left China were unaccompanied males who intended to return after they had 'made good', chain migration of individual family members also continued to occur as the pioneer sent for relatives or took them back with him after one of his periodic returns to China. In addition, as coastal and treaty port Chinese became more aware of opportunities outside China, large numbers of Chinese began to leave in response to the Californian and Australian goldrushes, to seek further education or to escape political upheavals within the home country (Wickberg 1994: 13).

Given the diversity of Chinese migration, it is not surprising that Chinese patterns of settlement and employment, as well as host community responses, show great variation. In eighteenth-century Borneo, Hakka immigrants formed locally powerful, self-governing groups (*gongsi*) which obtained the right to farm and mine from local rulers (Fitzgerald 1972: 147), while in Malacca, Penang and Singapore, the 'Baba' or Straits Chinese formed an acculturated minority. Originally the offspring of Malay–Chinese unions, most were highly educated traders who were Chinese in religious and social identity, but closely resembled Malays linguistically (Pan 1990: 169–72; Freedman 1960–1: 27–8). In nineteenth-century Thailand, in part because there were so few female migrants, inter-marriage between Chinese and Thai was common, and by the third generation many 'Chinese' were totally assimilated. In addition, Chinese were appointed merchants, seamen, accountants and officials to the Siamese court and many liaisons occurred between successful Chinese merchant families and the Thai aristocracy (Pan 1990: 29). In contrast, in the Philippines under Spanish rule and in Indonesia under the Dutch, the Chinese were considered essential to the economy but 'culturally repugnant, economically overbearing and politically unreliable' (Wickberg 1994: 23). This resulted in the Chinese being treated as a distinct community which paid higher taxes and had fewer legal rights than the indigenous population. They also suffered enforced ghettoization and restrictions on occupations and styles of dress. Resentment against the Chinese in Manila resulted in physical violence in 1603, when approximately 23,000 Chinese were massacred by the Spanish, and again in 1639, when a further 22–24,000 Chinese were killed. In Indonesia the Chinese also became the focus of local resentment, and over 10,000 Chinese in Batavia (Jakarta) and Java were massacred in 1740 (Pan 1990: 31–6, 158–61). As emigration of Chinese was prohibited, the Chinese government did not react to these massacres. On the contrary, in 1712, the Chinese authorities issued an edict which called upon 'foreign governments to have those Chinese who have been abroad repatriated so that they may be executed' (Pan 1990: 8). In 1799, an even more strongly worded edict declared that:

> All officers of government, soldiers, and private citizens, who clandestinely proceed to sea to trade, or who remove to foreign islands for the purpose of inhabiting and cultivating the same, shall be punished according to the law against communicating with rebels

and enemies, and consequently suffer death by being beheaded.

(Pan 1990: 8)

CHINESE EMIGRATION IN THE NINETEENTH CENTURY

Throughout the first half of the nineteenth century the Chinese were perceived in the metropolitan states of Europe and North America as an industrious, cheap, but unassimilable labour force. As a result, the entry of unaccompanied male workers was encouraged as they would be less likely to settle permanently. The experience of the Chinese in North America is a representative example of Chinese migration of this type. The majority of Chinese went as sojourners rather than permanent settlers, and in the words of Leland Stanford, president of the Central Pacific Railway Company, Chinese labourers were 'quiet, peaceable, patient, industrious and economical. . . . More prudent and economical [than white labourers], they are contented with less wages' (Tsai 1986: 17). By the late 1860s, as recession set in, the Chinese were increasingly employed as a cheap labour force and as strike breakers. White labourers accused the Chinese of causing unemployment, and political demands were exerted on Congress to ban Chinese immigration. This pressure culminated in the 1882 Exclusion Law preventing the entry of Chinese labour into the United States and barring Chinese immigrants from seeking naturalization. The immediate impact of this legislation was a reduction in the size of the Chinese population in America. Those who remained began to congregate in what would later be termed Chinatowns, establishing themselves as small independent entrepreneurs, but avoiding employment in unionized industries (Takaki 1989; Daniels 1988; Kim 1994; Bonavia 1978: 17–24).

THE ROLE OF GUILDS AND ASSOCIATIONS

The lineage organization, which assumed its present form in the Song Dynasty (960–1279) was an extension of the family in that it linked all those of patrilineal descent. Although a chief task was to record lineage genealogy, often tracing descent to a mythological ancestor, wealthy lineages owned land and supported education, rites and charity for members (Dikötter 1992: 69–70). Wealthy lineages in south-east China often dominated entire regions economically. As sojourning grew increasingly common in the eighteenth century, lineage organizations came to be supplemented by other types of voluntary associations, the most common of which were based on proximity of residence, although a great range of patterns appeared. In some localities individuals emphasized solidarity through temple associations, while in others coalitions of surname groups divided collective responsibilities. In addition, as government funding for public services began to diminish under the Qing dynasty, wealthy associations began to fund charitable organizations and provide public institutions such as orphanages and schools. Businesses carried out in an alien environment, either within Chinese cities or abroad, were organized according to similar principles as lineage and voluntary associations. To ensure their loyalty, workers were employed on the basis of lineage or common place of origin, though 'native place' could be interpreted in terms of village, town, prefecture or province. Moreover, as communities often specialized in the production of certain goods or the provision of particular services, native place ties often supplemented occupational ties and consequently natives of specific communities often filled an occupational niche. These occupational and native place associations, which emerged in the Ming and had become commonplace in the Qing dynasty, were organized into corporate organizations (*huiguan*) which, like lineage organizations, were run by the well-to-do members who managed communal property. As well as providing members with a meeting ground, financial assistance and storage facilities, the *huiguan* functioned as a monopolistic means of controlling trade (Skinner 1976: 343–6; Jones 1974; Naquin and Rawski 1987: 36–49).

The *huiguan*, then, was an organization which provided economic protection, services and social support to its members in an alien environment. The formation of many separate *huiguan* did not, however, imply a fragmentation of the Chinese community. Membership was not limited to any one organization, so that it was possible for an individual to simultaneously hold membership in dialect, surname, occupational or other associations. In the absence of support from either the host or Chinese authorities, *huiguan* were the earliest and most enduring types of organization formed by overseas Chinese emigrants. As in China, occupational guilds were often monopolized by immigrants from one region, although this did not necessarily reflect traditional regional expertise, but rather was determined by the economic opportunities available at the time of initial settlement.

JAPANESE PERCEPTIONS OF CHINA

Chinese intellectuals had long held a world-view in which China, *Zhongguo* or *Zhonghua* (the 'Middle Kingdom' or 'Civilized Centre') was the civilized (*hua*) central core surrounded by a barbarian (*yi*) periphery. This traditional Sinocentric world-view had been adopted by Japanese elites who regarded China as the primary source of high culture. The stability of the Tokugawa period encouraged the spread of education among the samurai elite and this led to an outpouring of literary works in Chinese. As in the past, Chinese was the language of the literati class and the medium of most classical learning, and Chinese books were imported into Japan via Nagasaki throughout the entire 'closed' period. Paradoxically, however, increased opportunities for study of the Chinese classics led to a rejection of Sinocentric views among many scholars. During this period, the social and moral order elaborated in Zhu Xi Confucianism was adopted as state orthodoxy. The increased emphasis given to Confucian theory, however, led Japanese scholars to re-evaluate the teachings of Confucianism as they began to analyse core Confucian texts directly instead of continuing to accept orthodox interpretation. By the eighteenth century Confucianism had taken on a wholly Japanese hue. Moreover, implicit in the Chinese *huayi* or civilized/barbarian dichotomy was the categorization of Japanese as barbarians: a dilemma that provoked a variety of responses as increasing numbers of Tokugawa intellectuals began to argue that *hua* referred to civilization as a concept rather than China as a nation. Japanese scholars noted that the Han had allowed themselves to be conquered by barbarians: first by the Mongols, then by the Manchus, while the Japanese had never been conquered by an alien race. Tokugawa intellectuals increasingly began to identify Japan also as a central, civilized country on a par with, or even superior to, China. By late Tokugawa, the term *Tō* ('Tang') was used as a generic term to refer to China, thus avoiding the Chinese expressions *Zhongguo, Zhonghua, DaMing, DaQing* ('Middle Kingdom', 'Civilized Centre', 'Great Ming', 'Great Qing') whose use implied Japanese acknowledgement of Chinese centrality and superiority (Harootunian 1980: 9–36; Jansen 1992; Toby 1984).

Further challenges to Chinese intellectual centrality arose in late Tokugawa. In Nagasaki, scholars of Dutch learning noted inaccuracies in Chinese anatomical and astrological texts and began to compare Chinese scientific rigour unfavourably with that of the West, while 'nativist' scholarship within Japan legitimized a rejection of

China and Chinese civilization by arguing that the pure and natural Japanese spirit had been contaminated by Buddhist and Confucian influence. Nativist scholars such as Motoori Norinaga and Hirata Atsutane called for renewed enquiry into the theological aspects of Shinto, stressing Japan's unique position in world history as a nation created by the Sun Goddess and distinguished by an unbroken Imperial line.

Traditional elite views of China altered abruptly in the mid to late nineteenth century. From the early period of Meiji modernization, Japanese intellectuals were deeply influenced by social-Darwinist assumptions concerning international relations. In this context, the weakness of the Qing and the consequent threat of China's partition among the foreign powers were a constant theme in Japanese writings on national security. Many feared that Japan would also be divided among the Western imperial powers, and Japanese leaders felt that if sovereignty were to be preserved, the Western powers would have to be countered by an equally strong Japan. National strength required not only a strong army and navy, but also a modern capitalist economy and a stable political system. To this end, Meiji leaders introduced institutional innovations, abolished legal distinctions between classes, removed restrictions on occupation and residence and introduced compulsory education and military conscription. China also tried to introduce reforms, and the Sino-Japanese war of 1895 was seen by both sides as a test of their country's modernization. Chinese defeat in that war led increasing numbers of Japanese to see China as weak, stagnant and corrupt.

Opinions varied as to what form Japan's relations with China should take. Some believed, as expressed by Fukuzawa Yukichi in *Datsu-A-ron* (Dissociation from Asia), that Japan should dissociate itself from Asia and align itself with the Western nations. An alternative perspective held that the Chinese and Japanese shared a common cultural heritage (*dōbun* or *tongwen*). Moreover, as members of a common race (*dōshu* or *tongzhong*), they should unite so that the 'Asiatic yellow race will not be encroached upon by the white race of Europe' (Dikotter 1992: 57). Still others argued that, as China was powerless, Japan should take steps to assist its neighbour. Less benign was Sugita Teiichi's view that, in the inevitable partition of China by the Western powers, the danger was 'whether Japan will be served up as the main dish in the coming feast, or whether it should join the guests at the table'. If Japan's national interests were to be protected, it was 'better to sit at the table than to be part of the menu' (Hashikawa 1980: 333); Japan should itself become an imperial power and seize China. It was, moreover, possible to advocate elements of all three latter theses, as in the case of those who supported continental expansion while expressing a deep reverence for China as a cultural abstraction (Hashikawa 1980: 337). The prominent China scholar Naitō Konan typified this approach:

> To me, it seems that it would make little difference if the present Chinese state were to perish, for the brilliance of Chinese culture would spread throughout the world, and the glory of the Chinese people would thrive so long as there is a heaven and an earth.
>
> (Hashikawa 1980: 344)

The cession of Taiwan to Japan following China's defeat in the Sino-Japanese war of 1894–5 encouraged Japanese adoption of Western imperialist justifications based on the assumption of the superiority of 'advanced' colonial rulers over their 'lesser' subject peoples. In consequence, the Chinese of Taiwan came to be seen as an alien people who were to be civilized under Japanese rule. Yet throughout the entire colonial period, the Chinese were also seen in the light of 'common race and common cultural heritage' who were united with the Japanese against the 'white races'.

EMIGRATION TO JAPAN BEFORE 1853

From 1371, the Ming (1368–1644) prohibited Chinese from travelling overseas for private purposes. This restriction was intended to protect the dynasty from rebels who had their bases on the yet unpacified Chinese littoral. Official trade missions, however, were permitted, which were legitimized by visas issued by the Ming in the form of tallies (*kanhe*). Between 1404 and 1549 seventeen such missions took place between Japan and China, although, due to the depredations of the *Wakō* (Japanese pirates) who ravaged Chinese coastal cities throughout the sixteenth century, the Ming imposed a ban on all trade with Japan in 1547. When, in 1567, the state permitted private Fujianese merchants in Amoy (Xiamen) to conduct private trade in South-east Asia, commerce with Japan remained proscribed. Ming maritime prohibitions, however, could not be enforced. Merchants along the South China coast ignored the government's ban, often with the connivance of local officials, and Chinese trade, which was often indistinguishable from piracy, continued unabated with Japan (Elisonas 1991: 235–55). Chinese trading communities were founded in towns along the coast of Kyushu and even as far east as the Kantō region. Chinese artisans, such as tile-makers, were recruited by Japanese lords such as Tokugawa Ieyasu; some were even enfeoffed (Jansen 1992: 7–8).

In an abortive attempt in 1616 to revive *kanhe* trade with the Ming, Ieyasu directed that Chinese trade be centred at Nagasaki. As a result, between 1608 and 1618, the Chinese population of Nagasaki grew from 20 to over 2,000, with more than thirty Chinese ships visiting Nagasaki annually. By 1641 this figure had reached a record ninety-seven vessels and in 1646 the amount of silver leaving Japan annually in payment for Chinese goods had reached 17,000 *kan* (63,750 kg) (Iwao 1976: 11). Over three-quarters of these 'Chinese' vessels actually originated with Fujianese merchants in South-east Asia, and thirteen of the ships arriving in 1641 belonged to Zheng Zhilong, a pirate trader whose power base was Fujian, but who had married a Japanese woman and was former aide to the head of the Chinese community in Hirado (Jansen 1992: 26).

The collapse of the Ming dynasty and the Qing (Manchu) conquest in 1644 led Ming loyalists to seek refuge in Fujian, South-east Asia and Taiwan. The principal leader of the Ming rebels was Koxinga (Zheng Chenggong) son of Zheng Zhilong, who selected the pirate stronghold of Taiwan as his base. During his struggle against the Ming, most of the ships that arrived in Nagasaki were from areas held by the Zheng regime, whose resistance was funded by exports of silk and sugar to Japan (Jansen 1992: 27–8). He petitioned the bakufu for military assistance on more than a dozen occasions between 1645 and 1685. Although the Tokugawa avoided direct involvement, they gave practical expression of support for Ming loyalists in 1646 by banning Nanjing merchants who wore their hair in the Manchu pigtail, telling them that they would be permitted to trade only if they came 'in Chinese style' (Toby 1984: 139). In addition, the Tokugawa also allowed Japan to serve as a haven for several thousand Ming intellectuals who preferred life among the Japanese 'Eastern Barbarians' to life under the Qing. The best known of these was the Confucian scholar Zhu Shunshui who became adviser to Tokugawa Mitsukuni, lord of Mito.

When the Tokugawa policy of national isolation was implemented in 1639, Chinese traders congregated in Nagasaki, the one port remaining open to foreign commerce. Earlier, payment for foreign goods with silver ingots had caused such a drain on Japanese silver reserves that the bakufu had placed a general ban on the export of silver and promoted the export of copper in its stead. When the Qing regained control of Taiwan in 1683, commerce with China increased rapidly. In 1685, eighty-five Chinese vessels visited

Nagasaki, and by 1698 this had grown to 193 vessels. The result was a huge outflow of copper, and efforts to limit this led to large-scale smuggling. In 1689, in an effort to control this, the Tokugawa bakufu ordered the Chinese merchant community confined to a residential quarter (*Tōjin yashiki* or 'Chinese residence'). Whereas the Dutch, who were few in number and conducted limited trade with the Japanese, were restricted to the small man-made island of Deshima, the size and location of the *Tōjin yashiki* reflected the scale of Chinese trade with Japan. The *Tōjin yashiki* was a spacious compound located on the Japanese mainland, which included warehouses and offices in addition to residential quarters which housed 4,888 people in its first year, and in the years which followed averaged in excess of 2,000 (Jansen 1992: 28–30; Uchida 1949: 101–22). Liaison between Chinese merchants and Japanese authorities was conducted by the Nagasaki Office of Chinese Interpreters, a hereditary office of nine interpreters and over one hundred translators held by people of mixed Sino-Japanese parentage. These interpreters worked from their own homes until the creation of a separate office in 1762 (Uchida 1949: 97–9). Each of the four groups of provincial traders (Sanjiang, Cantonese and North and South Fujianese) had constructed Buddhist temples in the 1620s, before the creation of the *Tōjin yashiki*. These were situated far from the Chinese residence and although official permission was initially required to visit the temples, restrictions gradually loosened so that the total isolation from Japanese life imposed on the Dutch did not occur in the case of the Chinese. These temples evolved a system of shared responsibility for major festivals, and assumed tasks similar to those carried out by Chinese associations in other countries, such as organizing the shipment of the dead back to China for permanent burial (Uchida 1949: 58–87).

Officially the Japanese ranked the Chinese merchants as 'barbarians' whose status was lower than the Dutch. Whereas the Dutch were to travel once a year to Edo to be 'viewed' by the Shogun, the Chinese were allowed no such 'privilege', and instead were informed of Japanese laws and edicts by staff interpreters in Nagasaki. Explaining why dealings with the Chinese were handled only through the Nagasaki magistracy, Hayashi Razan, councillor to Ieyasu, stated that: 'Dealing with barbarians is like dealing with slaves, which is the reason why these matters were handled by low-ranking vassals' (Toby 1984: 197). This attitude obscures the continuing importance of Sino-Japanese trade, which continued in such volume that in 1715 the bakufu adopted new regulations designed to limit the export of

Japanese specie. Chinese trade with Japan was made subject to acceptance of credentials similar to the Ming *kanhe*. These were issued via the Nagasaki Office of Chinese Interpreters, and those absent from Nagasaki when credentials were issued were no longer permitted to trade (Toby 1984: 198).

Apart from these formal restrictions, the Chinese trading community appears to have enjoyed a far higher degree of acceptance than their Dutch counterparts. Chinese merchants, who were referred to as *Acha-san*, a title which implied respect, were seen as wealthy and generous. In the famines of 1680 to 1682 Fujian temples distributed rice porridge to the Nagasaki populace, while in the famine of 1690, Fujian and Cantonese merchants contributed rice and money. By late Tokugawa, Chinese merchants mingled freely with the local Nagasaki population, Chinese peddlers hawked their wares in the streets of Nagasaki, and Chinese songs, sung in Chinese with Japanese verses attached, were highly popular. Believing that their children would receive a good education, destitute Japanese often offered them for adoption by Chinese merchants. Even after the Meiji Restoration this practice was so widespread that in 1870 the Nagasaki authorities passed an edict banning the sale of children to Chinese under the guise of adoption (Kamachi 1980: 63).

IMMIGRATION 1853–94

Chinese communities in the modern era arose as a result of the opening of Japan to the West in 1853. Although these new immigrants had no legal right to remain in Japan until the first Sino-Japanese treaty was concluded in 1871, they were brought in under the legal protection of treaty power nationals. Western merchants who had been trading in the Chinese treaty ports brought their Chinese employees to work as servants, stevedores and overseers. They supervised Japanese workers and provided expertise in processes such as tea production. Other labourers and merchants entered, for a fee, by becoming the nominal dependant or servant of treaty power nationals. By 1875 the Chinese population in the concession areas numbered approximately 2,500 out of a total foreign population of about 5,000. The Chinese, who were willing to work for lower wages than the Japanese, often constituted a large proportion of the police force in the foreign concessions. In addition they established shops, hotels, gaming houses and restaurants. By the late 1870s thousands of foreign seamen were passing through Japanese ports. European shipping lines had begun to use a high proportion of Chinese sailors in their Far Eastern lines and many of the 10–15,000 seamen who passed through Yokohama in 1878 alone were Chinese (Hoare 1977). After the opening of Nagasaki in 1859, the Tokugawa lost control over the entry of Chinese, and numerous Fujian and Sanjiang merchants, their families and employees settled in the environs of or within the Chinese residence. Few of these immigrants were Cantonese, reflecting their minimal involvement in earlier trade in Nagasaki, and those who did arrive were generally labourers and artisans who settled within the foreign settlement. By 1880, 549 Chinese, fifty-nine of them women, resided in Nagasaki (Kamachi 1980: 60).

The Chinese made a significant contribution to Japan's early indus-trializing efforts by bringing skills which had been acquired in the Chinese treaty ports. Chinese tailors passed on the techniques asso-ciated with the production of Western-style clothing, and Chinese hairdressers taught knowledge of Western hair-cutting skills. The Chinese also taught the Japanese how to process black tea and intro-duced the first kerosene lanterns into Japan. The Chinese in Nagasaki requested, and received, permission to install the first gas lights in the streets of that city (Kamachi 1980: 64). None the less, the Chinese were not the social equals of the Westerners and the two did not mingle. In Kobe the Chinese area arose next to, rather than within, the foreign concession. In Nagasaki, most Chinese remained in the vicinity of the former *Tōjin yashiki*, while in Yokohama the Chinese were concentrated in one distinct region. The poor hygiene in the Chinese areas, the cheap hotels, restaurants and grog-shops, and the drunken sailors they attracted, led Westerners and Japanese to avoid Chinese areas. When the Japanese permitted enlargement of the foreign concessions the Chinese remained in the original residential areas. In Yokohama, for example, Westerners moved to a healthier area on higher ground while the Chinese remained in the original settlement, which had been built on swampland (Hoare 1977: 28–30).

The majority of the new arrivals in Japan were unaccompanied males from the traditional areas of Chinese emigration, Guangdong and Fujian, although others made the journey from treaty ports such as Shanghai and Ningbo and a number of Chinese immigrants came from North China. New immigrants sponsored the immigration of relatives and people from their place of origin, initiating a pattern of chain migration. As a consequence, Chinese from Fujian came to dominate the Nagasaki community, those from Shanghai, Jiangsu and North China settled in Osaka, while Chinese from Guangdong were concentrated in Yokohama (Uchida 1949: 156–66).

Foreign traders, taking advantage of extraterritoriality and superior knowledge of international conditions, dominated overseas trade in the early Meiji era, controlling over 95 per cent of Japanese imports and exports (Uchida 1949: 25). Western traders in the Chinese treaty ports had employed Chinese compradores to manage local employees and act as intermediaries in business affairs, and they brought Chinese compradores with them to Japan. In many cases they received only nominal wages, earning the bulk of their income from fees which they exacted for arranging both purchases and sales (Uchida and Shiowaki 1950: 22–3; Uchida 1949: 32–4). Compradores also engaged in business on their own account and, together with independent Chinese merchants, enjoyed an almost exclusive monopoly on trade between Japan and China (Uchida and Shiowaki 1950: 11–13). In contrast to this wealthy minority, the majority of residents in the Chinatown areas were labourers, most of whom did not have steady employment. The Chinese population of Yokohama in 1869 was 1,002, of whom thirty-six were compradores or merchants and sixty-three were workers or servants, while the remaining 903 comprised women, children and daily labourers (Kamachi 1980: 60; Sugawara 1991: 48).

Merchants began to form provincial and occupational associations immediately after their arrival in Japan. Fujianese merchants from the Nagasaki *Tōjin yashiki* also established new branches in the foreign concessions. In common with Chinese associations in other countries, these organizations provided support to members, exploited trading links with their home province and developed a monopoly within the Chinese community on particular goods or services. This provincial specialization ensured that, in any particular city, whichever regional group was in the majority enjoyed a superior economic position. In the Meiji period, Guangdong immigrants were mostly restaurant owners or small-scale merchants, the Fujianese were barbers, while the clothing industry was dominated by those from Fujian and Shanghai (Uchida 1949: 156–66; Yamashita 1979: 44).

One factor prompting the early formation of associations was an 1867 agreement between the Tokugawa bakufu and the treaty powers concerning foreign nationals whose governments had no treaties with Japan. In 1868, the Japanese government announced that resident Chinese would be placed under its jurisdiction and that registration would be required. The Cantonese in Nagasaki subsequently requested permission to organize a Cantonese association which would be legally responsible for its members. Permission was granted and Chinese in other cities promptly followed suit (Kamachi 1980: 61–2). Under the Sino-Japanese Treaty of 1871 the Chinese acquired extraterritorial status, and like their Western counterparts were placed under the jurisdiction of their own diplomatic mission and subject to Chinese law. However, they were to remain formally under Japanese control until the Chinese government appointed diplomatic representatives in 1877. In October 1874 the government ordered that all Chinese register annually and carry registration documents, simultaneously placing restrictions on their movement between the foreign concessions (Hoare 1977: 23–4). Certain incidents in this period highlighted the need for a Chinese consul: in 1870 Chinese employees of the British consulate in Yokohama were arrested, tried and executed for attempting to forge Japanese currency (Sugawara 1991: 49). In 1872, when the Peruvian coolie vessel *Maria Luz* put into Yokohama harbour for repairs, some of the Chinese aboard tried to escape. The ship was forbidden from leaving port and the 231 Chinese labourers were taken ashore and later returned to Macao. In the absence of a formal representative, both incidents were adjudicated by the foreign chargés d'affaires (Sugawara 1991: 1–53; Satō 1990: 82–3).

Even after gaining extraterritorial status, the treatment received by the Chinese often differed to that of Westerners. The suppression of opium formed the basis for most conflicts between the Chinese and Japanese. Many Chinese were opium addicts and the Japanese authorities were anxious that the habit should not be imported. When the first Chinese consul arrived in December 1877 he was presented with a proposal which would empower Japanese police to enter private Chinese dwellings to search for and seize opium. Despite his objections, the Japanese government notified the prefects in the treaty ports of its intention to enforce this measure. The issue developed into open conflict in Nagasaki in 1883 when police raided a Chinese house to arrest an opium smoker. The suspect objected to his arrest and other Chinese attempted to release him from police custody. In the ensuing struggle one Chinese died and a number of others were injured. When Chinese residents protested, the prefect of Nagasaki maintained that, where suppression of opium was concerned, Chinese did not have the same rights as other treaty nationals (Kamachi 1980: 67–9). A similar incident occurred three years later in Kobe when police entered the house of a Chinese merchant and arrested him for smoking opium. When the Chinese consul in Kobe complained to the prefect of Hyogo that this was in violation of an 1879 agreement, in which Chinese houses bearing a door plate with the consul's stamp would be immune to police entry, the prefect replied that immunity did not apply in the case of opium use and applied only to gambling and sanitary offences (Kamachi 1980: 71–2).

After the arrival of the Chinese consul, the Chinese associations assumed the role of intermediaries between the consul and their individual members. They also continued to take responsibility for the economic and social well-being of their community. Merchant associations in Osaka constructed a temple in 1883 and a hospital in 1886, while the Guangdong, Fujian and Sanjiang merchants in Kobe who had united in 1873 to form a single association, founded a school in 1880 and in 1887 constructed a temple, expanded their headquarters and built a hospital. In 1891, an overarching organization, the *Zhonghua huiguan* ('Chinese Guild') was established in Yokohama with 863 members. The association provided general services such as the organization of religious and social events, burials and the shipment of remains to China for permanent burial. In subsequent years, as the Chinese community grew in size, merchant associations continued to sponsor the construction of new schools, temples and hospitals (Shiba 1983: 497–601).

Anti-Chinese sentiments grew as the immigrant population increased. By the late nineteenth century the Chinese in Nagasaki were being called *chankoro*, which was possibly a corruption of the Chinese word *Zhongguoren* ('Chinese'). Other epithets were added such as *chan-chan* and *chan-chan bōzu*. *Chan-chan* ranges in meanings from the female sexual organs to an onomatopoeic reference to the sound of small coins being jingled together, suggesting perhaps that the Chinese were concerned only with money. Certain epithets centred on physical difference, particularly the shaven head and long pigtail worn by the Chinese in conformity with Manchu sanctioned practice. The term *bōzu* ('monk') referred to the shaven forehead, while another epithet, *tonbi*, was a literal translation of the English word 'pigtail'. This gave rise to further taunts that the Chinese smelled or acted like pigs. By the 1870s Japanese newspapers increasingly referred to the Chinese as *tonbi, chan-chan* or *chan-chan sensei* (Mr Chan-chan), depicting them as sly and given to criminal behaviour (Jansen 1992: 87; Kamachi 1980: 66; Keene 1971: 139). Between 1872 and 1876 the *Yokohama Mainichi Shinbun* carried a monthly summary of local criminal activity. Although criminal activity among resident Chinese was about one-eighth that of resident Westerners, newspaper reports highlighted Chinese offences while those committed by Westerners were rarely mentioned (Itō 1991: 22).

THE SINO-JAPANESE WAR

The impact of the Sino-Japanese War of 1894–5 on the status of the Chinese community was both immediate and far-reaching. In Japan there was great enthusiasm for the war which was projected as a conflict between the forces of civilization and those of a decadent 'oriental' despotism. Accounts of the war dominated all newspapers. Dramas were written about Chinese defeats, while the *Yomiuri Shinbun* offered a prize for war songs which would encourage patriotism and feelings of hatred for the enemy. Although the first songs emphasized Japanese righteousness in fighting the war, the tone of the songs soon changed to denigrating the Chinese as weaklings and cowards. Anti-Chinese sentiment was exacerbated by the decision of the Minister of Education that these songs be taught in schools. *Nishikie* (wood block prints) portraying the war also became extremely popular. Most depicted gory war scenes in which the Japanese were presented as erect and dignified, dressed in sombre clothing and posing in heroic stances. The cringing Chinese, who were depicted in garishly bright dress and with gaping mouths and pigtails, were uniformly shown running away or allowing themselves to be bound by Japanese troops. Chinese prisoners of war were brought back to Japan and displayed to the general public. When the first Chinese prisoners arrived in Tokyo in October 1894, a jeering crowd waited for them at Shinbashi Station, and a woman in the crowd was reported to have shouted, '*Chanchan no heitai wa anna mono ka?*' (Is that what Chinese soldiers are like?) (Keene 1971: 135–8).

Letters from the battlefront and the wartime experiences later recounted by veterans to family and friends also had a profound impact on public opinion. Japanese soldiers had been imbued with a sense of national purpose and superiority which led them to interpret the poverty and backwardness of China as proof that the Chinese were lacking in the spirit which had led to development and modernization in their own country. Most Chinese troops were untrained and often fled at the beginning of battle. This was taken as further evidence of innate Chinese cowardice: where they did fight, it was considered that they must have received foreign training. To the soldiers, Chinese soldiers were cowardly and incapable, the merchants venal, and the peasants, when they welcomed the Japanese soldiers, foolish, unpatriotic and untrustworthy (Lone 1994: 64–5).

As 'enemy nationals', the extraterritorial rights of the Chinese in Japan were revoked and they were required to register with Japanese authorities. The war also resulted in the immediate departure of many Chinese residents who feared mass deportation or the imposition of punitive taxes to cover the costs of the war. The number of resident Chinese fell from 5,343 in 1893 to 1,576 in 1894, but the economic boom brought about by the war led many more Chinese to venture to Japan, and by 1897 the Chinese population stood at more than 5,000. The establishment of new shipping routes between Osaka and Shanghai in 1895, and between Osaka and ports in North China such as Shandong, Niuzhuang and Zhifu in 1899, also resulted in a rapid increase in the number of Chinese immigrants from North China and Shanghai. Most settled in Osaka and Kobe, where the majority of Chinese residents had hitherto come from Guangdong or Fujian (Shiba 1983: 547–51).

Victory in the Sino-Japanese War increased Japan's stature as an imperial power and led to a revision of the unequal treaties. With the abolition of extraterritorial privileges in 1899, foreign residents were permitted to live wherever they wished, while foreign companies, no longer confined to the free trade areas of the treaty ports, became subject to the same conditions as their Japanese counterparts. These new conditions would not, however, be applied to the Chinese, who had already lost extraterritorial status during the Sino-Japanese War. The Ministry of Agriculture and Commerce and the Home Ministry opposed 'mixed residence' for Chinese labourers, arguing that they would spread the habit of opium use among the general population, that their involvement in gambling and grog-shops was a threat to public morality, and that their lower requirements in wages, food and housing made them an economic threat to Japanese labourers. The Foreign Ministry, on the other hand, argued that the Chinese should be treated equally with other foreign nationals. Chinese merchants feared that their economic activities would be confined to the treaty ports while other foreign merchants had a free hand elsewhere in Japan. In June 1898, they sent petitions to the Chinese embassy, and Chinese merchants in Yokohama, Kobe, Nagasaki and Hakodate sent representatives to the *Zhonghua huiguan* in Yokohama. *Zhonghua huiguan* representatives held press conferences in Tokyo and argued their case with leading government officials such as the Home and Foreign Ministers (Itō 1995: 437–40). Imperial Ordinance No. 352, introduced in July 1899, allowed for Chinese 'mixed residence', but general labourers engaged in agriculture, fishing, mining, construction, engineering, manufacturing and transportation were prohibited from taking up employment outside the foreign concessions without the express permission of the prefectural authorities. The Home Ministry clarified the need for these restrictions in a supplemental ordinance which read:

> Imperial Ordinance No. 352 is concerned primarily with the maintenance of discipline over Chinese workers, since they are not only apt to vitiate public morals, but are also likely to enter into conflict with Japanese workers through competition, thereby causing disorder to industry and society and ultimately disturbing public peace and order.
>
> (Naimushō Keihokyoku 1979: 357)

This ordinance, by preventing the immigration of labourers and people from rural areas, profoundly altered the class composition of the Chinese community, which thereafter was dominated by skilled labourers, artisans and merchants residing only within Chinatowns. For its own part, moreover, the wealthy Chinese merchant community represented by the *Zhonghua huiguan* welcomed the possibility of 'mixed residence' and the exclusion of Chinese labourers whose activities, they felt, cast the Chinese community in a poor light. In fact, in February 1890, Chinese merchants from all over the country invited 300 leading Japanese political figures, including members of the House of Peers, the mayors of Yokohama and Nagasaki, and the Home, Foreign and Education Ministers, to a banquet in Tokyo to express their gratitude (Itō 1995: 442–3).

Following the cession of Taiwan to Japan in 1895, restrictions on the entry of Taiwanese were removed, and throughout the period of Japanese colonial rule there was a constant flow of Taiwanese into Japan. In 1922 there were over 2,400 Taiwanese students in Japan, and by 1942 this figure had risen to an estimated 7,000 (Tsurumi 1984: 292). Study in Japan reflected the lack of opportunities for secondary and tertiary study in Taiwan. The first Taiwanese middle school was not opened until 1915, and although rudimentary training in forestry, education and medicine was offered to Taiwanese, systematic discrimination in favour of Japanese children made it easier for those who could afford it to obtain admission to Japanese rather than Taiwanese schools (Tsurumi 1984: 281–90). In addition to students, labourers travelled freely to Japan and by the end of 1943 Taiwan had supplied about 150,000 men for military labour service in Japan. A further 3,505 Taiwanese were recruited for active military service between 1938 and 1943 (Chen 1984: 232–3).

After 1895 the Chinese revolutionary Sun Yatsen used Japan as a base from which to plot the overthrow of the Qing dynasty. The inability of this 'alien' dynasty to defend China was one factor leading to an upsurge of Chinese nationalism, and Chinese revolutionaries sought financial and moral support among overseas Chinese communities throughout Asia and North America. The revolutionaries competed for support with reformers such as Kang Youwei, who sought to maintain but reform the Chinese Imperial system. Following the failure of his first attempt at revolution in Canton in 1895 Sun Yatsen fled to Japan and, after a brief spell in London, returned to Japan in 1897, where he turned for support to left-wing liberals such as Miyazaki Torazō. Idealists like Miyazaki were often motivated by a missionary zeal to reform the 'corrupt civilizations' of Asia through their individual efforts. Although Sun Yatsen cooperated with these liberals, he failed to recognize the arrogance of their view that China was so inferior that it could not improve itself without outside help. Miyazaki, for example, saw himself as the 'manager' of the Chinese revolution and dreamt of 'entering the Chinese continent in front of a host of Chinese' (Miyazaki 1982: 197, 73).

In contrast to revolutionaries such as Sun Yatsen, who saw Chinese failure in the Sino-Japanese War as proof that the Qing should be overthrown, reform-minded intellectuals in the Qing government such as Liang Qichao and Kang Youwei interpreted Japanese success as evidence that Meiji policies of national development were more effective than those undertaken in China. They began to stress the advantages of study in Japan: it was close, had a similar cultural background and had shown itself capable of adapting Western knowledge to an Eastern culture (Sakane 1991: 42). Chinese officials adopted the slogan *Zhongxueweiti, xixueweiyong* ('Chinese learning for the essential principles and Western learning for practical use') and envisioned Chinese students in Japan as learning only Western science and technology while remaining 'unsullied' by Western thought. The advantages of study in Japan were also stressed by leading Japanese such as Ōkuma Shigenobu who believed that Japan's responsibility was to educate its neighbours. The number of Chinese students in Japan grew steadily from the turn of the century. The first to study in Japan were thirteen students sent by the Qing government in 1896. Coming as they did so soon after the Sino-Japanese War, Japanese derided their pig-tails and taunted them as *chan-chan bōzu* and four of the thirteen returned to China within the first three weeks (Sanetō and Sanetō 1961: 55).

None the less, the abolition in China of the Civil Service Examinations in 1905, as part of China's own attempts to modernize, had an immediate effect on study abroad, as this now became the basic requirement for entry into government service. Estimates of the number of Chinese students in Japan in 1906, the peak year, vary from 6,000 to 20,000. Existing educational institutions were unable to cope with the influx of students and the education most Chinese students received was poor: many did not enrol in regular courses at all, or attended 'cram schools' where courses lasted only a few weeks or months (Sakane 1991: 44; Sanetō and Sanetō 1961: 95). Most students lived in the Kanda district of Tokyo, and Chinese businesses, such as restaurants and printing shops, sprang up to cater to their needs. Students were issued upon their arrival in Japan with instruction booklets telling them how to behave: they should not shout or stand idling in the street, should treat maids with dignity and keep their clothes clean (Jansen 1980: 353). None the less the Japanese still objected to Chinese behaviour. In an article entitled 'The Problem of Chinese Students' which appeared in the journal *Chūō Kōron* in 1905, the anti-social behaviour of Chinese in student lodgings was condemned:

> The amount of noise coming from there is outrageous. They spit from their windows into the freshly swept yard and wantonly toss away waste paper so that one corner of the garden is piled high with their waste paper and spittle.
>
> (Sanetō and Sanetō 1961: 94)

The 'problem of Chinese students' was not confined to public disapproval of their behaviour. By 1905 Qing authorities were becoming more and more worried by the increasing radicalism of students in Japan and the poor academic accomplishments of returnees from Japan compared with those from Europe and America. In the same year, the Qing authorities began to formulate guidelines regarding the selection of students and approved courses of study. In this they were assisted by Japanese educational authorities who issued a set of regulations concerning Chinese students which stipulated that they reside in authorized dormitories and that schools monitor their conduct. This aroused student indignation against both the Qing and Japanese governments, and the provincial associations that had sent Chinese students to Japan began to withdraw them in protest. Several thousand returned home, while many of those who remained went on strike. The regulations concerning residence were relaxed and by January 1906 the strike was over. As in China, however, the student movement continued to be an important source of radicalism (Jansen 1980: 359–60).

Sun Yatsen turned increasingly for support to the Chinese students in Japan. At first he had found little: the first generation of students had been sponsored by the Qing government and were committed to its reform. Moreover, they considered themselves a chosen elite and regarded Sun Yatsen as an inferior. This attitude changed as a wider range of students came to Japan, and when Sun Yatsen formed the *Tongmenghui* (Revolutionary Alliance) in 1905, virtually all of the seventy people present were Chinese students, representing seventeen of the eighteen Chinese provinces (Jansen 1980: 370). Many students returned to China after the overthrow of the Qing dynasty in 1911 and by 1912 their numbers had fallen to about 1,500. Merchants also returned to China during the same period. While there had been over 6,000 Chinese resident in Yokohama alone before the 1911 revolution, this dropped to 4,000 in 1912. Numbers of Chinese increased once more in 1917 with the arrival of several thousand labourers who were recruited to alleviate the labour shortage caused by Japan's economic boom. Many were recruited from a single area, Wenzhou county in Zhejiang province, and were either related or from the same villages. These Chinese, who were perceived as temporary workers, were employed mostly as stevedores and coolies. By 1923 over half of the 4,000 Chinese in Tokyo were labourers, while there were over 7,000 labourers throughout the whole of Japan (Niki 1991: 42). By 1922 the need for Chinese labour had diminished. Entry was refused to new labourers, while many in Japan were unemployed or worked as daily labourers. They were seen as competing with unskilled Japanese labour and in 1923 scuffles occurred between Chinese and Japanese unloading coal from ships in Yokohama, and local Japanese labour contractors requested shipping companies and factories not to use Chinese labour (Niki 1991: 42–3).

In the Great Kantō Earthquake of 1923 the Yokohama Chinatown was destroyed and one-third of the Chinese in Tokyo and Yokohama were killed. Many didn't die in the earthquake itself, but were killed by Japanese in the days which followed. Although rumours of arson, rape and insurrection centred upon the Korean community, many Chinese, allegedly mistaken for Koreans, were also murdered by vigilantes, police and soldiers (Niki 1991: 26). Many of the Chinese labourers lived in the Tokyo ward of Ōshima. Although over 450 Chinese were taken from their dormitories there on the third day after the earthquake and killed by civilians, police and soldiers wielding axes, bamboo spears and swords, Japanese authorities denied the occurrence of this incident and the bodies of these victims were never recovered (Niki 1991: 22). The government ordered the establishment of reception centres to safeguard the lives of both Chinese and Koreans, and Chinese associations such as the Wenzhou Provincial Association organized the return of their members to China. Other survivors fled to Kobe, which had a resident Chinese community of 6,000, and returned to China from there. However, over the next five years, the number of Chinese in Yokohama rose again to 4,000, as many merchants returned to Japan where economic conditions were more favourable. The Chinese who remained in Yokohama throughout were among the first to re-establish business. The various Chinese associations and *hui* (revolving credit unions) played a vital role in financing rebuilding work. Most Chinese business had, of necessity, been established with relatively little capital and required less outlay than Japanese enterprises to re-establish. Chinese traders remained in the Chinatown area and re-established their import–export companies, while others continued to run small restaurants, barber shops or printing works. A few were tailors, painters or made caneware, while many from Fujian and Sanjiang were peddlers who sold clothing (Yamashita 1979: 37–9).

After the Manchurian Incident of 1931, most mainland Chinese students still in Japan returned home. Many expressed their intention to return to fight the Japanese and, like their predecessors, many became influential in the nationalist movement in China. Over 50 per cent of the Chinese merchants in Kobe, Osaka and Yokohama also left. Merchants who chose to remain in an 'enemy' country were influenced by a number of factors: they were well-established in Japan and had trading contacts with other overseas Chinese communities in South-east Asia; political instability in China made business difficult; and many lacked the ability to re-establish their businesses in China. In 1930, there had been 30,836 Chinese in Japan, by 1938 this had fallen to 17,043, although it is important to note that the overall number of men of working age actually increased gradually throughout this period (Uchida 1949: 6–7).

The degree of control exerted over the Chinese community increased during the late 1930s. In 1936 Chinese schools in Osaka, Kobe, Kyoto, Tokyo, Yokohama and Nagasaki were compelled to use textbooks approved by the Japanese. Three years later most existing Chinese associations were disbanded and replaced by a single organization, which in turn was responsible to the Japanese authorities. Many more Chinese merchants left during this period as the Chinese boycott of Japanese goods caused the volume of overseas Chinese trade with Japan to decrease in value from ¥75 million to

¥19 million between 1935 and 1940. Trade was further reduced by the disruption of maritime services and the loss of ships during the Pacific War (Shiba 1983: 580–1).

During the war the Chinese who remained were treated as enemy nationals by the Japanese, kept under surveillance and often forbidden to leave the Chinatown areas (Yamashita 1979: 38). Chinese residing in areas deemed militarily sensitive were forcibly relocated (*Asahi Shinbun*, 11 August 1992). None the less, the number of Chinese present in wartime Japan rose. As the labour situation deteriorated, Japan supplemented domestic labour mobilization with the conscription of colonial workers drawn mainly from Korea. Although the use of conscripted Chinese labour was never on the same scale as that of Korean, the Japanese authorities announced in 1942 that Manchurian Chinese were also subject to labour conscription. The first transports of 'coolie' labour were subsequently brought on a trial basis from the harbour of Dalian in Manchuria. Although theoretically on a one-year contract, most could not leave Japan until the end of the war. In addition, the regional authorities in Manchuria were ordered to provide a fixed quota of workers. This was accomplished by recruiting Chinese labour from other areas of North China as well as Manchuria. Some were volunteers, but most labourers were prisoners of war or peasants 'rounded up' from their villages in North China and Shandong specifically to fulfil labour quotas. All these labourers were taken to reception centres on the Chinese coast before being transported to Japan to work in mines, handling cargo and in civilian or military-related construction (Ishitobu 1973). Prisoners of war, soldiers, peasants and volunteers were treated alike: most were housed in camps surrounded by barbed-wire fences and far from other habitation. Food was far from adequate: men engaged in heavy manual labour were issued only one *mantou* (a Chinese steamed bun made from wheat flour) a day. As provisions grew increasingly scarce towards the end of the war, these often contained grass, rice bran or wheat bran, and even clay. The combination of physical hardship and poor living conditions led the weight of most labourers to drop from an average of 40–42 kg to 24–25 kg within several months (Nukii 1968: 15). Resistance against the Japanese included sabotage, the scrawling of anti-Japanese slogans on walls within the camp and attempted uprisings and escape. Many did in fact manage to escape, often in search of food, but as they knew no Japanese and had no geographical knowledge, they were usually recaptured within a few days. The Japanese authorities usually lynched recaptured escapees although in some cases they forced other Chinese prisoners to beat them to death (Nukii 1968: 18). As many had been in the army, they comprised both Guomindang and communist soldiers, and most incidents were a result of conflict between the two factions. In all, approximately 42,000 Chinese were transported from the mainland between 1943 and 1945. The death rate in certain camps exceeded 50 per cent and by the end of the war there were only 31,000 survivors. Most died from malnutrition or in work-related accidents, although others perished in uprisings against the Japanese, the most notorious of which occurred at the Hanaoka mine site in Akita Prefecture where over 400 Chinese labourers were killed (Hiraoka 1973).

Both Taiwanese and Chinese labourers were repatriated by the American occupation authorities between 1945 and 1949. All labourers from the mainland, with the exception of ninety-nine who chose to remain, were repatriated. In addition, there were approximately 28,000 Taiwanese in Japan at the end of the war. They were given the option of repatriation, but China was still in the throes of civil war and, in addition, the Supreme Command Allied Powers (SCAP) had issued a directive forbidding repatriates to take back more than 1,000 yen or objects of equivalent value. As a result over 14,000 Taiwanese elected to remain in Japan, so that in 1948 the total number of resident Chinese was 34,000 (Uchida 1949: 7).

In the immediate post-war period some Taiwanese and Koreans were engaged in smuggling and black-market activities. SCAP authorities claimed Taiwanese gangs were so powerful that police could not enter some areas of Tokyo. In July 1946 a number of Taiwanese were arrested in Shibuya in Tokyo for black-marketeering and there was an armed clash between Taiwanese and police (SCAP, 10 September 1946, SCAP, 10 February 1947). Anti-Korean and Taiwanese sentiments were also aired by the media. In August 1946 Shiikuma Saburō, Progressive Party member of the House of Representatives, blamed Taiwanese and Koreans for acts of 'unspeakable violence' and their domination of the post-war black market. In fact, there were relatively few acts of violence committed by Chinese, although many Taiwanese took advantage of their links with Taiwan to engage in the illegal import of sugar and to found large-scale enterprises producing sweets and confectionery (Uchida and Shiowaki 1950: 14–16). Other Chinese also established new businesses. As early as November 1945, Chinese in Yokohama had erected makeshift stalls selling fruit and vegetables and Chinese business generally flourished during the immediate post-war period. The Chinese in Yokohama derived their major income from the American occupation and later the Korean War by establishing night clubs and cabarets which catered to American servicemen at nearby military and naval bases (Yamashita 1979: 39–40).

In May 1947 the Japanese government enacted the Alien Registration Law, under which both Taiwanese and Koreans, hitherto classified as Japanese subjects, were legally classified as aliens, although they would retain Japanese nationality until the signing of the San Francisco Peace Treaty in 1952. Japanese policy focused on Koreans, who constituted 91 per cent of the foreigners in Japan, but, as aliens, Chinese and Taiwanese were also disenfranchised, obliged to register, and were excluded from a wide range of social and welfare benefits as well as employment in the public sector. These and other exclusions reinforced traditional reliance on Chinese associations and areas of employment. Before the war, many Chinese had been artisans, painters, peddlers or employees in Chinese-run enterprises. Although many of these occupations disappeared in the post-war period, mainland Chinese generally remained in Chinatown enclaves as self-employed shopkeepers and restaurateurs. Like mainland Chinese, a number of Taiwanese owned restaurants or sold groceries or general merchandise, while others were merchants, barbers, or sold clothing (Uchida 1949: 12–14). Employees and business contacts continued to be drawn from among either relatives or Chinese from the same province of origin, while Chinese enterprises continued to raise capital using provincial ties (Uchida and Shiowaki 1950: 19). The provincial associations maintained their traditional functions as social clubs and benevolent societies, providing hospitals, Chambers of Commerce and schools. When Chinese businessmen found it difficult to obtain loans from Japanese banks, Chinese associations sponsored the foundation of a Chinese bank in 1952 (Sugawara 1991: 170).

Despite these apparent similarities, clear distinctions can be drawn between Taiwanese and mainland Chinese patterns of settlement and employment. In the pre-war period, the Taiwanese, as colonial subjects, had not been affected by formal occupational restrictions. Due to the successful implementation of linguistic assimilation, Taiwanese often had a greater mastery of the Japanese language than other Chinese. Moreover, many had originally come to Japan in order to further their education and had remained in Japan as educated professionals. As a consequence, they had few links with Chinese from the mainland. In Kanagawa in 1952, for example, most of the 1,134 resident Taiwanese resided outside the old Chinatown area. By comparison, most of the 4,075 Chinese from the mainland lived and worked within the traditional residential area (Yamamuro and

Kawamura 1963: 16). None the less, the majority of Taiwanese and mainland Chinese alike resided in the major urban centres. In 1952, of the 44,000 Chinese living in Japan, 12,000 were in Tokyo, 9,000 in Kobe, 6,000 in Osaka and 5,000 in Kanagawa. Smaller communities were to be found in Kyoto and Nagasaki (Yamamuro and Kawamura 1963: 16). In addition to the traditional areas of Chinese employment outlined earlier, Taiwanese held occupations ranging from construction work to medicine, dentistry, teaching and journalism. Although the absence of Taiwanese from the traditional associations deprived them of the support and economic niches that these supplied, it also facilitated their expansion into new areas. Taiwanese enterprises, which were generally larger than those of other Chinese, included coffee-shops and cabarets, pachinko parlours, real estate, ownership of cinema halls and large-scale manufacture of food and beverages (Uchida 1949: 12–14; Yamashita 1979: 44).

After the foundation of the People's Republic of China (PRC) and the Taiwanese Republic of China (ROC) in 1949, both countries vied for the loyalty of overseas Chinese by sponsoring ethnic schools and cultural activities. The existence of two competing regimes subsequently caused a rift within the community in Japan. In the 1950s, for example, the Yokohama Chinese Association split along Taiwanese and PRC lines. In the 1970s a further rift occurred within the Taiwanese association which resulted in the establishment of a rival association advocating an independent Taiwan. Chinese schools were aligned with, and supported by, either the PRC or the Taiwanese Guomindang. In an effort to avoid being drawn into a PRC–ROC conflict, many parents began to send their children to Japanese schools (Yamashita 1979: 45–7). None the less, provincial associations continued to play an important, if somewhat reduced, role in Chinese social life. The Fujian Association, for example, offered general advice on problems in education, marriage and employment and promoted ethnic education. In 1962 it established a youth group and a marriage agency, and made efforts to maintain links with relatives in China and organized regular trips to the mainland (Luo 1989: 420–1).

Japan's recognition of the PRC rather than the ROC as the legitimate government of China in 1972 led many Chinese to seek naturalization as Japanese citizens. Taiwanese residents were initially fearful that Japan's normalization of relations with the PRC would result in the loss of Taiwanese citizenship and their reclassification as citizens of the PRC (Sugawara 1991: 207). Among the mainland Chinese rumours abounded that their assets would be confiscated by the PRC. Before 1972 only about 200 Chinese a year had become naturalized. In 1973 this increased to 7,338, and has since remained at over 1,000 a year (Kobe Shinbunsha 1987: 181). Many of the later Chinese to be naturalized did so in the hope of improving their own or their children's employment prospects (Kobe Shinbunsha 1987: 249–51). The normalization of relations with the PRC also sparked a Chinese boom in Japan. China became the object of a naïve romanticism which was later bolstered by television series such as *The Silk Road*. Chinatowns became tourist destinations and many small restaurants, bars and cabarets switched over to serving Chinese food. Increased trade with the PRC also facilitated the rise of small shops selling curios and ethnic items. The emergence of Chinatowns as tourist attractions also encouraged overt displays of Chinese ethnicity, usually in the form of public celebrations of traditional festivals (Yamashita 1979: 40–2).

By 1975, Chinese residents in Japan numbered almost 68,000. Of these, one-third, or 21,000 were living in Tokyo, 9,000 in Hyogo Prefecture, 7,000 in Kanagawa and 8,000 in Osaka. Aichi, Kyoto and Fukuoka each had a resident Chinese population of approximately 1,500, while Nagasaki had the smallest number of Chinese at 800. With the exception of Tokyo, where they comprised 63 per cent, and Nagasaki, where the comparable figure was only 19 per cent, Taiwanese accounted for between 35 and 45 per cent of the Chinese population elsewhere. As in the past, patterns of residence continued to reflect provincial clusterings; Kanagawa Prefecture was dominated by Cantonese (26 per cent), Hyogo Prefecture by those from Guangdong and Jiangsu (21 and 12 per cent respectively), Osaka also by those from Jiangsu (20 per cent), Kyoto and Fukuoka by Fujianese (22 and 19 per cent), while over half of the Chinese in Nagasaki came from Fujian (52 per cent) (Kobe Shinbunsha 1987: 249–51).

The 1980s witnessed a wave of new arrivals from both Taiwan and the PRC. The labour shortage and the lure of higher potential earnings in Japan were but two of the factors determining migration during the decade. In fact, prior to the introduction of economic liberalization programmes in China, only members of the party elite were permitted to travel abroad (Nagasawa 1994: 58). But the passage of a new law by the PRC in 1982 provided for the introduction of study–work exit visas, issued on proof of sponsorship from an official organization. This coincided with a decision taken by the Japanese Education Ministry in 1983 to increase the number of foreign students in the country to 100,000 by the year 2000 (Sakai

1989: 412). At first, the number of Chinese students entering Japan annually increased only gradually. In 1984, out of a total 4,329 foreign students in Japan, only 251 were Chinese nationals. By 1988, however, the number of foreign students in Japan had increased to 35,107, of whom 28,256 were Chinese. The Chinese need for proof of sponsorship, coupled with lack of regulation within Japan, led to the establishment of many schools which were little more than 'front' organizations to facilitate the entry of Chinese labour (Tanaka 1991: 174–6). The sponsorship requirement, coupled with a lack of effective monitoring, led to the establishment of many schools which were little more than employment agencies facilitating the entry of Chinese migrant labour. Since many bona fide students lacked sufficient financial support, it was common for them to work up to ten hours a day in restaurants, bars or as day labourers on construction sites. Still others remained in Japan to work after expiry of their visas (Sakai 1989: 409–11). After 1988, as Chinese authorities became more stringent in issuing student visas, the number of Chinese students arriving on these visas fell to an average of 10,000 per year. In addition to these working students (*shūgakusei*), the number of Chinese exchange students (*ryūgakusai*) also grew steadily throughout this period from 4,000 in 1984 to 9,000 in 1990 (Tanaka 1991: 175).

The attempted entry and subsequent repatriation of Chinese from Fujian masquerading as Vietnamese refugees in 1989 was widely publicized in the Japanese press. What this incident obscured, however, was a massive increase in the number of Chinese illegally attempting to enter Japan. In 1989, the number of apprehensions stood at 10,404, rising to 13,934 in 1990, and again to 27,137 in 1991 (Sassen 1993: 82). In addition, the number of Chinese from both the mainland and Taiwan entering the country on short-term visas and then overstaying also rose. By 1992, the number of visa overstayers was estimated at 25,737 mainland Chinese (19,266 male and 6,471 female) and 6,729 Taiwanese (3,427 male and 3,302 female), while, in 1991, the number of Chinese illegals who were apprehended was 1,162 from the PRC and 460 from Taiwan (Sassen 1993: 97–9).

In marked contrast to earlier patterns of migration and settlement, where new arrivals were assisted by a network of pre-existing mutual support organizations, there has been little interaction between the established Chinese community and the most recent arrivals from the PRC. Instead, Japanese local authorities and voluntary organizations have taken the lead in providing a range of legal and advisory services to Chinese immigrants. In fact, the lack of support provided through traditional Chinese sources is not all that surprising. Historically, these associations chiefly served and preserved the interests and privileges of the wealthier Chinese; representatives of the principal Chinese associations played an important role in ensuring the exclusion of Chinese labourers from Japan, and offered little or no assistance to labourer victims in the Great Kanto Earthquake and the conscripted labourers of the 1940s. Moreover, the function of these organizations was never to extend aid indiscriminately to all Chinese, but to family members or immigrants from the same region in China.

CONCLUSION

The objective here has been to provide a broad outline of the historical formation of the Chinese community in Japan. A major factor in determining this process has been, and remains, Japan's shifting role within the international economic and political order over the course of the past one hundred years. During the Meiji period, Chinese residents, for all their economic success, were never accorded the respect or status of their Western counterparts. By the turn of the century, moreover, Chinese labourers had come to be perceived as a threat to working-class interests. Thereafter, with the exception of Taiwanese students and labourers, Chinese immigration was restricted to merchants and skilled workers. As a result, the urban character of the Chinese community was reinforced, as was the influence of Chinese associations which continued to provide a range of services. The fact that Chinese residents of Taiwanese origin continue to exist as a distinct sub-group, in terms of areas of settlement, employment and relative economic success, is a further reflection of pre-war Japanese policies. None the less, the development of the Chinese community was not driven by Japanese policies alone. Nor were the Chinese passive participants in this process. Chinese immigrants brought with them well-developed mechanisms of social and economic organization which influenced both patterns of settlement and the maintenance of a distinct identity. It was these factors which also ensured relative economic success and served to distinguish the Chinese as a model minority community.

BIBLIOGRAPHY

Bonavia, D. (1978) 'The overseas Chinese', *Far Eastern Economic Review*, 16 June.

The Chinese community: a model minority 137

Chen, C. (1984) 'Police and community control systems in the empire', in R. Myers and M. Peattie (eds) *The Japanese Colonial Empire, 1895–1945*, Princeton: Princeton University Press.

Daniels, R. (1988) *Asian America*, Seattle and Washington: University of Washington Press.

Dikötter, F. (1992) *The Discourse of Race in Modern China*, Stanford: Stanford University Press.

Elisonas, J. (1991) 'The inseparable trinity: Japan's relations with China and Korea', in J. Hall (ed.) *The Cambridge History of Japan*, Vol. 4, Cambridge: Cambridge University Press.

Fitzgerald, C.P. (1972) *The Southern Expansion of the Chinese People*, London: Barrie and Jenkins.

Freedman, M. (1960–1) 'Immigrants and associations: the Chinese in nineteenth-century Singapore', *Comparative Studies in Society and History*, vol. 3.

Harootunian, H.D. (1980) 'The function of China in Tokugawa thought', in A. Iriye (ed.) *The Chinese and the Japanese: Essays in Political and Cultural Interactions*, Princeton: Princeton University Press.

Hashikawa, B. (1980) 'Japanese perspectives on Asia: from disassociation to coprosperity', in A. Iriye (ed.) *The Chinese and the Japanese: Essays in Political and Cultural Interactions*, Princeton: Princeton University Press.

Hiraoka, M. (ed.) (1973) *Chūgokujin wa Nihon de Nani wo sareta ka*, Tokyo: Ushio Shuppankan.

Hoare, J. (1977) 'The Chinese in the Japanese treaty ports, 1858–1899: the unknown majority', *Proceedings of the British Association for Japanese Studies 2*, 1: 18–33.

Ishitobu, J. (1973) *Chūgokujin Kyōseirenkō no Kiroku*, Tokyo: Taihei Shuppansha.

Itō, I. (1991) 'Yokohama Kakyō Shakai no Keisei', *Yokohama Kaikō Shiryōkan Kiyō* 9: 1–28.

—— (1995) 'Yokohama ni okeru Chūgokujin Shōgyō Kaigijo no setsuritsu wo megutte', in Yokohama to Shanhai Joint Editorial Committee (eds) *Yokohama to Shanhai – Kindai Toshi Keiseishi Hikaku Kenkyū*, Yokohama: Yokohama Shiryō Kaikan.

Iwao, S. (1976) 'Japanese foreign trade in the 16th and 17th centuries', *Acta Asiatica* 30: 1–18.

Jansen, M. (1980) 'Japan and the Chinese Revolution of 1911', in J. Fairbank and K.C. Liu (eds), *The Cambridge History of China*, Vol. 11, Cambridge: Cambridge University Press.

—— (1992) *China in the Tokugawa World*, Cambridge: Harvard University Press.

Jones, S.M. (1974) 'The Ningpo *Pang* and financial power at Shanghai', in M. Elvin and G.W. Skinner (eds) *The Chinese City Between Two Worlds*, Stanford: Stanford University Press.

Kamachi, N. (1980) 'The Chinese in Meiji Japan', in A. Iriye (ed.) *The Chinese and the Japanese: Essays in Political and Cultural Interactions*, Princeton: Princeton University Press.

Keene, D. (1971) 'The Sino-Japanese War of 1894–95', in D. Shively (ed.) *Tradition and Modernization in Japanese Culture*, Princeton: Princeton University Press.

Kim, H. (1994) *A Legal History of Asian-Americans, 1790–1990*, Westport: Greenwood Press.

Kobe Shinbunsha (ed.) (1987) *Sugao no Kakyō*, Tokyo: Jinbun Shōin.

Lone, S. (1994) *Japan's First Modern War*, London: St Martin's Press.

Luo, H. (1989) 'Shilun Riben Huaqiao Tongxianghuiguan de Yanbian', in C. Liang and M. Zheng (eds) *Huaqiao Huarenshi Yanjiuji (2)*, Beijing: Haiyang Chubanshe.

Miyazaki, T. (1982) *My Thirty-Three Years' Dream: The Autobiography of Miyazaki Tōten* (trans. S. Etō and M. Jansen), Princeton: Princeton University Press.

Nagasawa, T. (1994) 'Suginami no Chūgokujin', *Chiri*, March: 54–61.

Naimushō Keihokyoku (1979) *Gaiji Keisatsu kankei Rekishi-shū*, Tokyo: Ryūkei Shōsha.

Naquin, S. and Rawski, E. (1987) *Chinese Society in the Eighteenth Century*, New Haven and London: Yale University Press.

Niki, F. (1991) *Kantō Daishinsai Chūgokujin Daigyakusatsu*, Iwanami Bukkuretto, no. 217, Tokyo: Iwanami Shoten.

Nukii, M. (1968) 'Taiheiyō Sensōka ni okeru Chūgokujin Kyōseirenkō to Teikō', *Rekishi Hyōron* 217: 9–27.

Pan, L. (1990) *Sons of the Yellow Emperor*, London: Secker and Warburg.

Sakai, T. (1989) 'Chinese working students in Tokyo', *Japan Quarterly*, Oct.–Dec.: 409–16.

Sakane, K. (1991) 'Shinchō Nihon Ryūgakukō', *Tokai Daigaku Kiyō Ryūgakusei Kyōiku Sentā* 12: 41–52.

Sanetō, K. and Sanetō, T. (1961) *Nitchū Yūkōshi*, Tokyo: Awaji Shobō Shinsha.

Sassen, S. (1993) 'Economic internationalization: the new migration in Japan and the United States', *International Migration* 31, 1: 73–99.

Satō, T. (1990) 'The Maria Luz incident', in Y. Katō (ed.) *Yokohama Past and Present*, Yokohama: Yokohama City University.

SCAP, Office of Strategic Services (10 September 1946) 'Nationality and treatment of Formosans', *The Occupation of Japan, Part 3, Reform, Recovery and Peace*.

—— (10 February 1947) Intelligence Memorandum, 'Problems regarding the treatment of Formosans in Japan', *Post-war Japan, Korea and Southeast Asia*, Research and Analysis no. 3436.85.

Shiba, Y. (1983) 'Hakodate Kakyōshi Nenpyō', in Y. Yamada (ed.) *Nihon Kakyō to Bunka Masatsu*, Tokyo: Gannandō Shoten.

Skinner, G.W. (1976) 'Mobility strategies in Late Imperial China: a regional systems analysis', in C. Smith (ed.) *Regional Analysis: Volume 1 Economic Systems*, New York: Academic Press.

Sugawara, K. (1991) *Nihon no Kakyō*, Tokyo: Asahi Bunko.

Takaki, R. (1989) *Strangers from a Different Shore*, New York: Penguin.

Tanaka, H. (1991) *Zainichi Gaikokujin*, Tokyo: Iwanami Shinsho.

Toby, R. (1984) *State and Diplomacy in Early Modern Japan: Asia in the Development of the Tokugawa Bakufu*, Princeton: Princeton University Press.

Tsai, S.H. (1986) *The Chinese Experience in America*, Bloomington and Indianapolis: Indiana University Press.

Tsurumi, E.P. (1984) 'Colonial education in Korea and Taiwan', in R. Myers and M. Peattie (eds) *The Japanese Colonial Empire, 1895–1945*, Princeton: Princeton University Press.

Uchida, N. (1949) *Nihon Kakyō Shakai no Kenkyū*, Tokyo: Dōbunkan.

Uchida, N. and Shiowaki, K. (1950) *Ryūnichi Kakyō Keizai Bunseki*, Tokyo: Kawade Shobō.

Wickberg, E. (1994) 'The Chinese as overseas migrants', in J. Brown and R. Foot (eds) *Migration: The Asian Experience*, Basingstoke and London: The Macmillan Press.

Yamamuro, S. and Kawamura, M. (1963) 'Yokohama Zairyū Kakyō no Tokushitsu ni kansuru jakkan no kōsatsu (1), *Yokohama Kokudai Jinbun Kiyō*, September.

Yamashita, K. (1979) 'Yokohama Chūkakai Zairyū Chūgokujin no seikatsu Yōshiki', *Jinbun Chiri* 31, 4: 33–50.

6 Troubled national identity

The Ryukyuans/Okinawans

Koji Taira

At its peak of ethnic/cultural/territorial/administrative integrity, the Ryukyu kingdom governed the south-western two-thirds of the archipelago lying between Kyushu and Taiwan. The kingdom is no more, but the islands it governed are a constant reminder of the vanished kingdom. There are four island groups in Ryukyu: from north-east to south-west, Amami, Okinawa, Miyako and Yaeyama. Today 'Ryukyuan' culture, distinct from 'Japanese' culture, still survives in these islands (Shimono 1986).

As a single island, Okinawa is the largest in the Ryukyu archipelago. The Ryukyu kingdom arose in Okinawa and extended its rule over the rest of the Ryukyus. In 1609 the kingdom was invaded by Satsuma. In 1879 it was annexed by the Meiji state and incorporated as Okinawa Prefecture. Okinawa was reduced to rubble by the Battle of Okinawa in 1945. The Ryukyu Islands were under American occupation until 1972, when they were returned to Japan and reconstituted as Okinawa Prefecture.

Ryukyuans/Okinawans tend to compensate for a sense of historical melancholy through memories of the glory days of their lost kingdom. At a minimum they are reassured that although today's Okinawa is one of many prefectures of Japan, and a trivial one at that, it is not a mere prefecture, but something special and distinct. In the foreword to an Okinawa Prefecture publication (Okinawa Prefecture 1992), Governor Ōta Masahide expressed his pride in Okinawa's heritage, though with a touch of irony and hesitancy, in these words:

Although Okinawa is small in size, it is rich in culture and history. For four and a half centuries [before annexation by Japan in 1879], Okinawa existed as the Kingdom of the Ryukyus – independent and prosperous – playing an important role in the commerce of Asian nations. The tiny kingdom acted as the center of trade in luxury goods shipped from the markets of Southeast Asia to the ports of China, Korea, and Japan.

The phrase 'Kingdom of the Ryukyus' is a new coinage by the scholar-governor. It is quite apt as a description of what the Ryukyu kingdom was, based on the entire Ryukyu Islands. One correction is in order, however. Although the Ryukyu kingdom survived until 1879, it did not govern all of the Ryukyus after the 1609 Satsuma invasion. Amami Islands were lost to Satsuma at this time.

At this introductory stage, we would not quarrel over historical or contemporary details. The argument that informs this chapter is that Ryukyuans/Okinawans, who generated their own national monarchy and governed themselves, deserve a modern international certificate of collective dignity and self-respect: a nation-state of their own. A search for answers to the question of why they are submerged under Japanese political waters instead of standing proudly on their own in the community of nations may shed new light not only on the history and character of Ryukyu/Okinawa, but also on the well-concealed underside of the Japanese state and the impact of international geopolitics on Asia.

A ROUGH PERIODIZATION OF RYUKYUAN/OKINAWAN HISTORY

To prepare the reader for the detailed account of Japanese–Okinawan relations which follows, we offer a brief historical outline. Including prehistory, there are eight periods in Ryukyuan/Okinawan history:

1 Prehistory (40,000 BP–AD 1000).
2 Proto history (AD 1000 1310).
3 Three kingdoms (AD 1310–1429).
4 The Ryukyu kingdom (1429–1609).
5 Dual subordination (1609–1879).
6 Okinawa Prefecture I (1879–1945).
7 US occupation (1945–1972).
8 Okinawa Prefecture II (1972 to present).

THE STIGMA OF OKINAWAN IDENTITY IN MODERN JAPAN

Even a bare outline of Ryukyuan/Okinawan history like the one presented above suggests a lack of fit between it and Japanese history.

This has been the source of many relational problems between Okinawa and Japan and between Okinawans and Japanese. When a small nation is absorbed by a larger nation, it is likely to become a disadvantaged minority group in the new setting. Okinawa is a case in point.

The indigenous people of the Ryukyu Islands are ethnically distinct from the people of mainland Japan. Recently, this proposition has come to enjoy a measure of appreciation among both Japanese and Okinawans. Historically, this is an unusual development and its significance is still difficult to evaluate. Basically it contradicts Japanese notions of political correctness based upon assumptions of 'racial' homogeneity and superiority. The entry into Japanese vocabulary, though still in *katakana*, of the concept of 'ethnicity' as distinct from 'race' or 'nation' is new. 'Race' and racial purity were particularly powerful mobilizing forces in pre-war Japan. 'Nation', by contrast, has enjoyed popular appeal since Meiji, though its usage has often been confused with 'state'. The flip side of this emphasis on 'racial' homogeneity is an unusually keen awareness of the apparent differences between Japanese and non-Japanese. When foreigners visit Japan, their reception is still determined by the position they occupy in an assumed hierarchy of races and nations. Historically, contempt for persons belonging to 'inferior' races or nations has co-existed with adulation for those from 'superior' races or nations. During the pre-war period Okinawans were regarded as members of an inferior race. Nearly forty years ago George Kerr noted that:

> In 1941, the Okinawans formed the largest minority group within Japan's forty-seven prefectures. Prejudice corroded Okinawan relations with Japanese . . . Students at the universities and higher schools in Japan met with discrimination and heard Okinawa referred to in contemptuous terms.
>
> (Kerr 1958: 459)

In Japan today, there are several groups of people ethnically distinct from the majority Japanese. Okinawans constitute the largest minority group of this type, with a population of about 1.3 million in their home base (Amami Islands and Okinawa Prefecture). An estimated 300,000 Okinawans can be found in other parts of Japan, with a similar number scattered elsewhere – mostly in Hawaii and the Americas. The second largest national ethnic group are Koreans, who, counting both naturalized and alien-status residents, would exceed one million. These are followed by the several tens of thousands of Chinese, Ainu, and a host of other nationalities and ethnicities. Both the Ainu and the outcast, Burakumin populations have historically been subjected to diverse forms of discrimination and prejudice. The relational patterns which developed in the pre-modern period between the majority Japanese on the one hand and Burakumin and Ainu on the other provided norms of ethnic relations when neighbouring nations were conquered by modern Japan and their peoples became subjects of the Japanese empire. Japan allocated status, opportunities and resources to them on terms no better than those traditionally imposed upon Burakumin or Ainu. At the same time, attitudes and practices of discrimination learned in relation to Burakumin and Ainu were replicated when these colonial subjects migrated to Japan and established new minority communities.

The sequence of the territorial expansion of imperial Japan is instructive. Ryukyu, annexed in 1879, was the first foreign country absorbed by imperial Japan. Taiwan came next, acquired in 1895, followed by Korea which was annexed in 1910. In these countries which were cut off from the rest of the world and marginalized within the Japanese empire, centuries-old national systems of government, justice, education, honours, etc. were destroyed and replaced with double-decker colonial societies where the Japanese military, administrators, educators, professionals, and businessmen dominated disenfranchised natives. When these new imperial subjects migrated to Japan proper, they were incorporated at the bottom of the Japanese social stratification, equivalent in status to the Burakumin. Segregation and discrimination were the terms imposed on ethnic minorities in Japan proper.

Pointing to 'the ugly problem of social discrimination against the Okinawans', Kerr writes: 'In Japanese eyes the Okinawans stood somewhere between the former outcastes, the Eta of pre-Restoration days, and full-fledged membership in the nation-family' (Kerr 1958: 448). He goes on to state:

> An outstanding example of differentiation was the Okinawan use of pork as a main article of diet. This was part of the Chinese cultural heritage; many Okinawans established themselves in the metropolitan centers of Japan (and in Hawaii) as proprietors of piggeries. This, in Japanese eyes, placed them almost on a level with the despised Eta, the butchers and tanners and shoemakers of the old days.
>
> (Kerr 1958: 448–9)

There were many other distinctive Okinawan cultural characteristics that the Japanese misunderstood and used as justifications for discrimination against Okinawans.

We consider the degradation of Okinawan identity during the period of Okinawa Prefecture I (1879–1945) a defining characteristic of Okinawan–Japanese relations. Discriminatory exclusions were in part a product of the national ethos of Japan during the age of imperialism. Japan began its modern history under a series of humiliations at the hands of Western powers, first illustrated by the 'black ships' of Commodore Perry of the United States Navy. The injured pride could only be mended by becoming powerful enough to return the 'favours' in kind. Rage at the humiliation by the West was also displaced on to neighbouring countries. For the Meiji state, Okinawa was the first step towards demonstrating its ability to engage in the imperialist game.

ETHNIC ORIGINS OF RYUKYUANS AND JAPANESE

Among Japanese academics, the current mainstream view holds that the Ryukyuans and the Ainu are direct descendants of the prehistoric Jōmon people. The Jōmon people were subsequently conquered, eliminated or assimilated by the ancestors of the modern Japanese who immigrated from Korea in several waves during the millennium preceding the Nara period, i.e., 300 BC to AD 700 (Umehara and Hanihara 1982; Hanihara 1991, 1993; Baba 1993; Baba and Narasaki 1991; Ueda 1976). The present-day Japanese are seen to range over an ethnic gradient from the purest 'immigrant (*toraijin*) type' to the purest 'Jōmon type', with different mixes of the two stocks in between. The conventional view is that the 'immigrant type' pervades the upper classes, headed by the imperial clan, while the 'Jōmon type' more often characterizes the lower classes (Hanihara 1984).

Fossils of prehistoric humans have been found at several sites throughout the Ryukyus (Baba and Narasaki 1991). They are dated by radiocarbon, fluorine content or faunal stratigraphy. Radiocarbon dates are ascertained for finds at three sites: Yamashita-cho, 32,000 years BP; Pinza-abu, 25,800–26,800 years BP; and Minatogawa, 16,600–18,250 years BP. Of these various human types, the Minatogawa humans are generally considered direct ancestors of modern Ryukyuans. Palaeolithic hunter-gatherer-fishers of Minatogawa evolved into neolithic Shell-Mound Period Ryukyuans who in turn evolved into modern Ryukyuans.

The origins of the Minatogawa people are somewhat ambiguous. The most definitive statement on this issue has been made by Christy Turner (Turner 1989). According to Turner, the common area of origin for all East Asians, American Indians, and Oceanic peoples was the Sunda Shelf which, though under water today, was dry during the Ice Age and which was then a centre of great population growth. One stream of migrants went into the interior of China, while the other stream moved up north along the coast. The Sunda Shelf was flooded by 12,000 years BP. The rise of the sea-level, compounded by seismic upheavals, broke up the Ryukyu peninsula of the Ice Age and formed the Ryukyu Islands (Kimura 1991).

The migrants to the interior of China developed different tooth characteristics through micro-evolution as they adapted to the extremely cold climate of this region. Turner refers to this group as *Sinodonts*, as opposed to the *Sundadonts* who migrated along the coast of China and retained their original tooth characteristics. To add Baba's terminology, Sinodonts were New Mongoloid, while Sundadonts who populated the Ryukyu/Japan area during the Ice Age remained Old Mongoloid or even an earlier Proto-Mongoloid. The Minatogawa humans, who were forebears of the Jōmonese, were Sundadonts or Proto- (or Old) Mongoloid. The Ainu and Ryukyuans are directly descended from the Minatogawa humans and Jōmonese.

The migrants from Korea to Japan beginning around 2,300 years BP were Sinodonts, from whom the modern Japanese are descended. By the time Sinodonts (New Mongoloid) began to migrate to Japan, they and the Jōmonese had undergone separate micro-evolutions for 30,000 years. The two groups of humans were physically and culturally – that is, ethnically – distinct. Comparison of prehistoric earthenwares found in Japan and Ryukyu suggests that culture may have been similar in Japan and Ryukyu, but that the earlier similarities subsequently broke down and differentiated. By the end of the Jōmon period (the beginning of the Yayoi period) in Japan, Ryukyuan culture and Jōmon culture had diverged considerably (Takamiya 1990, 1994). During the Yayoi period (300 BC– AD 300), there was active trade between Kyushu and Okinawa (Pearson 1990). The political hegemony of the Yamato state of the Kofun period (AD 300–710) did not reach the Ryukyu Islands, nor was there an influx of New Mongoloid immigrants into the Ryukyus.

Historical linguistics has not uncovered evidence of the languages spoken in Ryukyu or Japan during the Jōmon period. Serafim hypothesizes that Hayato-Jōmonese of southern Kyushu, which was influenced by Yayoi culture, diffused to the Ryukyu Islands, taking time as it travelled south-west from island to island (Serafim 1994). The linguistic diffusion from southern Kyushu to the Ryukyus was intense during the Yayoi period, but weakened during the Kofun period as southern Kyushu was increasingly dominated by the Yamato state. The political barrier between Kyushu and the Ryukyus hindered further lingustic diffusion.

The Yamato state was formed by migrants from Paekche. Their language, ancient Korean, largely replaced languages previously spoken in the Yamato area and became the direct ancestor of modern Japanese (Hong 1994: 160–4). On the other hand, the languages of the Ryukyu islands retained considerable Austronesian elements and evolved in relative isolation from Kofun-Japanese influences. By the Nara period, something distinct that might be called proto-Ryukyuan, though with numerous dialects, had emerged. The above suggests that prehistoric Ryukyu was evolving into a distinct area with few cultural or genetic influences from China or Japan. The next stage in Ryukyu's social evolution was the formation of an independent state.

STATE FORMATION AND ITS IMPLICATIONS

That an autochthonous state arose in the Ryukyu islands is an important indicator of the social evolution of the Ryukyus. During its prehistoric and protohistorical periods, the Ryukyu Islands were relatively isolated and the forces of endogenous development gradually worked towards state formation without major external interference. By the historical accident of being left alone by the relatively advanced states which surrounded the islands, the Ryukyus became an ideal laboratory for the observation of the forces leading to state formation. The evolutionary process observed in the Ryukyu islands conforms to the general pattern of social evolution culminating in an archaic state proposed by Johnson and Earle (1987). In this section, we attempt a generalized narrative on the rise of the Ryukyuan state with the help of the Johnson–Earle paradigm.

According to Johnson and Earle, societies go through stages like foraging families, clan-based villages, local villages comprising different clans and families, village collectivities controlled by 'Big Men', rise and growth of 'chiefdoms', and finally, the 'archaic State'. The origins and growth patterns of Ryukyuan villages, noted meticulously in encyclopedias and gazetteers (e.g., Okinawa Taimususha 1983; Takeuchi 1986), and various works on the history of Ko-Ryukyu (especially, Ryukyu Shinpōsha 1991, vol. 1) provide a wealth of material for testing the Johnson–Earle paradigm in a Ryukyuan setting.

Not much is known about Ryukyuan life in the foraging-family stage. Mythological accounts generally suggest migrants landing on an island, settling and establishing villages. Each major island group boasts its own mythological account about the origins of its people and society, and these are contained in a number of works: Majikina (1923) on Okinawa, Nobori (1949) on Amami, Kiyomura (1929) on Miyako, and Kishaba (1953) on Yaeyama. In an idealized spatial layout of a Ryukyuan village, the founder family builds its house near a wooded hill or a grove and the houses of its offspring spread out like a fan riveted on the founder's house. The spatial pattern correlates degrees of kinship and spatial distance from the founder family. The hill or grove behind the founder family's house is a sacred space where the guardian deities reside and religious functions are performed. This is the origin of the '*gusuku*'. The sister of the male founder assumes the role of a village priestess (*nīgan*). The founder himself is considered the 'root' of the village-clan (*nīcchu*). The founder's house is called 'root house' or 'original house' (*nīyā* or *mutuyā*).

Latter-day villages often contained multiple origins and their offspring. At the time of founding, however, the founder houses may have been sufficiently isolated by the standards of the time, but, with population growth, the space separating them was filled in and separate villages eventually formed what appeared to be a single village unit. Even so, the most senior among the founder families was the most prestigious one and provided the services of the *nīcchu* and *nīgan* for the expanded village. The village was no longer a clan village, but a local village integrating families of different origins. Spatial constraints were often solved by spinning off some families and founding new villages. These villages then were appropriately ranked over the gradient of consanguinal degrees issuing from the original founder family. Supra-village clan networks were formed in this fashion. The extent and structure of government became complicated by the interactions between local villages and supra-village clans.

During the *gusuku* period, competition for and maintenance of existing resources demanded new leaders identified by new criteria like charisma, valour, popularity, innovativeness, ability to administer, etc. 'Politics' was born, with 'power' becoming an additional dimension of social order. Many *nīcchu* together with *nīgan* must have made the transition to new political leadership. The newly powerful men were variously called: big man, renowned one, big father, chief, head, lord, or, where merits were extraordinary, the Sun (*tida*). The generic title by which they came to be widely known was *aji*. The dignity of titles evolved in association with the accumulation and concentration of power. The *aji* appropriated sacred hills and woods and fortified them. These fortifications marked the first appearance of *gusuku*. The usual attributes of political power emerged: ruler (*aji*), citadel, troops, territory. During the twelfth and thirteenth centuries, the Ryukyus were studded with *gusuku* of various sizes, reflecting the wealth, status and power of their rulers (Asato 1990). An *aji* ruling several villages did so by subordinating their *nīcchu* and *nīgan*. Such an *aji* created *nuru* as a head priestess to oversee various village *nīgan*. Alliances and competition among *aji* produced numerous large and small political units which, as if through a tournament, were progressively eliminated as aggregation and concentration of power over larger areas escalated. The upward spiral of competition for power reached its logical culmination: the ultimate winner (*aji sui* – ruler of rulers). Another glorifying title was *yu-nu-nushi* (lord of the world – sovereign).

In common usage, the size of 'the world' was flexible. An *aji* with only a village to govern was a *yu-nu-nushi* if the village was the world itself for the inhabitants. Eventually, the perception of 'the world' expanded to connote the whole of the Ryukyus, and *yu-nu-nushi* applied only to the paramount ruler of these islands. Formal kingship (*wang* or *ō*) was then granted by the emperor of China. The Muromachi shogun of Japan used *yu-nu-nushi* (*yo-no-nushi* in Japanese reading) in letters to the Ryukyu king. Even at this early stage, the Japanese avoided addressing the Ryukyu ruler as 'king' (*ō*). The Japanese tendency to look down upon Ryukyu became progressively worse as history progressed.

The process of aggregating power in kingship in Ryukyu was concentrated in a relatively short period: the twelfth to fifteenth centuries. Since it is also relatively recent, the process of Ryukyu's state formation is highly visible and easily comprehended without reliance on the blurring effects of mytho-history. Partly because of the rapidity of Ko-Ryukyu state formation, there were many loose ends to tighten up. Unitary administrative structure under the king and reaching down to the village level throughout the Ryukyus appeared only towards the end of the fifteenth century. Villages, clans, and local *aji* remained largely autonomous up until then. Power struggles among *aji* were incessant. Established *aji* could be toppled by new leaders emerging from nowhere. In sum, the relationships among *aji* as well as those between *aji* and people were highly volatile.

Thus, in Ko-Ryukyu, ruling dynasties rose and fell in quick succession. After the end of the mythic dynasty of Heaven's Offspring in the twelfth century, in *Chūzan* of Okinawa, four ruling dynasties rose and fell: Shunten (1187–1260), Eiso (1260–1349), Satto (1349–1406), and First Shō (1406–70). Stabilization began with Shō En (king, 1470–77), whose own name was Kanimaru and who served the First Shō kings in various capacities. He was 'elected' king by an assembly of lords and officials that decided to dethrone the sitting Shō king for a lack of governing virtue.

Shō En was not related to the Shō dynasty he succeeded. But as a means of concealing the revolution for diplomatic reasons, he took on the former dynasty's surname and reported to China that he was the heir to the late king. Ko-Ryukyu state building was completed during the lengthy reign of Shō En's son, Shō Shin (king, 1477–1527). The second Shō dynasty lasted more than four hundred years, until its last king, Shō Tai, was deposed by the Meiji state in 1879.

KO-RYUKYU AND LONG-DISTANCE TRADE

Towards the end of the Shell Mound period, in the tenth century, Ryukyu began to participate in East Asian trade. Archaeological finds suggest that Ryukyu's import of Chinese ceramics began around the middle of the twelfth century and became widespread in the thirteenth century (Pearson 1990: 273). Trading activities were probably initiated by Chinese merchants, although there is evidence that some of the powerful *aji* also sent their ships to China and South-east Asia. In the latter part of the thirteenth century, Japanese merchants also became active in Ryukyuan trade. By the time the tributary relationship with China began in the late fourteenth century, Ryukyu was already practising entrepôt trade, moving goods among different areas of Asia such as China, South-east Asia, Japan, and Korea. Throughout the fifteenth century, Ryukyu prospered through vigorous entrepôt trade underwritten by the official suzerain/tributary gift exchanges with China.

After King Satto accepted Ryukyu's tributary status with China in 1372, the emperors of China generously rewarded Ryukyu's submission and loyalty. They granted Ryukyu massive economic, technical, and educational assistance and contributed greatly to Ryukyu's material and cultural progress. They permitted the enrolment of

Ryukyuan scholars at Chinese academies with expenses paid in full. The emperors also sent their emissaries to Ryukyu to invest the Ryukyuan rulers with the honours and powers of kingship. The emissaries and their entourages often remained in Ryukyu for months and promoted the hands-on transfer of Chinese culture and technology to Ryukyu. A Chinese community (*Kuninda*) grew up and prospered in Naha, taking responsibility for navigation, documentation, negotiation, and other matters essential to the conduct of Ryukyu's relations with China and South-east Asia. Initially, *Kuninda* was autonomous and neutral with respect to the three Ryukyu kingdoms, offering technical services for their tributary transactions with China. Shortly after the First Shō dynasty replaced the Satto in 1406, however, the Chinese community came under the direct control of the *Chūzan* kingdom.

The First Shō kings appointed a Chinese, Huai Ji, as their prime minister. Huai Ji, whose earlier and later years are unknown, came to Ryukyu as a young man at about the beginning of the Yongle era (1403–25) and served the Shō dynasty with distinction until about 1450. Historians speculate that Huai Ji may have been dispatched to Ryukyu as a part of the Yongle emperor's grandiose plan to publicize the superiority of Chinese culture abroad. Huai Ji was an able administrator, city planner, civil engineer, and military strategist. The consolidation of power in the hands of the Shō kings owed much to Huai Ji's stewardship. He formalized the administration of the royal government at Shuri, managed Ryukyu's tributary relations with China as well as international trade with Asian countries, undertook major public works, built temples and shrines, and sent students to China. Designed by Huai Ji, Shuri *gusuku* became an impressive castle with a Chinese-style palace within it for royal residence and government offices. He also engineered the construction of a long causeway connecting Naha (hitherto an offshore island) to the main island of Okinawa.

Ryukyuan ships called at many ports throughout East Asia and South-east Asia. Sansom writes in this context:

> The voyages of the Luchuan craft were quite remarkable, for they reached as far as Siam, Burma, Sumatra, and Java. Every year the Luchu traders would collect Chinese porcelain and silk and Japanese swords, fans, and sulphur, and exchange them for tropical products, such as the spices and perfumes of Indonesia. They made use of the monsoons, and in order to find favourable winds the ships went by way of the Fukien coast to Malacca and thence

to their several destinations across the seas east and west of Malaya.

(Sansom 1961: 180)

Entrepôt trade produced Ko-Ryukyu's golden age. It was in great part stimulated by Ming China's withdrawal from maritime expansion in the fifteenth century. China's demand for foreign goods was filled by overseas Chinese and others. This worked to the advantage of Ryukyu. Curtin points out:

> Off the Chinese coast in the late fifteenth century, the small kingdoms [*sic*] on Okinawa in the Ryukyu Islands stepped into the picture and began to play a commanding role in trade between China and Japan and Melaka, incidentally providing the economic base for a kind of Okinawan golden age.

(Curtin 1984: 127)

With the advance of the Portuguese into Asia, Ryukyuan ships retreated. Malacca was captured by the Portuguese in 1511. In 1512, two Ryukyuan ships reached Singapura, but at the news of Malacca's fall did not proceed any further. The last travel document issued to a ship going to Sunda-Karapa (today's Jakarta) is dated 1518. Ayudhaya of Siam fell to Burma in the 1560s, and Ryukyuans lost profitable opportunities there. Nearly two hundred years of trade relationship with Siam thus ended. Before trade with Siam was severed, commercial relations with other South-east Asian ports were terminated at varying dates (Kobata and Matsuda 1969). The reduction in long-distance trade doomed Ko-Ryukyu.

DUAL SUBORDINATION TO CHINA AND JAPAN

A new age of centralized feudalism dawned in Japan in the late sixteenth century. With no more areas in Japan left for military conquest, Toyotomi Hideyoshi undertook prolonged military aggression against Korea in the 1590s. Ryukyu's unwillingness to support Japan in this war provided the daimiate of Satsuma in 1609 with an excuse to subsequently 'punish' Ryukyu. King Shō Nei (1564–1620), failing to repulse the Satsuma invasion, was taken prisoner, retained in Japan for two years, and allowed to return home upon signing a pledge of feudal fealty to Satsuma. Satsuma demoted the king (*koku-ō*) to 'governor' (*koku-shi*). The restoration of the royal title did not take place until 1712. Ryukyu, a commercial state, was in part transformed into a Japanese-style agrarian feudal province. Out of the assessed annual yield of about 90,000 *koku* (revised up or down in later years), Ryukyu paid an annual tax equivalent of 15,000 *koku* to Satsuma. However, Ryukyu's international status as China's tributary state was recognized and allowed to continue by Satsuma and the bakufu in Edo. With great determination, Ryukyu maintained this status as an expression of its independent identity.

Between the Satsuma invasion of Ryukyu in 1609 and the fall of the Ming in 1644, despite internal difficulties in China and Ryukyu, Ryukyu's tributary relations with China were maintained with some changes in the delivery schedule of the tribute. Political and economic relations, disrupted by the Ming–Qing transition in China, were restored by the era of the Kangxi emperor's reign (1661–1722), and Ryukyu's cultural, social and economic renaissance began. The Kangxi emperor treated Ryukyu with imperial benevolence, thus reinforcing images of a generous China and a rapacious Japan. But dual subordination also encouraged a process of dual acculturation among Ryukyuans. During the eighteenth century (the eras of the Kangxi, Yongzheng and Qianlong emperors overlapping in large part with the relatively stable reign periods of the Ryukyu kings, Shō Kei and Shō Boku, 1713–94), Ryukyuans attained a new level of social and cultural development, discarding much of the Ko-Ryukyu legacy. A variety of new cultural forms were created in architecture, fine arts, music, performing arts, literature, poetry, education, etc., blending Chinese and Japanese influences. Many distinct aspects of Ryukyuan culture that are highly prized today are the bequests of the cultural flowering of the eighteenth century.

In the late eighteenth century, Ryukyu suffered an unprecedented series of natural disasters. Most damaging were the 1771 *tsunami* in Miyako and Yaeyama which killed more than 10,000 people. In these areas, the population did not recover the pre-*tsunami* levels for a hundred years. Productivity fell throughout the Ryukyus, and the government sent special inspectors to tax-defaulting villages to implement economic recovery measures. In the nineteenth century, Satsuma also encountered fiscal difficulties. By the Tenpo era (1830–44), Satsuma's debt to Osaka merchants had grown to 5 million *ryō*, necessitating drastic revenue-raising measures as well as special strategies to deal with the creditors (Sumiya and Taira 1979: ch. 6). Satsuma's Tenpo Reform reinforced the economic exploitation of Ryukyu. The poll tax on the people of Miyako and Yaeyama, in particular, acquired notoriety as a cruel and inhumane tax during this period (Stinchecum 1988–9). Ryukyu's socio-economic vitality had greatly declined by the era of the last king, Shō Tai (1843–1901; reign: 1848–79).

Ryukyu's woes were compounded by the arrival of Western ships. The formal independence of Ryukyu coupled with its *de facto* subordination to Japan greatly tested Ryukyu's diplomatic capability. The major event that defined this phase in Ryukyuan history was the conclusion in 1854 of a treaty with the United States under Commodore Perry's coercion. This was followed by treaties with France in 1855 and the Netherlands (1859). Historians believe that Ryukyuan skills in dealing with foreign powers at least avoided a potential major catastrophe in the form of outright Western occupation. Ryukyu was fortunate to have an able scholar-official, Itarajichi (or Makishi) Chōchu, who acquired Western language skills on his own and singlehandedly took charge of Ryukyu's Western diplomacy. However, the benighted officialdom of the Shuri Court failed to respond effectively to this new opportunity, which, if correctly seized upon, could have resulted in international recognition of Ryukyu as an independent state. In contrast, shocked by Perry, Japan began a rapid transformation into a modern industrial state. Ironically, the new Japan was brought into being by major western *han*, among them Satsuma as a *primum mobile*! To Ryukyuans, the Meiji state was in effect a Satsuma writ large, foreboding continued misfortune for them.

RYUKYU SHOBUN AND OKINAWA PREFECTURE I

In 1866, the long-awaited Qing imperial emissaries came to Ryukyu and declared Shō Tai king. In 1867, the Tokugawa shogun returned powers of government to the emperor, and, in 1868, the era name, Meiji, was proclaimed. In 1879, after several self-serving steps taken by the Japanese government, the Ryukyu kingdom was finally 'disposed of' (Ryukyu *shobun*) under Ryukyuan protest. The process of disposition of Ryukyu was the beginning of modern Japan's less than honourable international dealings which later snowballed into sabre-rattling diplomacy and wars of imperialist expansion.

In the wake of Japan's *haihan chiken* (abolition of *han* and establishment of prefectures) and the disappearance of Satsuma as a *han*, Ryukyu's dual subordination required redefinition. Japan sought to abolish this duality by completely absorbing Ryukyu, but China and Ryukyu desired the continuation of their traditional relationship. Since China was officially ignorant of Ryukyuan–Japanese relations, its view of Ryukyu as a tributary needed no revision. China considered Japan's territorial claims over Ryukyu outrageous and unjustified. To sever Ryukyu completely from China, Japan resorted to a series of highly questionable manoeuvres. In 1872, the Ryukyu king sent a mission to Tokyo to congratulate the Meiji emperor on his enthronement. On this occasion, the emperor made Shō Tai a 'king of Ryukyu *han*' (Ryukyu-*han* ō) and admitted him to the ranks of Japan's peerage (*kazoku*). The royal title was retained, but Ryukyu was downgraded to a fictitious *han*, when all *han* of Japan had already disappeared. However, on the basis of the traditional sinocentric notion of emperor–king relationships, the Ryukyu mission interpreted the Japanese imperial awards to their king as the Japanese-style investiture of a king by an emperor. Japanese intentions were quite different. Ryukyu was now a *han* of Japan subordinate to the Japanese government and therefore abolishable as were all *han*. Japan lost no time in announcing to the world that Ryukyu was its province. At the same time Japan assured the United States, France and the Netherlands that Japan would assume and honour all international obligations arising from Ryukyu's treaties with them. The Western Treaty Powers acquiesced, but China refused to recognize Japan's rights over Ryukyu.

Japan's diplomacy towards China over Ryukyu was governed by the laws of the jungle and characterized by deceit and bad faith. In 1874, Japan undertook a military expedition to Taiwan to punish its aborigines who had murdered or otherwise harmed shipwrecked 'Japanese subjects'. Japan later claimed that the 'Japanese subjects' in question were mainly the sixty-nine Ryukyuans who had been shipwrecked off the east coast of Taiwan in 1871 (one year before the 'investiture' of the Ryukyu king by the Japanese emperor), fifty-four of whom were murdered by Taiwanese aborigines. The 'Japanese subjects' also included four seafarers from Oda Prefecture (now part of Okayama Prefecture) who Japan insisted were robbed and nearly killed by Taiwanese aborigines in 1873.

The Sino-Japanese treaty in the wake of the Taiwan expedition contains no indication of the identity of the 'Japanese subjects' on whose behalf Japan sent troops to Taiwan. Considerable controversy exists among researchers on this point. Did Japan inform China specifically that the 'Japanese subjects' in question referred to Ryukyuans? And, if so, did China agree that Ryukyuans were Japanese subjects? Two recent research findings (Leung 1983; Zhang 1992) indicate that Japan did not mention Ryukyuans either in the treaty or during the negotiation leading up to it and that China was under the impression that Japan was referring only to Japanese subjects from Oda Prefecture.

There were good reasons for Japan's failure to specify that the purpose of the Taiwan expedition was to establish that Ryukyuans were Japanese. The Chinese position on the status of Ryukyuans was all too well known to the Japanese negotiators. What is more, the 1871 incident had already been settled between China and Ryukyu. The Ryukyuan survivors of the incident were protected and cared for by Chinese residents and authorities in Taiwan. They safely returned to Ryukyu via Fuzhou in 1872, and the Ryukyu king thanked the Chinese emperor and officials for the rescue, care and repatriation of his subjects. China and Ryukyu had resolved the matter amicably on the basis of well-established rules and procedures. There was nothing in the incident that even remotely concerned Japan. Recent research also indicates that the alleged harm received by the Oda seafarers was a Japanese fabrication. The truth was that the shipwrecked Japanese in this case were rescued by a Taiwanese aboriginal chief on the north-east coast and repatriated via Shanghai, for which the Japanese government expressed thanks to China (Zhang 1992: 112). The Japanese negotiators in 1874 were either ill-informed or simply lied.

Japan then reproduced the fabrication internationally by announcing that China recognized Japanese claims to the Ryukyus. Encouraged by the tacit approval of the Treaty Powers, Japan proceeded to take over the islands, despite Ryukyuan claims to the contrary. China also protested Japanese actions through diplomatic channels (Kamachi 1981: ch. 4). After the disposition of Ryukyu in 1879, Ryukyuan exiles in China succeeded in gaining Li Hongzhang's sympathy (Leung 1991). As a consequence, disputes again flared up between China and Japan over Ryukyu, now Okinawa Prefecture. The disputed status of the Ryukyus, though never formally resolved, disappeared from the agenda following the defeat of China in the Sino-Japanese War of 1894–5. The illegitimate incorporation of the Ryukyus as Japanese territory had come about as a result of three interrelated factors: (1) Japan's well-planned imperialist designs on Asia based upon its correct understanding of the Western rules of international relations; (2) China's failure to appreciate these rules and its consequent failures to counteract Japanese actions; and (3) Ryukyuan inability to defend itself from Japanese aggression.

Although the reasons are unclear, between 1879 and 1895 the Meiji government soft-pedalled the Japanization of Ryukyu. Because many institutional features of the former Ryukyu kingdom were retained, this period is often referred to as *Kyūkan onzon jidai* (period that preserved old custom). Hundreds of Ryukyuans went into exile in China and lobbied the Chinese government for the restoration of the Ryukyu kingdom. In Okinawa itself, things began to change with the arrival in 1892 of Governor Narahara Shigeru (1834–1908: governor 1892–1908). Reforms (Japanization) accelerated after the Sino-Japanese War, moulding Ryukyu into a Japanese prefecture. The last Ryukyu king, Shō Tai, died in 1901. Narahara's autocratic Japanization of Ryukyu, while encouraging economic progress through the introduction of private property and a market economy, also brought hardship and tragedy to many Okinawans. Exiles to China were among the obvious losers, as were many members of the traditional gentry. Even among the new men of Meiji Okinawa, Narahara's politics turned out to be a curse. One of the best-known victims is Jahana Noboru (1865–1908), an agronomist, who was one of the first Okinawans to study and obtain a degree at Tokyo Imperial University. Jahana opposed Narahara's plans to privatize community lands and forests, and, in 1898, went to Tokyo where he almost succeeded in having Narahara removed as governor of Okinawa by the Japanese cabinet of Prime Minister Okuma Shigenobu. Narahara's recall was only prevented by the collapse of the Okuma cabinet. Jahana then led a not-too-successful anti-Narahara movement in the name of people's rights and liberties (*jiyū minken undō*).

But something good also came out of Narahara's repressive policies. In response to the imposition of an inferior status in his own country, Tōyama Kyūzō (1868–1910), Jahana's political ally, found a radically new future for Okinawans in emigration. Narahara's interest in ridding himself of potential troublemakers coincided with Tōyama's plans. The first contingent of twenty-seven Okinawan emigrants left for Hawaii in December 1899, and annual emigration to Hawaii peaked at 4,467 in 1906, just before the US–Japanese Gentlemen's Agreement to limit Japanese emigration went into effect. Emigration to Latin America began in 1904 with 223 Okinawans going to Mexico. In the same year, 360 Okinawans went to the Philippines, followed by 387 to New Caledonia in 1905. Okinawans also spread out within the Japanese empire, first to nearby Taiwan and later to Micronesia (Nan'yō). The volume of emigration from Okinawa fluctuated from year to year. There were four statistical peaks in Okinawan emigration (*Okinawa kenshi*, vol. 7: 38–54). The leading destinations are different each time. An overwhelming majority of emigrants at the first peak (1906) went to Hawaii. Slightly more than a half at the second peak in 1918 went to Brazil. At the third peak in 1929, most went to the Philippines, followed by Brazil and Argentina. At the fourth peak, the Philippines again dominated. The fluctuating volume and shifting destinations of Okinawan emigrants reflected a complex interplay of various factors: socio-economic conditions in Okinawa, Japan and receiving countries, as well as policy shifts in Japan and receiving countries.

Japanization of Okinawa and global dispersion of Okinawans went hand in hand. In 1935, there were 42,669 Okinawans settled overseas, 32,335 on the Japanese mainland, and a further 17,614 in the Japanese dependencies (Ishikawa and Taira 1991). Okinawans outside the prefecture constituted more than 15 per cent of the then prefectural population. Emigration continued between 1935 and 1945, Nan'yō becoming the most popular destination (*Okinawa kenshi*, vol. 7: 397; Peattie 1988). By 1945, Okinawans had built several diaspora communities, which after the holocaust of the Battle of Okinawa, contributed considerably to the reconstruction of their homeland.

THE AMERICAN OCCUPATION AND OKINAWA PREFECTURE II

In June 1945, roughly two months before the surrender of Japan, the United States won the Battle of Okinawa and occupied it as a hard-won prize of war, placing it and Okinawans under military government (Fischer 1988). Okinawa was regarded as a piece of enemy territory seized by the victor before the ceasefire. How America occupied Okinawa was quite different from how Japan proper was administered under the Allied Occupation. This basic difference influenced the attitudes and policies of both the United States and Japan towards Okinawa. Okinawans remained under American occupation until 1972, while the peace treaty with the Allied Powers, though partial, ended the occupation of Japan in 1952.

Post-war Okinawa's experience indicates that Okinawa is not an 'inherently integral territory' of Japan (*Nihon koyū no ryōdo*), a description that some Japanese and Okinawans still prefer. The fact is that Okinawa is separable from Japan or integrable with it depending on Japan's national interest and the international environment. Under the Potsdam Declaration of 26 July 1945, which demanded Japan's 'unconditional surrender', Japanese sovereignty was to be 'limited to the islands of Honshu, Hokkaido, Kyushu, Shikoku and such minor islands as we determine'. There was no mention of the Ryukyus or Okinawa in this declaration. But since the Ryukyus were obviously not part of any of those major islands (Honshu etc.), they must have been included with the 'minor islands' whose status would be determined at the discretion of the Allies.

The Showa emperor was well aware of the ambiguous nature of Okinawa's relationship to Japan, and, in September 1947, Hirohito sent a message to General MacArthur which argued in favour of the long-term US occupation of Okinawa. Displaying considerable forethought, the emperor advised MacArthur that since the United States had no territorial ambitions in the region, the occupation of Okinawa might be effected on the basis of 'the legal fiction of a long-term lease . . . with sovereignty reserved to Japan' (Ota 1990: 314–20; Sodei 1990: 4–5). In advancing this argument, the Showa emperor pioneered the doctrine of 'residual sovereignty' and acted as an architect of the long-term American occupation of Okinawa. The legality of the emperor's intervention in territorial issues at this time was questionable in the light of the Constitution of 1947 which defined the role of the emperor as 'symbolic'. The United States improved on the emperor's suggestion by a flexible adaptation of the concept of United Nations trusteeship: i.e., 'Pending the making of such a proposal [to place the Ryukyus under the United Nations' trusteeship system] and affirmative action thereon, the United States will have the right to exercise all and any powers of administration, legislation and jurisdiction over the territory and inhabitants of these islands, including their territorial waters' (Article 3 of the San Francisco Peace Treaty). At the same time, and behind the scenes, the United States recognized Japan's 'residual sovereignty' over the Ryukyus.

Between 1945 and 1950, the United States placed the Ryukyus under military government, but neglected civilian rehabilitation and reconstruction. The beginning of the Cold War and the communist victory in China impressed the strategic value of Okinawa on policy-makers in Washington and the General Headquarters of the Allied Powers in Tokyo. A permanent foothold in Okinawa became a military necessity for the United States. This required a degree of economic, political and social progress for the Ryukyuans if for no other reason than to gain a measure of popular support for the expropriations of land and the expanded construction of military bases which followed.

In 1950, the United States experimented with a loosely structured form of federal system of government by designating each of the four island groups (Amami, Okinawa, Miyako, and Yaeyama *guntō*) an area with its own popularly elected governor and legislature.

A judicial system was also established for each island group. These civilian governments were overseen by a restructured military government called the United States Civil Administration of the Ryukyus (USCAR). In the gubernatorial and legislative elections in July 1950, candidates and their supporters expressed divergent views on the future status of the Ryukyus, ranging from independence, to self-government under the United States, to co-operation with the military government, and to a United Nations trusteeship. A view not expressed was that of reversion to Japan (Nakachi 1989: 38). In Okinawa, Taira Tatsuo (1892–1969) won the gubernatorial race by opposing independence, self-government or trusteeship. But once elected, Taira openly promoted the idea of reversion. The Okinawa *guntō* legislature promptly passed a resolution calling for reversion to Japan. The other island groups followed suit.

In spring 1952, the 'island-group (*guntō*) governments' were abolished and absorbed by a centralized Government of the Ryukyu Islands (GRI). The chief executive of the administrative branch of the GRI was appointed by the USCAR, while the legislature was popularly elected. The judicial system was also consolidated for the entire Ryukyus. The three branches of civilian government with limited autonomy under the supervision of the USCAR remained the basic feature of Ryukyuan government until 1972. At its first session in March 1952, the newly elected legislature passed a resolution in favour of the expeditious reversion of the Ryukyus to Japan.

The USCAR–GRI setup under the remote control of Washington smacked of a conventional Western colonial system in which a metropolitan power's agency ruled an alien territory and population through a hand-picked native government (Taira 1958; Selden 1971). Under the circumstances, the rise of an anti-colonial movement seeking independence from colonial domination had to be expected. In Okinawa, this would have implied the elevation of the GRI to the status of a newly independent Ryukyuan national government. However, the movement for Okinawa's liberation from 'alien rule' took the form of a movement to demand reversion to Japan which had itself only regained independence in 1952. In mainland Japan, irredentism arose in response.

By opting for reversion, Okinawans lost a potential opportunity to regain full independence. Today, more than twenty years after the reversion of 1972, independence from Japan appears to be a widely shared dream (Miki 1992). But in view of Japan's national ethos, it is not 'politically correct' to openly advocate independence for an area that is already part of Japan. Once again Okinawans have manoeuvred themselves into a catch-22 situation which they dislike but cannot escape from. Why, from among all alternatives, Okinawans chose reversion to Japan requires an understanding of how the international environment during the 1950s and 1960s, especially US–Japanese relations, constrained Okinawan choices. The Cold War made any political stance in Okinawa other than co-operation with the *status quo* a subversive and therefore repressible one. Any criticism which likened US rule to that of a colonial power was regarded by USCAR as part of an imagined communist conspiracy. This threat effectively choked off the freedom of speech for Okinawans. The extension of political autonomy for Okinawa was denounced as a myth by the longest serving High Commissioner, General Caraway (in office, 1961–4).

It was clear that civil liberties under the USCAR–GRI regime were inferior to those enjoyed by citizens in any prefecture of Japan under the 1947 Constitution. A matter of symbolic importance was that governors of Japanese prefectures were popularly elected, while the chief executive of the GRI was not. Bills passed by the Ryukyuan legislature were also subject to a USCAR veto. Decisions of the Ryukyuan courts were sometimes reviewed, reversed, or removed from their jurisdiction by USCAR. Public officials, elected or not, were removable at the discretion of USCAR. The US eventually made a concession on the chief executive by allowing for popular elections to determine who should fill the office. But this gesture was not made until 1968, when US–Japanese negotiations for Okinawa's reversion to Japan were already under way.

Why the United States opposed the implementation of a Japanese prefectural level of democracy in Okinawa for so long is a fascinating question. A widespread interpretation among Okinawans was that USCAR denied democracy to Okinawans due to 'racist' prejudices; i.e., the belief that Okinawans unlike Japanese were incapable of governing themselves. American insistence on an Okinawan identity, as opposed to a Japanese identity, was also interpreted by Okinawans as a thinly veiled 'racist' contempt for Okinawans as an inferior people. The Okinawan response was, more often than not: 'We are Japanese', 'we are entitled to the same extent of democracy and civil and human rights as the Japanese enjoy in the mainland', etc. In the heat of reversion politics, 'mainland' was even called 'fatherland' by many Okinawan reversionists, while reversionists and irredentists alike promoted the notion that Okinawa was an inherently integral part of Japan proper. From a historical perspective, it is curious that Okinawans should have claimed that they were Japanese or that Japan was their 'fatherland'. It was a stance which implied a rejection of their own ethnic and cultural identity as Ryukyuans. A partial answer can be found in the twists and turns in the psychology and rhetoric of contemporary Okinawan politics. Okinawans knew that the United States respected Japan. They also knew that the United States distinguished Okinawans from Japanese. From this, they then inferred that any distinction made by the United States implied a denial of equal respect to Okinawans. Thus, *vis-à-vis* the Japanese, Okinawans would claim distinctiveness for themselves, but *vis-à-vis* Americans they would claim that whatever they felt towards the Japanese was none of the business of the United States: i.e., it was wrong for Americans to manipulate Japanese–Okinawan differences in ways prejudicial to Okinawans. From this, then, the most convenient weapon against American racism was to insist that Okinawans were Japanese.

Japan's 'residual sovereignty' over the Ryukyus as stipulated in the San Francisco Peace Treaty implied that when the United States no longer required the use of these islands, Japanese sovereignty would be restored. The advantages of this arrangement to Japan were obvious. Less obvious was an alternative interpretation: i.e., the United States should not allow Okinawans to gain sufficient autonomy as to aspire to an independent nation-state claiming sovereignty over the Ryukyus. Other than the US, Japan was the only state that could claim sovereignty over these islands, a factor which clearly ruled out any other country, even a newly independent Ryukyuan state, as a legitimate claimant to sovereignty over the Ryukyus. This further implies that the Peace Treaty obligated the United States to discourage, or even suppress, any Okinawan independence movement. The formal language of international law coincided neatly with the ideological language of the Cold War in emasculating anti-colonial independence movements among Okinawans.

The agreement on Okinawa's reversion to Japan was only an extension of the doctrine of Japan's residual sovereignty. Logically and actually, Okinawans had no influence over the status of the Ryukyu Islands at the time of reversion, just as they had no role in the earlier process that produced the doctrine of residual sovereignty. Since the primary interest of the United States in the Ryukyus was the use and maintenance of its military bases, provided this was guaranteed by Japan after reversion, the United States basically had no objection to returning the islands to Japanese administration. In taking them back, the Japanese government merely sought the reinstatement of the *status quo ante* prior to the defeat in the Pacific War.

The reversion movement had political *raison d'être* and vitality so long as the United States did not want to give up the Ryukyus. When US policy shifted to support for reversion, the movement lost meaning. The question of what exactly was gained through the reversion movement remains an unresolved question for many Okinawans. They may not agree that it was superfluous, but whether they like it or not, the reversion was only a bilateral transaction between the United States and Japan without any input from Okinawa. There is evidence that from the very beginning of speculation and then negotiation over Okinawa's reversion, the Japanese government was adamantly opposed to Okinawan participation in the discussion (National Diet Library 1971: 18).

None the less, the remodelling of the GRI as a prefectural government and the conversion from a dollar-based to a yen-based Ryukyuan economy required extensive negotiations involving Okinawans so as to safeguard their interests. There was a nominal machinery for tri-lateral (US–Japan–Ryukyu) consultation, but once the United States secured what it wanted, the remainder of the consultation amounted to little more than the imposition of Japanese terms on Okinawans. Throughout the preparatory years, 1969–72, Okinawan opposition to reversion under terms that unfolded in this process intensified significantly. The reversion movement almost became an anti-reversion movement!

Ideas on alternatives to the prefecture system also filled books, journals, and the media. These ranged from an independent republic to a 'free state', to a commonwealth, to a special prefecture, to 'Okinawa for Okinawans', and to the rejection of the agreed date for reversion in favour of a later date (Taira 1974). What all these ideas had in common was the traditional Okinawan suspicion of Japanese intentions. Indirectly, at least, 'opposition' to reversion had some influence over Japanese policy. Japan offered generous transitional measures to minimize Okinawa's reversion shock or to advertise the benefits of reversion. A cabinet-level Okinawa Development Agency was set up in Tokyo to handle economic aid to Okinawa.

However, the most important goal of the reversion movement as a reaction against alien rule was never realized. That was the elimination of the American military presence. Neither Japan nor the United States paid much attention to Okinawan concerns in their 1971 bilateral agreement on reversion. Japan made the matter worse by deciding to send units of Japan's Self Defence Forces to Okinawa upon reversion. To dramatize Okinawan disapproval of the reversion terms, the popularly elected chief executive of the GRI, Yara Chōbyō (1902–present), an avowed reversionist himself, declined the invitation to attend the signing ceremony for the reversion agreement.

In historical perspective, by ignoring or obstructing the expression of Okinawan views, the reversion agreement amounted to another Ryukyu *shobun*, unilaterally formulated and imposed by Japan on Okinawa. Excluded from the preparatory process between 1969 and 1972, the reversion turned out to be a lamentable event for many Okinawans. On Reversion Day, 15 May 1972, the Okinawa Reversion Council, the group that had worked long and hard for bringing it about but felt betrayed by the Japanese and US governments, staged a massive rally under the slogan: '"no" to SDF deployment, "no" to land lease for military use, "no" to *Ryukyu Shobun*, down with the Sato government' (Matsuda 1981: 862–5; Miyamoto 1989: 314–22). Thus the era of Okinawa Prefecture II emerged in an atmosphere of heightened Okinawa–Japan conflict over a wide range of unsettled issues arising from twenty-seven years of 'alien rule'.

In terms of civil and human rights, however, Okinawan life under Japanese rule, if still 'alien', is incomparably better than it was under US occupation. The reversion agreement states that 'Japan is willing to assume full responsibility and authority for the exercise of *all powers of administration, legislation and jurisdiction over the territory and inhabitants of the Ryukyu Islands and the Daito Islands*' (Preamble: emphasis added). Okinawans would have said: 'There you go again!' These were the same 'all powers' over the Ryukyus and Ryukyuans that the United States appropriated by virtue of the San Francisco Peace Treaty. When the United States exercised these powers, the result was a colonial dictatorship exercised through a military government in the Ryukyus. On the other hand, Japan's exercise of these powers is bound by the 1947 Constitution which states that 'we, the Japanese people . . . do proclaim that *sovereign power resides with the people*' (Preamble; emphasis added). The critical difference between American and Japanese rule, then, is that the Constitution of the United States, arguably the best model for the legal guarantee of civil and human rights, was not applied to Okinawans, while the Constitution of Japan is. The people of Okinawa Prefecture are now part of the people with whom the 'sovereign power' of Japan resides. A sheer technical comparison of the laws, pre- and post-reversion, leaves no room for doubt as to which system of government has provided Okinawans with better opportunities.

WHITHER RYUKYUAN ETHNICITY/NATIONALITY?

Okinawa Prefecture II is more than twenty years old. However, in light of the historical volatility of Okinawa's international political status, one can never be sure how long Okinawa will retain its present form as a prefecture of Japan. Historically, 'self-determination' has never been a controlling principle for resolving Okinawa's international political status. Okinawans have historically had to accommodate themselves to the shifting configuration of external forces for a temporary settlement of the status question. At the level of individual psychology, moreover, Okinawans' quest for a stable, satisfying sense of self-identity has never been allowed to achieve its desired natural solution. Below we comment on the nature of Okinawan identity and explore the direction in which the subjective world of Okinawans is evolving.

Subject to the objective reality that Okinawa is part of Japan and that ethnic diversity is not an official Japanese value, the overriding question for Okinawans is how they can maintain a sense of personal integrity (the feeling of being true to themselves) under the challenge of a dual, Okinawan–Japanese, identity. The ideal solution to this conflict is Okinawan independence. As early as the tenth anniversary of the reversion, Okinawans and their Japanese supporters held symposia and study meetings to draft a constitution for a Republic of the Ryukyus and to explore all conceivable problems and promises of Ryukyuan independence (Nishino 1982).

In such aspects of life as culture, language, and social relations, Japan is not an easy country for Okinawans to adjust to. Instances of overt discrimination against Okinawans are fewer in post-reversion Japan than in pre-war Japan, although the problem has not totally disappeared. Okinawans seeking a Japanese identity often despair of their ability to become fully Japanese. An instructive example of this kind of disappointment is offered by a former, three-term (1978–90) governor of Okinawa, Nishime Junji (1922–present).

Despite personal and professional achievements that, had he been Japanese, would have been trumpeted as an unconditional Japanese success story (a University of Tokyo degree, a member of Japan's House of Representatives, a ranking member of Japan's Liberal Democratic Party, and so on), Governor Nishime of Okinawa is reported to have said that although he attempted to be Japanese, he eventually failed to assimilate Japanese identity. Diverse reactions of the readers and extensive comments by Okinawa's opinion leaders filled the newspapers' culture and education pages for days in 1985.

The governor attributed his failure to become Japanese to his Okinawan 'nationalism' (*minzokushugi*) (*The Ryukyu Shinpō* 1985).

In the language of psycho-cultural analysis, this is a problem of 'passing'; that is, an individual from a disadvantaged minority group rejects the stigmatized original identity and acquires the more acceptable majority group identity (DeVos 1992: ch. 8). Among Okinawans in Japan proper, several successful cases of 'passing' have been catalogued. Ashamed of their Okinawan identity, and feeling that it stands in the way of their career objectives, those who 'pass' change names, move or disguise permanent domiciles, and cut off all connections with Okinawa and Okinawans: family, kin, and friends. To compound the irony, however, some of the children of these successful converts re-discover their true ancestry, become ardent Okinawans and proudly display an Okinawan identity.

Asked about a possible contradiction between Okinawan nationalism and the reversion movement initiated and sustained by Okinawans themselves, Governor Nishime replies that reversion was a reaction (*hanpatsu*) to the American occupation of Okinawa. He then makes an important observation: 'although *vis-à-vis* Americans, Okinawans insisted that they were Japanese, they felt that in Japanese society they were a different kind of people (*ishitsu no mono*) from the Japanese'. He adds that the basic determinants of a national character – history, tradition, climate, etc. – are vastly different between Japan and Okinawa. (At the first popular election for the GRI chief executive in 1968, Nishime campaigned for a more gradual reversion and lost to Yara Chōbyō who supported immediate reversion.) In the final analysis, however, Nishime approves Okinawa's being part of Japan and Okinawans' status as Japanese nationals. Obviously he distinguishes between Okinawan nationalism as subjective experience and Japanese nationality for Okinawans as a matter of law and government. His image of Okinawa fits that of a 'sub-nation', which is 'a unit smaller than a nation but otherwise similar to it' (Petersen *et al.* 1980: 3). Further, 'a nation is a people linked by common descent from a putative ancestor and by its common territory, history, language, religion, or way of life' (*ibid.*). By this definition, Okinawans clearly constitute a nation.

When a bona fide nation is absorbed by another larger nation, becoming a sub-nation in the process, there arise questions like whether and to what extent the members of the sub-nation can or will accept a broader national identity. It is not unusual that a sub-nation's identification with a larger nation is only partial and ambiguous tinged with hostility and resentment against the larger entity (Kampf 1976). The attitudes of a sub-nation are highly complex, percolate through a variety of contexts, and range from hostility to attachment, from rejection to admiration, from alienation to identification, from differentiation to integration, from separatism to unification, and so on. Okinawan attitudes towards Japan have shifted back and forth over these spectra.

'Ethnicity' is definitely part of Governor Nishime's concept of Okinawan nationalism. He calls Okinawans *Uchinānchu* and Japanese *Yamatunchu*. These are Okinawan words by which Okinawans establish a boundary between Japanese and themselves. Open, public use of these terms by Okinawans, acquiesced to or even welcomed by the Japanese, is an outstanding social phenomenon of recent years in Okinawa, indicating what might be interpreted as 'ethnic equality' between Japanese and Okinawans, or more generally, as Japanese tolerance of ethnic diversity. The media have also played a major role in dignifying Okinawan ethnicity. Curiously, it is the Okinawa branch of Japan's Broadcasting Corporation (Nippon Hōsō Kyōkai NHK) that has been most active in promoting the distinctiveness and respectability of Okinawan culture. On the 15th anniversary of Okinawa's reversion to Japan, 15 May 1987, a day-long symposium sponsored by the NHK and the *Ryukyu Shinpō* featured a keynote speech on possibilities and problems of Ryukyuan independence (Taira 1987). The title of the symposium was *Mānkai [ga] Uchinā* (Whither Okinawa?). On 17 May 1990, another NHK–*Ryukyu Shinpō* joint programme presented a talk show to examine the strengths and weaknesses of Okinawa's national character (*Ryukyu Shinpō* 1990).

In the course of animated discussions among participants, a new category of people emerged: long-term Japanese residents of Okinawa, who were now called *Uchitunchu* (cross of *Uchinānchu* and *Yamatunchu*). A Japanese author, Mrs Kishimoto Machiko, a long-term resident of Okinawa with numerous books on Okinawan subjects to her credit, questioned why she was still an *Uchitunchu* in the eyes of *Uchinānchu*, while she herself always felt that she was an *Uchinānchu*. A *Yamatunchu* taking on Okinawan identity is surely an unprecedented reversal of 'passing' in identities.

Recently Okinawan newspapers reported extensively on findings by physical and cultural anthropologists on Okinawan ethnic origins. A most impressive explication of the different ethnic origins of the Japanese and Okinawans was offered by Hanihara Kazuo in a fifteen-part article which appeared in the *Ryukyu Shinpō* between January and February 1993 (Hanihara 1993). The public expression of such views would have embarrassed Okinawans enormously a few decades ago. Today, by contrast, Okinawans seem to be pleased with scientific evidence which points to: (a) their descent from a people related to both the Jōmon of the prehistoric period and the Ainu of today; and (b) that they are physically distinct from the Japanese who are descended from migrants who entered Japan from Korea only 1,300–2,300 years ago. Once an immovable physical basis of ethnicity is confirmed, it appears that other cultural and historical differences easily fall into place completing the image and definition of an ethnic group.

Okinawan ethnic pride has also been buoyed by interactions with overseas ethnic Okinawan communities all over the world, though relatively concentrated in the Americas. As would have been expected, Governor Nishime during his multiple terms was particularly active in promoting connections with overseas *Uchinānchu*. Emigration of Okinawans began in the years 1899–1900. Now the overseas *Uchinānchu* are estimated at about 300,000, in addition to a similar number in Japan proper (*Ryukyu Shinpō* 1995). They are residents or citizens of ethnically diverse nation-states and, like other 'ethnics', are fiercely proud of their Okinawan roots.

In August 1990, Okinawa hosted a convention/festival for overseas *Uchinānchu* to commemorate the 90th anniversary of the beginning of Okinawan emigration. Home-country Okinawans were impressed and pleased with the worldwide expansion of their kin. To the stunned pleasure of the spectators, the *Uchinānchu* of the world paraded in the streets of Naha wearing colourful national costumes of their respective adopted countries. Feelings that 'we are not alone' but a part of the entire world boosted ethnic pride further. The 90th anniversary of Okinawan emigration was also celebrated by Okinawan communities in Hawaii, Peru, Bolivia, Brazil, and other countries. A second home-country convention/festival of the *Uchinānchu* of the world was held in the autumn of 1995.

To paraphrase Governor Nishime, Okinawa's reversion to Japan was a utilitarian choice in favour of a legal, political, and economic system that offered advantages in terms of civil and human rights and secured better opportunities for political participation and economic achievements than the system imposed on Okinawans by the United States. Despite a national consciousness that apparently prevents Okinawans from becoming fully Japanese, the price one has to pay for being Okinawan in terms of discrimination and blocked career opportunities is much lower today than before the war. Thanks to democratization and economic development since 1945,

Japanese society has also become more tolerant of different peoples, cultures, and beliefs.

But will Okinawan nationalism ever see its fulfilment in the form of a fully independent Okinawan nation-state? Or will it remain a subnational state of mind, subordinate to the Japanese nation-state? Very few scholars discuss these questions explicitly and seriously. Governor Nishime, while emphasizing Okinawan nationalism, affirms Okinawa's existence as part of a culturally heterogeneous Japan. Nishime, a consummate politician, can be forgiven for seeking a pragmatic resolution to a potentially dangerous ideological dilemma, though some may regard his position as ambiguous or even disingenuous.

Nishino Terutaro, a former high-ranking research officer in the National Diet Library, was responsible for basic research on choices Okinawa faced regarding its international political status during the waning years of US occupation (National Diet Library 1971). Ten years after the reversion, Nishino admitted that when writing the earlier report, he 'was privately thinking that Okinawa should not revert to Japan in the usual form of a prefecture like any other prefecture, but choose to become an independent nation-state' (Nishino 1982: 49). But now he 'cannot help thinking that at present, the freedom to choose a new political status is no longer available to the people of Okinawa Prefecture' (Nishino 1982: 49). He laments Okinawa's missed opportunity for independence, but now equates independence to 'separatism' and points out how ferociously any duly constituted nation-state, Japan not excluded, would contest and suppress separatist movements. This is but one of the dangers inherent in current nationalist politics in Okinawa.

Nishino's final thought on these issues is: 'The only available choice that the people of Okinawa Prefecture today can plan for is a status within the framework of local autonomy' (Nishino 1982: 51). But he does not elaborate what status within the 'framework of local autonomy', other than that of a prefecture, is available to Okinawans. In addition, he appears to be highly pessimistic about the nature and scope of 'local autonomy' in Japan. Ironically, there lies the last hope for Okinawan independence.

In the 1990s, the concept of local autonomy has become highly dynamic among Japanese scholars and opinion leaders, even involving politicians and decision-makers. 'Re-structuring the Japanese state' has become a fashionable idea (Ozawa 1993). 'Local revolt against central government' was urged by one political figure who later became Japan's prime minister (Hosokawa and Iwakuni 1991).

Deregulation, which includes devolution of regulatory powers on 'local' (prefectural and municipal) governments, has also been in progress. In May 1995, the Diet passed a law to promote power sharing with local governments (*chihō bunken suishinhō*). But only in its most radical form does autonomy offer a real opportunity for an independent Okinawa.

1995: FIFTY YEARS AFTER THE PACIFIC WAR
(by K. Taira and M. Weiner)

The year 1995 marked the fiftieth anniversary of the Battle of Okinawa. To celebrate this important juncture in Okinawan history, the prefectural authorities had planned a number of major commemorative projects: one was unveiled on 23 June 1995 at the Peace Memorial Park located at the southern tip of the Okinawa Island, Mabuni, where the Battle of Okinawa had ended precisely fifty years earlier. The memorial, called the Cornerstone of Peace, consists of a number of granite screens inscribed with the names of 234,183 persons who died directly, or indirectly, as a result of the battle. It includes both military personnel and civilians regardless of nationality – American, Japanese, Korean, Okinawan and Taiwanese. Included among the 147,110 Okinawan dead are those who perished during the Fifteen Years' War which began with the Manchurian Incident of 1931. Saipan alone contributed 6,217 Okinawan names. As Higa Teruyuki has noted: 'Saipan and Okinawa have much in common . . . [B]oth suffered attack, invasion and occupation by the U.S. military, and both share the nightmare of "suicide cliff" experiences' (Higa 1995: 197). It is believed that many more Okinawan dead remain unaccounted for. Since the unveiling of the memorial additional names have been confirmed.

During the Battle of Okinawa, the Japanese and American forces suffered enormous casualties. The Cornerstone of Peace records the names of 72,907 Japanese and 14,005 American servicemen who lost their lives. The memorial also bears the names of 133 Koreans and twenty-eight Taiwanese. In fact, the number of Koreans confirmed to have died during the Battle of Okinawa is almost three times greater than that which appears on the memorial. This underrepresentation was brought about by the refusal of many Korean families to allow the names of relatives to be associated with a Japanese war memorial. The reasons for their non-cooperation are not difficult to comprehend. Many of the Koreans who died in the Battle for Okinawa had been conscripted into the Imperial Army as colonial levies. For their families, it is no honour to have their names appear on a 'Japanese' memorial. Indeed, since Okinawa is a part of Japan, many Koreans perceive little if any difference between the memorial tablets at Yasukuni Shrine in Tokyo and inscriptions on a memorial on Okinawa.

None the less, there is a profound difference between Japan's Yasukuni Shrine and Okinawa's Cornerstone of Peace. Governor Ōta Masahide, himself drafted as a student into the Iron Blood Corps attached to the Imperial Army, had been spared death by accident and contrary to his wishes in 1945. In conceiving of and completing the construction of the Cornerstone of Peace, Okinawa Prefecture, under the leadership of Ōta, sought to create a physical reminder of both the immense suffering caused by Japan's misguided imperial ambitions and of Okinawa's enduring commitment to peace. In this sense, the Cornerstone of Peace is the antithesis of Yasukuni Shrine. For Okinawans, the bloody battle for their homeland in 1945 serves as a stark reminder that death in war makes no distinction on the basis of combat status, national origin, race or gender. Okinawans generally feel that by praying for the peaceful afterlife of the dead and sharing the painful memories of the Battle of Okinawa, the living find strength to renew their commitment to peace. As Governor Ōta observed:

> The monument was made to convey the peace-cherishing heart of Okinawa and its yearning to live in peace with all. It is my wish, as we contemplate the Cornerstone of Peace, that the brutal typhoon of steel experienced fifty years ago will be transformed into a warm breeze of peace that will gust to every corner of the world.
>
> (*Ryukyu Shinpō*, 27 June 1995)

Within a few months, however, these noble sentiments were shattered by an incident whose repercussions extended well beyond the islands. On 4 September 1995, a 12-year-old Okinawan girl was abducted, beaten and raped by three US servicemen. The suspects were quickly apprehended, placed under house arrest on their base, and subsequently handed over to the local authorities for trial. All were found guilty, and, on 7 March 1996, two of the defendants were sentenced to seven years and the third to six and a half years imprisonment with hard labour (*chōeki*). In passing sentence, the presiding judge noted that the crime had been premeditated, carefully planned and vicious. On the other hand, he acknowledged the remorse shown by the accused, their lack of criminal record, and the offer of compensation from their families.

The ramifications of this case were far-reaching, intense and entangled. The sense of outrage among Okinawans unleashed dormant resentment against the decades-long American military presence. In the minds of many, had there been no US bases on Okinawa then they would have been spared this and many other serious crimes committed by American servicemen. The answer was clear: rid Okinawa of US troops and return military-occupied land to its rightful Okinawan owners. The rape of a young girl had become a political metaphor for the continued despoliation of Okinawa by the United States.

The 1995 rape case was not the first serious crime committed by American service personnel. Since reversion to Japan in 1972, Americans have committed nearly 5,000 serious offences, including more than ten murders of Okinawans. During the occupation period, 1945–72, such crimes were even more frequent, the most notorious of which was the Yumiko-chan Incident of 1955. An American serviceman abducted, raped and murdered Yumiko, a 6-year-old girl. On 3 September 1955 her body was found abandoned on a beach near Kadena Air Base. A non-commissioned officer was subsequently arrested, court-martialled, convicted and sentenced to death. Although later repatriated to the United States, the reasons for this decision were never made public.

History apparently repeats itself. The Yumiko-chan Incident of 1955 took place against the backdrop of Okinawan struggles against the military appropriation of land. By 1955, the United States Far Eastern Command in the Ryukyus had forceably appropriated vast tracts of Okinawan land, much of it privately owned by farming families. The compensation offered by the military fell far short of current market value. At that time, neither the US nor Japanese Constitution protected the property rights of Okinawans. Although the Fifth Amendment to the US Constitution states that the 'taking' of private property for public use requires *due process* and *just compensation*, such safeguards were not extended to Okinawans during the occupation. The Japanese Constitution, under Article 29, provides similar protection: 'The right to own or to hold property is inviolable. Property rights shall be defined by law, in conformity with the public welfare. Private property may be taken for public use upon just compensation therefor.'

Although a *due process* clause is absent from the Japanese version, it can be inferred from Article 31, which states, 'No person shall be deprived of life or liberty . . . except *according to procedure estab-lished by law*' (emphasis added). The Land Appropriation Law (*tochi shūyō hō*), which implements Article 29, makes the 'promotion of the public interest' (*kōkyō no rieki no zōshin*) the legal basis for the appropriation of privately held land (Article 1). These governing principles were in effect in the US and mainland Japan when Okina-wan land was taken for use by the American military. During the 1950s, however, Okinawan land rights were excluded from any form of legal protection. Whenever the US military required land, a decree was sufficient to mobilize troops to evict the owners and appropriate the land.

Extensive military bases have been constructed on land, the appro-priation of which has no legitimacy under the Japanese Constitution. The US military presence, currently 30,000 personnel stationed on sites equivalent to 20 per cent of the land area of Okinawa Island and Iye Shima (Yoshizawa 1994: 39–42), includes a minority who with statistical regularity commit crimes against Okinawan persons and property. The US–Japan Mutual Security Treaty, whose Cold War *raison d'être* has disappeared, also accords a measure of extra-territorial privilege to the military bases, in effect transforming them into both a breeding ground and a sanctuary for criminal elements among service personnel.

However, the United States alone is not to blame. Although Okinawans are Japanese nationals, as far as land use is concerned, the Japanese and US governments have colluded against Okinawan interests. From an Okinawan perspective, the injustices and inequal-ities fostered by the Mutual Security Treaty have acted as a structural constraint in a triangular relationship. Following on from the post-war military occupation, Okinawa Prefecture, with less than 1 per cent of Japan's total territory and population, has been compelled to accommodate 73 per cent of the American troops in Japan and to provide 75 per cent of the land used by the US military. Given this arrangement, it is no wonder that Okinawans have suffered dispro-portionately from crimes perpetrated by US servicemen in Japan. This discriminatory pattern has been legitimated by a Mutual Secur-ity Treaty designed to protect Japan's 'public interest'. The obvious question is whether the 'Japan' referred to in the treaty includes Oki-nawa. In the context of national security, Okinawa has clearly been factored out, ensuring that mainland Japan gains peace at Okinawan expense. Neither Japan nor the US has indicated a willingness to con-front this uncomfortable truth which underpins both the Mutual

Security Treaty and the accompanying Agreement on the Status of the United States Armed Forces in Japan.

For fifty years, Okinawans have endured a basic injustice, and many fear that unless current security arrangements are renegotiated they may be forced to endure a further half century of bases, troops and 'base crimes' (*kichi hanzai*). The 1995 rape case crystallized Okinawan fears and fuelled popular demands for the closure of all US bases. On 21 October 1995, a massive demonstration, attended by 90,000 Okinawans representing all strata, was held near Kadena Air Base. Similar rallies were held elsewhere in the prefecture. Subsequently, caravans travelled the length of the mainland informing the Japanese public of the Okinawan situation. Okinawan law-makers and women's groups also visited the United States, either to lobby Washington, or to alert the general public to the bases issue. The most significant appeal came from Governor Ōta, who sought to heighten public awareness by directly confronting the central government on the bases issue.

Under the Land Appropriations Law, *due process* requires that records of land and property to be taken for public use be signed by the owner/s. Should the owner/s refuse, the mayor of the relevant municipality is required to appoint a witness (*tachiainin*) to sign the documents in lieu of the owner/s. In the event that the mayor is unwilling to perform this task, responsibility falls to the Governor of the Prefecture. The refusal of thirty-five Okinawan landowners, and subsequently the mayors, to sign the required documents placed Governor Ōta in an awkward position. He eventually refused to sign the documents in lieu of the owners, thus opening the possibility of an illegal seizure of land by the central government. As a means of forcing Ōta's compliance, the prime minister, citing a provision of the Local Autonomy Law which requires prefectural governors to carry out duties delegated by state, took legal action against the governor. Although the Naha branch of the Fukuoka Higher Court ruled in favour of the central government in March 1996, Governor Ōta has appealed to the Supreme Court.

While the central government has maintained its right to enforce its will under the Local Autonomy Law, Governor Ōta has argued that in its decades-long dealings with the US military the government has acted unconstitutionally and in ways prejudicial to the 'public welfare' of Okinawans (Ōta 1996). The conceptual separability of Okinawa's 'public welfare' from that of the Japanese mainland is implicit in the US–Japan Mutual Security Treaty which imposes a disproportionate burden upon the citizens of Okinawa. Okinawans

174   Koji Taira

also remember that the Battle of Okinawa was part of a defensive strategy which explicitly sacrificed the interests of their homeland in favour of Japan 'Proper'. In other words, the thousands of Okinawan names inscribed on the Cornerstone of Peace refer to Okinawans killed by the Japanese state.

BIBLIOGRAPHY

Asato, S. (1990) *Kōkogaku kara mita Ryukyushi* (Ryukyuan History as Seen from Archaeology), 2 vols, Naha: Hirugisha.
Baba, H. (1993) 'Ainu, Ryukyujin wa Jōmonjin no chōkkei shison ka' (Are the Ainu and the Ryukyuans Direct Descendants of the Jōmonese?), in K. Suzuki (ed.) *Sōten Nihon no rekishi* (Controversy: History of Japan), vol. 1: 106–22, Tokyo: Shin-Jinbutsu Ōraisha.
Baba, H. and Narasaki, S. (1991) 'Minatogawa Man, the Oldest Type of Modern *Homo sapiens* in East Asia', *The Quarternary Research* 30, 3: 221–30.
Curtin, P.D. (1984) *Cross-Cultural Trade in World History*, New York: Cambridge University Press.
De Vos, G.A. (1992) *Social Cohesion and Alienation*, Boulder: Westview Press.
Fischer, A.G. Jr. (1988) *Military Government in the Ryukyu Islands 1945–1950*, Washington, DC: Center of Military History, United States Army.
Hanihara, K. (1984) 'Gyakuten shikō no Nihonjin kigenron' (Origins of the Japanese Examined Upside Down), *Rekishi to jinbutu* (History and People), November: 126–39.
—— (1991) 'Dual structure model for the population history of the Japanese', *Japan Review*, no. 3: 131–9.
—— (1993) 'Uchinānchu wa dokokara kitaka' (Where Have Okinawans Come from?), 15-part essay, *The Ryukyu Shinpō*, 5 January–4 February.
Higa, T. (1995) 'Three islands in the Pacific, each one seeking happiness', *Transactions of the Institute of General Industrial Research at Okinawa International University*, no. 3: 197–8.
Hong, W. (1994) *Paekche of Korea and the Origin of Yamato Japan*, Seoul: Kudara International.
Hosokawa, M. and Iwakuni, T. (1991) *Hina no ronri* (The Logic of the Countryside), Tokyo: Kobunsha.
Ishikawa, T. and Taira, K. (1991) 'The geographical distribution of emigrants by place of origin: the case of Okinawa', pp. 109–25 in J.G. Scoville (ed.) *Status Influences in Third World Labor Markets*, Berlin and New York: Walter de Gruyter.
Johnson, A.W. and Earle, T. (1987) *The Evolution of Human Societies*, Stanford, Calif.: Stanford University Press.
Kamachi, N. (1981) *Reform in China: Huang Tsun-hsien and the Japanese Model*, Cambridge, Mass.: Harvard University Press.

Kampf, H.A. (1976) 'Okinawan attitudes towards Japan: a case study in the nationalist feelings of a disadvantaged minority', *Asian Profile* 4, 2 (April): 115–37.

Kerr, G.H. (1958) *Okinawa: The History of an Island People*, Tokyo: Charles E. Tuttle Co.

Kimura, M. (1991) *Mu tairiku wa Ryukyu ni atta* (The Mu Continent Was in Ryukyu), Tokyo: Tokuma Shoten.

Kishaba, E. (ed.) (1953) *Yaeyama rekishi* (Yaeyama History), Ishigaki: Yaeyama Rekishi Henshu Iinkai.

Kiyomura, K. (1929) *Miyako shiden* (History and Legends of Miyako), Hirara: Nanto Shiseki Hozonkai.

Kobata, A. and Matsuda, M. (1969) *Ryukyuan Relations with Korea and South Sea Countries*, Kyoto: Kawakita Printing Co.

Leung, E.P.-W. (1983) 'The quasi-war in East Asia: Japan's expedition to Taiwan and the Ryukyu controversy', *Modern Asian Studies* 17, 2: 257–81.

—— (1991) 'China's dispute with Japan over Liu-Ch'iu: the role of Li Hung-chang, 1871–81', Paper presented at the First International Symposium of the International Society for Ryukyuan Studies, Naha, Okinawa.

Majikina, A. (1923) *Okinawa issennenshi* (One-Thousand-Year History of Okinawa), Fukuoka: Shin-Minposha.

Matsuda, Y. (1981) *Sengo Okinawa shakai keizaishi kenkyū* (A Study of Post-war Okinawan Social and Economic History), Tokyo: University of Tokyo Press.

Miki, T. (1992) *Okinawa: Datsuwa no jidai* (Okinawa: Time to Get Out of Japan), Naha: Niraisha.

Miyamoto, K. (1989) *Keizai taikoku* (An Economic Power), Tokyo: Shōgakukan.

Nakachi, K. (1989) *Ryukyu–U.S.–Japan Relations 1945-1972*, Quezon City, Philippines: Hiyas Press.

National Diet Library (ed.) (1971) *Basic Problems on the Reversion of Okinawa* (The Research Material Series 71-1 June 1971; content in Japanese), Tokyo: National Diet Library.

Nishino, T. (1982) 'Taiheiyō shominzoku no dokuritsu to Okinawa no sentaku' (Independence of Pacific Nations and Choices for Okinawa), pp. 39–51 in M. Arasaki, S. Kawamitsu, Y. Iiga and S, Harada (eds) *Okinawa jiritsu eno chōsen* (Challenges to Okinawan Independence), Tokyo: Shakai Shisōsha.

Nobori, S. (1949) *Dai Amamishi* (History of Greater Amami), Naze: Amamisha.

Okinawa Prefecture (1992) *Keys to Okinawan Culture*, Naha: Okinawa Prefectural Government.

Okinawa Taimususha (ed.) (1983) *Okinawa dai-hyakka jiten* (Encyclopedia of Okinawa), 3 vols and index vol., Naha: Okinawa Taimususha.

Okinawaken Kyōiku Iinkai (ed.) (1974) *Okinawakenshi*, vol. 7: *Imin* (History of Okinawa Prefecture, vol. 7: Migration), Naha: Okinawaken Kyōiku Iinkai.

Ota, M. (1990) *Shōwa no Okinawa* (Okinawa of the Showa Era), Naha: Naha Shuppansha.

—— (1996) '"Dairi shomei kyohi" saiban ni okeru Ōta Okinawaken-chiji no dai ichi junbi shomen' (The first brief of Okinawa Governor Ōta in preparation for the trial on the refusal to 'sign in lieu'), *Nihon no shinro* (Direction for Japan), no. 42: 12–39. Kawasaki: Kohan na Kokumin Rengō.

Ozawa, I. (1993) *Nihon kaizō keikaku* (Plans for Reinventing Japan), Tokyo: Kōdansha.

Pearson, R.J. (1990) 'Trade and the rise of the Okinawan state', *Indo-Pacific Prehistory* 1: 263–81.

Peattie, M. (1988) *Nan'yo: The Rise and Fall of the Japanese in Micronesia 1885–1945*, Honolulu: University of Hawaii Press.

Petersen, W., Novak, M. and Gleason, P. (1982) *Concepts of Ethnicity*, Cambridge, Mass.: Harvard University Press.

Ryukyu Shinpō (1985) 'Nihonjin ni naroutoshite narikirenai' (Tried but failed to be fully Japanese), 23 August.

—— (1990) 'Kenjin katagi dai-kenkyū' (A Thorough Study of the Character of Okinawans), Part I, 21 May; Part 2, 5 June.

—— (1995) 'Sekai no Uchinānchu' (Uchinānchu of the World), 15 May.

Ryukyu Shinpōsha (ed.) (1991) *Shin Ryukyushi* (A New History of Ryukyu), 4 vols, Naha: Ryukyu Shinpōsha.

Sansom, G. (1961) *A History of Japan 1334–1615*, Stanford, Calif.: Stanford University Press.

Selden, Mark (1971) 'Okinawa and American colonialism', *Bulletin of Concerned Asian Scholars*, Spring: 50–63.

Serafim, L.A. (1994) 'Linguistically, what is Ryukyuan? – synchronic and diachronic perspectives', Paper presented at the Second International Symposium of the International Society for Ryukyuan Studies, Harvard University.

Shimono, T. (1986) *Yamato bunka to Ryukyu bunka* (Japanese Culture and Ryukyuan Culture), Tokyo: PHP kenkyūjo.

Sodei, R. (1990) 'Democratization and the reunification of Okinawa with Japan', Paper presented at the 1990 Annual Meeting of the American Political Science Association, San Francisco.

Stinchecum, A.M. (1988–9) 'Textile production under the poll tax system in Ryukyu', *Textile Museum Journal* 27/28: 56–69.

Sumiya, M. and Taira, K. (eds) (1979) *An Outline of Japanese Economic History 1603–1940*, Tokyo: University of Tokyo Press.

Taira, K. (1958) 'Ryukyu Islands today: political economy of a U.S. colony', *Science and Society* 22, 2 (Spring): 113–28.

—— (1974) *Nihonkoku kaizō shiron* (Experiments in the Reconstitution of the Japanese State), Tokyo: Kōdansha.

—— (1987) 'Soto kara Okinawa no shinro wo tou' (To Ask about the Future Direction of Okinawa Looking in from Outside), *Ryukyu Shinpō*, 7-part essay, 16–23 May.

Takamiya, H. (1990) *Senshi kodai no Okinawa* (Prehistoric and Ancient Okinawa), Tokyo: Daiichi Shobō.

—— (1994) *Okinawa no senshi iseki to bunka* (Prehistoric Remains and Culture of Okinawa), Tokyo: Daiichi Shobō.

Takeuchi, R. (ed.) (1986) *Nihon chimei daijiten*, vol. 47: Okinawaken (An Encyclopedia of Japanese Place Names, vol. 47: Okinawa Prefecture), Tokyo: Kadokawa Shoten.

Turner, C.G. II (1989) 'Teeth and prehistory in Asia', *Scientific American* 260, 2: 88–97.

Ueda, M. (1976) *Wakoku no sekai* (The World of the Wa Country), Tokyo: Kōdansha.

Umehara, T. and Hanihara, K. (1982) *Ainu wa gen-Nihonjin ka* (Are the Ainu Original Japanese?), Tokyo: Shōgakukan.

Yoshizawa, H. (1994) *Okinawa no beigun to kichi* (The American Troops and Bases in Okinawa), Haebaru, Okinawa: Akebono Shuppan.

Zhang, Q. (1992) 'Nisshin gokan jōyaku ni oite Ryukyu no kizoku wa kettei saretaka' (Was the Status of Ryukyu Determined in the Sino-Japanese Agreement?), *Okinawa bunka kenkyū* (Studies in Okinawan Culture) 19: 95–129.

7 *Nikkeijin*

The phenomenon of return migration

Yoko Sellek

INTRODUCTION

Unlike most European labour importing countries which launched foreign labour schemes to solve a shortage of labour in the 1960s, Japan managed to achieve high levels of economic growth without relying on foreign manual workers until the early 1980s. However, the high economic growth in Japan over the last two decades has brought about the necessary conditions for migration and, since the mid-1980s in particular, Japan has been chosen by migrant workers as one of the major destination countries. Although the 'Immigration-Control and Refugee-Recognition Act'[1] in Japan provides that the government only accepts foreigners who possess some special skill which is not held by Japanese nationals (Japan Immigration Association 1990: 24–40), there has been an increasing number of foreigners working as manual labourers in the so-called unskilled job sector. Most of these foreigners are illegal migrant workers who are forbidden from entering the country by the Immigration Control Law.[2] These workers include those who have engaged in an activity other than that permitted by the status of residence granted them (visa abusers) and overstayers continuing in such activities. The number of overstayers was 293,800 in May 1994 and it is assumed that most of them worked illegally (Japan Immigration Association, 1994f: 13–14). However, there is one group of foreigners who are allowed to work *legally* in the unskilled job sectors – the *Nikkeijin*. *Nikkeijin* in Japanese refers to descendants of Japanese who emigrated abroad between 1868 and 1973, but in the context of the issue of foreign migrant workers in Japan, the term *Nikkeijin* refers specifically to South American-Japanese descendants up to the third generation and their spouses, mainly those from Brazil and Peru, the number of which was 175,118 in 1993 (Japan Immigration Association 1994e: 40–1).

With the presence of a large number of foreign migrant workers including *Nikkeijin*, Japan is now facing the problem of how to incorporate foreign workers into its society. For a country which is already home to nearly 600,000 Korean residents, themselves a legacy of the massive migration from Korea to Japan between 1910 and 1945, the arrival of 'new' migrant workers has presented another serious challenge to the prevailing conceptualization of Japanese racial and cultural homogeneity.

This chapter focuses on the *Nikkeijin* in Japan. It aims to detail the current state of the *Nikkeijin* and discuss the possibility of them becoming a new minority group in Japanese society. If the major concern behind governmental reluctance to accept migrant workers is the possibility of permanent settlement, an investigation of the *Nikkeijin* will be useful in terms of predicting the various social costs that might be associated with the settlement of other migrant workers in Japan. After a brief introduction, the issue of foreign workers since the late 1980s is addressed to provide a general idea of the context in which the *Nikkeijin* first entered Japan. The next section is concerned with the pattern of foreign-worker entry into Japan since the late 1980s, followed by an overview of the *Nikkeijin* in Japan. We then consider the impact and social costs associated with *Nikkeijin* in Japan, including the possibility of settlement and the emergence of a new minority group. Next, we discuss the ideological significance of *Nikkeijin* immigration in Japanese society. A number of concluding points are drawn at the end.

THE CHANGING SITUATION OF FOREIGN WORKERS IN JAPAN: *NIKKEIJIN* AND OTHER MIGRANT WORKERS

The initial stage

Table 7.1 shows the trends in the number of apprehended illegal migrant workers by nationality and gender between 1981 and 1993. Three different stages can be distinguished in the influx of foreign workers into Japan. The first stage began in the late 1970s and ended around 1986; this period is characterized by the influx of a large number of female illegal migrant workers from South-east Asia (Thailand, the Philippines) and East Asia (South Korea, Taiwan). Until 1985 the majority of illegal migrant workers apprehended were

Table 7.1 Trends in the number of apprehended illegal migrant workers broken-down by nationality and sex (1981–93)

Nationality/region	1981	1982	1983	1984	1985	1986	1987	1988	1989	1990	1991	1992	1993
South Korean	37	132	114	61	76	119	208	1,033	3,129	5,534	9,782	13,890	11,865
	(12)	(35)	(24)	(34)	(35)	(69)	(109)	(769)	(2,209)	(4,417)	(8,283)	(11,204)	(8,473)
Iranian	–	–	–	–	–	–	–	–	15	652	7,700	13,982	8,886
									(13)	(648)	(7,611)	(13,781)	(8,730)
Malaysian	–	–	–	–	–	–	18	279	1,865	4,465	4,855	14,303	11,913
							(15)	(265)	(1,691)	(3,856)	(3,892)	(11,301)	(8,932)
Thai	223	412	557	1,132	1,073	990	1,067	1,388	1,144	1,450	3,249	7,519	12,654
	(28)	(25)	(39)	(54)	(120)	(164)	(290)	(369)	(369)	(661)	(926)	(2,408)	(5,160)
Filipino	288	409	1,041	2,983	3,927	6,297	8,027	5,386	3,740	4,042	2,983	3,532	4,617
	(14)	(13)	(29)	(96)	(349)	(1,500)	(2,253)	(1,688)	(1,289)	(1,593)	(1,079)	(1,466)	(2,246)
Mainland Chinese								7	39	481	1,162	3,167	4,989
								(5)	(26)	(428)	(981)	(2,599)	(3,964)
Taiwan	641	775	528	466	427	356	494	492	531	639	460	656	674
	(107)	(84)	(85)	(136)	(125)	(161)	(210)	(223)	(275)	(351)	(225)	(374)	(347)
Hong Kong								3	18	22	43	144	114
								(2)	(15)	(20)	(36)	(125)	(91)

Pakistani	—	7	—	3	36	196	905	2,497	3,170	3,886	793	1,072	1,406
		(7)		(3)	(36)	(196)	(905)	(2,495)	(3,168)	(3,880)	(793)	(1,068)	(1,403)
Sri Lankan	—	—	—	—	—	—	—	20	90	831	307	451	782
								(20)	(87)	(821)	(295)	(415)	(719)
Bangladeshi	—	—	•	0	1	58	438	2,942	2,277	5,925	293	390	717
				(0)	(1)	(58)	(437)	(2,939)	(2,275)	(5,915)	(292)	(387)	(712)
Peruvian	—	—	—	—	—	—	—	—	—	—	172	580	1,908
											(133)	(424)	(1,375)
Indonesian	—	—	—	—	—	—	—	—	—	—	180	625	924
											(156)	(571)	(778)
Other	245	154	99	138	89	115	150	267	590	1,957	929	1,850	2,892
	(47)	(20)	(23)	(27)	(20)	(38)	(70)	(154)	(374)	(1,586)	(648)	(1,398)	(2,214)
Total	1,434	1,889	2,339	4,783	5,629	8,131	11,307	14,314	16,608	29,884	32,908	62,161	64,341
	(208)	(184)	(200)	(350)	(687)	(2,186)	(4,289)	(8,929)	(11,791)	(24,176)	(25,350)	(47,521)	(45,144)

Source: Immigration Control Office, Ministry of Justice.

Notes: 1 Figures in parentheses indicate the number of males included in the total.
2 Dashes indicate that a separate figure for the number of nationals is not available. In such cases these nationals are included in the figure for the category entitled 'Other'.

female, most of whom had been recruited as singers and entertainers but actually working as hostesses and prostitutes, and were concentrated in the sex-related industry. Because of their specific occupational concentration – and because there is a tendency for people to consider a woman's primary role to be that of a housewife/mother and not that of a wage earner – the first wave of foreign workers was not recognized as a migrant worker phenomenon (Itō 1992: 294). None the less, this type of migration has continued and constitutes a significant proportion of the current population flow to Japan.

THE SECOND STAGE: MASSIVE INFLOW OF MALE WORKERS

The second stage began in the latter half of the 1980s and ended in 1990; this period is characterized by a shift towards the predominance of male illegal migrant workers, drawn primarily from the Philippines, Pakistan, Bangladesh, China, South Korea, Malaysia, Thailand and Iran. In 1988 the number of male illegal migrant workers surpassed that of females for the first time. Since the mid-1980s the sharp increase in illegal migrant workers has resulted mainly from the increase in the number of *male* illegal migrant workers. Since 1988 the gender ratio has not changed significantly, with males accounting for 70 to 75 per cent of the total.

There are several 'pull' factors influencing the influx of migrant workers to Japan. These include the existence of wide wage differentials between Japan and the sending countries, Japan's strong economic and cultural presence in Asia, and a severe shortage of certain types of labour in the domestic labour market. During the period between the late 1980s and the beginning of 1991 Japan experienced an economic upswing followed by a severe shortage of labour, which generated a massive inflow of male foreign workers into Japan. They found employment mainly in medium- and small-sized companies in labour-intensive industries, such as manufacturing, construction and services where the shortage of labour was particularly serious. Jobs such as metal processing and fabrication, plastic processing, building and road construction and demolition, retail trade and restaurant work have provided them with many job opportunities. These jobs had been shunned by younger native workers not only because of the '3D' (dirty, dangerous and difficult) nature of the work, but also because of the rapid expansion of industrial activity, irregular working hours and, above all, because these were 'bottom-wage' and 'dead-end' jobs (Mori 1995: 59–60; Sellek and Weiner 1992: 215–17). Foreign migrant workers stepped in to fill these undesirable positions and have started to become an indispensable part of the workforce which supports the basic structure of the Japanese economy.

It was only during the second stage that the issue of foreign workers came to be discussed as a major social problem. In the late 1980s there was a heated public debate on whether Japan should be 'open' or 'closed' to foreign workers. People in industry were enthusiastic about introducing foreign workers within the unskilled job sector at that stage, whereas the government remained exceedingly reluctant to legalize the introduction of foreign migrant workers. However, a rising flow of illegal migrant workers has posed a complex dilemma for successive Japanese governments. On the one hand, Japan requires a low-cost and flexible workforce to serve in its labour-intensive industries. In addition, the Japanese population is ageing rapidly and the birth-rate is low. At the same time, many young Japanese are no longer interested in manual labour. In the late 1980s, when the number of foreign illegal workers increased dramatically, all of these factors dictated the urgent implementation of a policy to supplement the existing pool of unskilled labour (Yamanaka 1993: 72). On the other hand, the government was worried, based on the experiences of Western European nations, that the introduction of temporary foreign workers might lead to the creation of permanent immigrant communities, and that these could become a source of political, economic and social tension.

THE THIRD STAGE: THE REVISION OF THE IMMIGRATION CONTROL LAW

In conjunction with the increase in the number of illegal migrant workers, infringements of human rights have become widespread, quite often involving criminal syndicates both in Japan and in the sending countries where criminal elements function as brokers. In order to respond to the infringements of human rights of illegal foreign workers and the shortage of labour, the government revised the Immigration Control Law. The revised Immigration Control Law of 1 June 1990 marked the onset of the third stage in the absorption of foreign workers into Japan. The revised law, on the one hand, broadened the scope of legal activities for foreigners in certain skilled and professional categories to meet the requirements of Japanese companies, while simultaneously introducing severe penalties against employers who illegally employ foreign workers who entered Japan on or after 1 June 1990 as well as against brokers who found jobs for these workers.[3] But, to meet the labour requirements of small and medium-sized enterprises, which might otherwise have been forced to close due to severe labour shortages, the government granted formal status of residence to *Nikkeijin* and their spouses via the revised Immigration Control Law, thus enabling them to work in Japan *legally*. The government also decided to accept a larger number of foreigners in the 'trainee' visa category.

In principle, the entry of foreigners who intend to take up employment is only permitted in accordance with the professional-occupation categories enumerated in the revised Immigration Control Law. In effect, therefore, foreign workers working in the unskilled job sector were rendered invisible by the government. However, once the scale of illegal labour migration became significant, the government reacted to it in an *ad hoc* way and tried to respond to employers' short-term labour requirements without any form of long-term labour-market planning.

The third stage, dating from the introduction of the revised Immigration Control Law, is characterized by a diversification of the foreign manual-worker population, and their employment under differing legal constraints and employment conditions. It should also be noted that, prior to the 1990 revision, the problem of foreign workers implied the problem of illegal migrant workers who, in principle, should be excluded from Japanese society. However, owing to the acceptance of a large number of *Nikkeijin* and foreign trainees since around 1990, the problem has shifted towards a discussion of the consequences of having a large number of both legal- and illegal-migrant workers working in unskilled job sectors.

Excluding foreigners in the professional category (who comprise only a small fraction of the total),[4] these foreign workers can be categorized as follows:

1 *Illegal migrant workers.* Included are visa abusers and overstayers. The number of overstayers was 293,800 in May 1994 (Japan Immigration Association 1994f: 13–14).
2 *Female entertainers* who have entered the country on entertainment visas. Although these individuals are technically regarded as professional entertainers, in practice they are most often employed as manual workers, and as hostesses and prostitutes in the entertainment and sex-related industry. The number of foreigners entering

Japan on entertainment visas was 76,242 in 1993 (Japan Immigration Association 1994c: 45).

3 *Pre-college students* who are enrolled in either Japanese-language schools or vocational schools and are permitted to work a maximum of four hours a day if they report this fact to the Immigration Bureau. A large number of pre-college students take on part-time jobs, while many others are suspected of full-time employment under the guise of study (Komai 1993a: 83). The number of foreigners on pre-college-student visas was 44,418 in December 1993, and the number of overstayers who had entered Japan on pre-college-student visas was 23,995 in May 1994 (Japan Immigration Association 1995a: 18).

4 *Foreign trainees* on trainee visas. They are not permitted to work, but may be required by their employers to undertake manual labour as part of their 'on-the-job' training. The number of foreigners on trainee visas was 17,431 in 1993 (Japan Immigration Association 1994e: 43).

5 *Foreign trainees* under the 'Work Training Programme' scheme inaugurated in April 1993. This scheme allows trainees to work upon completion of 'training' for a period approximately one and a half times the training period (which, with the additional period, should not total more than two years) in order to make use of newly acquired skills and to acquire practical knowledge and skills. They are granted special status by the Ministry of Justice. The number of trainees under this scheme was ninety in October 1993 (Japan Immigration Association 1994b: 32–4).

6 *South Americans of Japanese descent and their spouses* (the *Nikkeijin*). These individuals are *legally* permitted to reside in Japan, with no job restrictions, for up to three years. The number of such people was 175,118 in 1993 (Japan Immigration Association 1994e: 40–1).

Foreigners in groups 2–6 have been accorded a formal status of residence by the government, and, in the case of pre-college students and foreign trainees in particular, they are in effect able to work under certain conditions, while not being recognized, *per se*, as foreign workers. There is a gap between the government's official line of not accepting foreign workers in the unskilled job sectors and the actual situation of having a variety of foreigners who may work in these sectors. In a very real sense, the government has tacitly recognized the entry of foreign workers into the unskilled job market through a variety of 'back-door' and 'side-door' options, one of which has been the creation of a special category for *Nikkeijin*.

The recession

Since late 1991 Japan's economy has been in recession. Whether Japan will follow the experiences of Western Europe after the oil crisis of 1973 will be the most interesting aspect in the migration movement in Japan. In other words, will labour migrants in Japan, both illegal and legal, pack up and go home if recession renders their labour unnecessary, or, as in the Western European experience, will the first phase of labour migration merge into a second phase of family reunification, a consequence of which has been a demand for increased expenditure on housing, schooling, and medical and social facilities?

The ongoing recession has clearly manifested itself in the foreign labour market; the number of job opportunities and overtime work in the manufacturing industry, in particular, have decreased substantially.[5] In terms of employment, there has been much less public enthusiasm for the introduction of foreign workers. The Cabinet consultation committee dealing with the issue of foreign workers, which was established in 1990 in order to examine the effect of a large influx of foreign workers on Japanese society, was adjourned in 1993. Similarly, people in industry who had enthusiastically supported the introduction of foreign manual workers during the economic boom of the late 1980s, have lost interest in the issue since the collapse of the 'bubble economy' in 1991.

Despite a decrease in the number of job opportunities for foreign labour, illegal migrant workers now tend to remain longer, and this has given rise to increased public concern with issues such as the provision of medical care and education and an apparent rise in crime (*Tokyo Yomiuri Shinbun* 1995: 15). In the past, the majority of apprehended illegal migrant workers had stayed in Japan less than one year (70.6 per cent in 1991, 58.8 per cent in 1992, respectively). But, in 1993 only 29.5 per cent had stayed in Japan less than a year, while the number who had stayed in Japan longer than five years had increased 2.4 times over the previous year (Japan Immigration Association 1994d: 40–1). The longer-term implication is clear. However much the government and employers may wish to regard migrant workers as a flexible and low-cost response to labour shortages, any short-term benefits are beginning to be outweighed by longer-term social costs.

ARRIVAL OF *NIKKEIJIN* – THE 'RETURN-MIGRATION' PHENOMENON

Historical background: the origin of *Nikkeijin* as emigrants from Japan

Most *Nikkeijin* working in Japan are second- and third-generation descendants of Japanese emigrants who settled in South America after 1899, a period when Japan was one of the major sources of Asian out-migration.[6] The total number of Japanese emigrants between 1868 and 1941 was 776,304 and, among these, 244,946 emigrated to South America (Suzuki 1992: 262). This migration was encouraged by the Japanese government in an attempt to counter a perceived population explosion, and a number of South American countries welcomed the Japanese as part of their drive to develop interior regions. Most of these emigrants were employed as contract labourers on sugar and coffee plantations and saw themselves as 'target earners', hoping to stay in their chosen country for only a short time.[7] However, low earnings in Brazil encouraged them to stay longer and eventually a significant number became landed farmers. Even though many managed to establish for themselves a reputation for honesty and hard work and succeeded in setting up their own independent farms, their hope was 'to return wearing brocade', the nineteenth century Japanese symbol of affluence acquired abroad. This desire was finally frustrated by the outbreak of the Second World War and the defeat of Japan. The number of *Nikkeijin* in Brazil has grown since then. Both the levels of education and social status for second- and third-generation *Nikkeijin* have also risen. The *Nikkeijin* community in Brazil is the largest in the world; in 1988 the Brazilian *Nikkeijin* population stood at approximately 1,230,000, comprising 8.9 per cent (110,000) of the first generation, 36.6 per cent (450,000) of the second, 40.7 per cent (500,000) of the third, 6.5 per cent (80,000) of the fourth, and 1.6 per cent (20,000) of the fifth (Suzuki 1992: 169).

Patterns of *Nikkeijin* migration to Japan

One of the most fundamental causes of *Nikkeijin* migration to Japan has been the considerable disparity in income and job opportunities between Japan and their home countries. South American and Caribbean countries have been suffering from declining levels of economic performance, high inflation rates and the burden of financing and repaying huge national debts. Downturns in economic performance have also exacerbated employment problems linked in part to rapid growth of the indigenous labour forces. Since the 1980s, political instability in their home countries has also contributed to further increases in emigration to North America, Europe and Japan.[8]

Nikkeijin *in Japan before 1990*

In the 1960s and 1970s, only a small number of *Nikkeijin*, mainly first- or second-generation emigrants who possessed Japanese or dual nationality, came to Japan to work. They participated in the huge construction projects for the 1964 Tokyo Olympic Games, while others, who had originally emigrated from Okinawa, were employed on construction projects relating to the Expo in Okinawa in 1972. The number of those who were able to work in Japan was, however, limited. Most first-generation *Nikkeijin* were too old for manual labour, while few second-generation emigrants held dual nationality.[9] In fact, during the 1960s and 1970s, second- and third-generation *Nikkeijin* faced greater difficulty in obtaining even short-stay visas for Japan than did their European counterparts who held dual nationality.

It was not until autumn 1985 that the influx of second-generation *Nikkeijin*, who did not possess Japanese nationality, became numerically significant. This was mainly because the government enlarged its interpretation of the category known as 'spouse or child of Japanese national'. This status can be granted to a person whose father or mother was/is a Japanese national. Previously, this status had only been accorded when both the parents and the grandparents of the applicant were Japanese, but from around 1985 applicants became able to obtain this status if a relative within the fourth degree of consanguinity, such as the applicant's cousins or the applicant's grandparents' brothers/sisters, guaranteed the applicant's status. Even if the applicant had already started working in Japan during the time when she/he sought to change status of residence from temporary visitor to 'spouse or child of Japanese national', the change could be approved. By implementing these very broad guidelines, the government tacitly permitted illegal employment (Maeyama 1990: 4).

The revised Immigration Control Law

Revision of the Immigration Control Law represented a compromise position between the government's previous closed-door policy, which excluded all foreign workers, and strong demands for foreign workers from industries facing massive labour shortages. The revised law created a new category of residence, namely that of the 'long-term resident'. This status became available to third-generation *Nikkeijin*, as well as to the spouses of second- and third-generation *Nikkeijin*, regardless of their ancestry. Moreover, under the revised law, if a relative within the sixth degree of consanguinity in Japan, such as a grandnephew or a grandniece of the applicant's grandparents, or a nephew or a niece of the applicant's great-grandparents, obtained a 'certificate of eligibility' from the local Immigration Office in advance, the issuance of a visa was effectively guaranteed (Kura 1992: 248).

As a result of the revised law, in São Paulo between 1988 and 1991, the number of visas issued jumped from 8,602 to 61,500, and in Peru about 15 per cent of Peruvian *Nikkeijin* are thought to have gone through the formalities for emigration (Stalker 1994: 251). Although the visa of 'spouse or child of Japanese national' or the visa of 'long-term resident' is not by definition a working visa, there are no restrictions on the activities these individuals can undertake in Japan. In a sense, therefore, these visas can be described as *de facto* working visas. The status of 'long-term resident' or 'spouse or child of Japanese national' allows them to stay in Japan for up to three years (Japan Immigration Association 1990: 34–7).

An overview of *Nikkeijin* in Japan

Trends in the number and origin of Nikkeijin

Once the law had been revised, intense competition developed among employers eager to employ *Nikkeijin*, rather than risk prosecution for employing illegal migrant workers. Opportunities for the *Nikkeijin* are such that Brazilian emigrants, who represent the biggest reservoir of *Nikkeijin*, have been joined by those from Argentina, Peru and Paraguay. Tables 7.2 and 7.3 show recent trends in the number of foreigners who have acquired the status of 'spouse or child of a Japanese national' and that of 'long-term resident'.

The number of Brazilians who had the status of 'spouse or child of Japanese national' was only 750 in 1986. This number increased after 1988, and in 1993 had reached 94,870 which represented an increase of approximately 120 per cent. Brazilians constituted 42.7 per cent of the total number of 222,353 in this category.

Table 7.2 Recent trends in the number of foreigners who have acquired the status of residence of 'spouse or child of a Japanese national', broken down by nationality, 1986–93

Country	1986	%	1988	%	1990	%	1992	%	1993	%
Brazil	750	1.8	2,003	3.5	40,384	31.0	91,816	43.9	94,870	42.7
China	13,085	31.7	16,812	29.5	23,051	17.7	29,008	13.9	32,382	14.6
Philippines	5,299	12.9	11,298	19.8	20,516	15.7	28,351	13.5	32,370	14.5
Korea*	7,841	19.0	11,532	20.2	19,999	15.4	21,855	10.4	22,025	9.9
Peru	218	0.5	271	0.5	5,276	4.1	10,455	5.0	10,692	4.8
Others	14,071	34.1	15,115	26.5	20,992	16.1	27,784	13.3	30,014	13.5
Total	41,264	100	57,031	100	130,218	100	209,269	100	222,353	100

Source: Ministry of Justice.

Note: *Korea indicates both South and North Korea.

Table 7.3 Recent trends in the number of foreigners who have the status of 'long-term resident', broken down by nationality, 1990–3

Country	1990	%	1992	%	1993	%
Brazil	12,637	23.2	51,759	42.1	55,282	42.7
China	15,263	28.1	23,877	19.5	26,267	20.3
Peru	4,202	7.7	14,845	12.1	14,274	11.0
Korea*	10,412	19.2	13,775	11.2	13,361	10.3
Vietnam	4,027	7.4	5,171	4.2	5,582	4.3
Others	7,818	14.4	13,387	10.9	14,740	11.4
Total	54,359	100	122,814	100	129,506	100

Source: Ministry of Justice.

Note: *Korea indicates both South and North Korea.

The number of Brazilians who held 'long-term resident' status was 12,637 in 1990. By 1993 this figure had risen fourfold to 55,282, over 40 per cent of the total number of 129,506. The Ministry of Justice estimates that in 1993 the number of *Nikkeijin* in Japan was approximately 196,000. It is considered that approximately 16 per cent of all Brazilian *Nikkeijin* have worked in Japan; this figure was 38 per cent in the case of Peruvian *Nikkeijin*.

As a result of the increase in the number of foreign workers, the number of foreign residents with alien registration permits in Japan increased by about 62 per cent from 1983 to 1,320,748 in 1993, comprising 1.06 per cent of the total Japanese population of more than 124 million (Japan Immigration Association 1994e: 36). It should be noted that until the influx of migrant workers in the late 1980s, the bulk of non-Japanese resident in Japan were Korean and Chinese permanent residents, the numbers of which were 592,471 and 26,065 in 1993, respectively (Japan Immigration Association 1994e: 40). In 1992, the number of so-called 'New Comers', comprising mainly legal and illegal migrant workers, surpassed the number of 'Old Comers' (Korean and Chinese permanent residents).[10]

Types, characteristics and motivation of Nikkeijin *working in Japan*

According to Kajita (1994a: 154), the characteristics of *Nikkeijin* living in Japan for reasons of employment differ depending on when they entered the country. In the case of first-stage *Nikkeijin* immigrants from Brazil, who began entering Japan around 1985, the majority were male farmers, had been low-income earners in Brazil, and wished to work in Japan in order to satisfy their households' basic needs. From 1988, as the advantages of working in Japan became widely known, the class composition of *Nikkeijin* working in Japan underwent a dramatic change; the majority were now highly educated members of the middle class. For these second-stage migrants, the motivation to work in Japan was almost entirely economic/instrumental – for example, to satisfy a desire for new houses or cars, or to enhance their actual or perceived standing in Brazil by starting a new business or enrolling in higher education.

The third, or current, stage started from around the time of the revision to the Immigration Control Law on 1 June 1990. During this stage the number of *Nikkeijin* working in Japan has increased dramatically. At the Japanese Consulate General in São Paulo, for example, 'family visitation' visas (temporary visitor visas) issued for 1990 to *Nikkeijin* totalled 22,426 as of 20 June 1990. This represents a fourfold increase on corresponding visas issued in 1987 (*Daily Yomiuri* 1990a: 2). The majority of those working in Japan were highly educated individuals, including around 21 per cent graduates and 15 per cent undergraduates (*Shizuoka Shinbun* 1992: 30). Many *Nikkeijin* have come to Japan with their entire families, including young children. Of those *Nikkeijin* who have dependants, the proportion whose families accompany them to Japan has risen to one in three (Komai 1993b: 192). At the same time, there has been a substantial increase in the number of young, and often single, third-generation *Nikkeijin* who wish to enjoy 'high-consumption' lifestyles in Japan rather than making remittances to their families at home.

Although the dominant factor drawing *Nikkeijin* to work in Japan remains economic, a variety of non-economic issues are also involved. The attraction of the 'bright lights' of Japan is one such non-economic factor. In spite of the geographical distance between Japan and South America, potential *Nikkeijin* migrants are made constantly aware of the attractions of affluent countries through advertising and stories relayed by *Nikkeijin* returning to their home communities. Some also wish to satisfy a desire to see the country where their ancestors were born. This desire to confirm their traditional and cultural images of Japan is heightened by the often imaginative, if not necessarily accurate, depiction of Japanese society transmitted by elderly relatives.

THE IMPACT OF *NIKKEIJIN* ON JAPAN

Impact on the Japanese labour market

The employment situation of Nikkeijin

More than 50 per cent of the *Nikkeijin* in Japan reside and work in Mie, Aichi, Shizuoka, Kanagawa, Saitama and Gunma prefectures, where there exists a heavy concentration of subcontractors and sub-subcontractors of giant manufacturing companies, such as Nissan, Fuji Heavy Industries, Yamaha and Kawai. According to an investigation carried out by the *Nikkeijin*'s Employment Service Centre, in 1993, 51.1 per cent of *Nikkeijin* worked on assembly lines in manufacturing industry, 25.1 per cent in the construction industry, and 13.2 per cent in the service industry, including hotels, hospitals and golf courses (Japan Immigration Association 1994a: 10; Watkins 1994: 59). More than 60 per cent of *Nikkeijin* are recruited and employed by Japanese labour contractors/brokers (Yoshimen 1992: 117).

The impact of Nikkeijin *in the labour market*

An important consequence of the entry of *Nikkeijin* in Japan has been the creation of a stratified labour market structure for foreign manual workers based upon the legal status of individual workers (Inagami *et al.* 1992: 125). It is worth noting in this context that *Nikkeijin* income levels increased rapidly following the *de facto* legalization of their status under the revised Immigration Control Law. Before June 1990, the position of *Nikkeijin* in the labour market was no better than that of other illegal migrant workers (Yamamoto and Chiba 1995: 76). Since the revision of the Immigration Control Law, however, legal migrant workers (i.e., *Nikkeijin*) have emerged as a sort of migrant labour 'aristocracy', with illegal migrant workers from Asia existing at the other end of the spectrum. The fact that the number of possible *Nikkeijin* emigrants is limited has led to an increase in wages, and, on average, the wage level of male *Nikkeijin* is the highest among all foreign migrant workers in Japan.[11] They are so-called 'target earners' who aim to earn a 'target' sum of money within a limited period of time. The economic climate was very healthy until autumn 1991, making it particularly easy for male *Nikkeijin* in their twenties or thirties employed by brokers to frequently change jobs in search of higher incomes (Yamamoto and Chiba 1995: 75–6).

In general, medium-sized companies or sub-subcontractors employ both *Nikkeijin* and illegal migrant workers, whereas small- or family-sized companies and sub-sub-subcontractors can, for financial reasons, only employ illegal migrant workers. Further stratification is reflected in the types of labour required by their employers. Until around the autumn of 1991 the *Nikkeijin* tended to be employed in the manufacturing or service sectors, whereas illegal migrant workers tended to be employed either in factories or in the construction industry where employment conditions were far worse than in the manufacturing and service industries.

Generally speaking, foreign workers provide additional and replacement labour during growth periods and a flexible source of labour during recessions – in other words, they represent a 'buffer' in the labour market. During the current recession, conditions of employment for foreign workers have declined. Many foreign workers employed in the car-manufacturing industry and the electrical-appliance manufacturing industry have either been dismissed or had their wages substantially reduced (*Daily Yomiuri* 1993a: 3; *Asahi Shinbun* 1993: 13). A large number of *Nikkeijin* have also had no choice but to seek jobs in the construction and the service industries where working conditions are poor by comparison with manufacturing industry. The general trend is that many *Nikkeijin* have left for regions other than those where the car and related industries are located. Some *Nikkeijin* have engaged, for example, in seasonal agricultural work and fish-processing work in the peripheral regions where the demand for manual labour remains substantial (Yamamoto and Chiba 1995: 76).

Compared with the position of Japanese full-time workers, *Nikkeijin*, as well as illegal migrant workers, occupy a subordinate position in the domestic labour market. This despite the fact that the costs incurred in employing Japanese labour – including mandatory elements, such as payments for health insurance and pension schemes – are much higher than the cost of employing *Nikkeijin*. The fact that more than 60 per cent of *Nikkeijin* are 'contract' workers employed by brokers indicates that their employers prefer indirect to direct employment, since the former pattern places fewer responsibilities on the employer while allowing for greater employment flexibility (Yoshimen 1992: 117). For many employers these advantages outweigh the additional costs that come from using labour contractors. In addition, owing to the temporary nature of their employment, the *Nikkeijin* are not paid the bonuses that are commonly awarded to Japanese workers. Nor can they rely on regular pay increases or promotion in accordance with length of employment as is the case with Japanese workers. Nevertheless, the shortage of available and affordable indigenous workers is so severe in certain industries that employers have no choice but to employ *Nikkeijin* if they can afford to do so.

Through the influx of *Nikkeijin* and other migrant workers, Japan has become structurally dependent on foreign workers, and a more extensive dependence on foreign workers will be difficult to avoid. Although there will be fluctuations in the number of foreign workers employed, Japan will face a structural shortage of labour due, *inter alia*, to the accelerated ageing of the population and a low birthrate. Around the year 2000 a labour shortage of approximately 5 million persons is anticipated even on the basis of a relatively moderate economic growth rate (Mori 1995: 61). In a situation where there is a limited supply of young Japanese workers, and where a large number of foreign workers are prepared to accept '3D' jobs and reduced wages, foreign workers will be required as soon as the economic recovery comes about.

Social 'expenditure' created by the *Nikkeijin* and other foreign workers: the possibility of *Nikkeijin* settlement in Japanese society

The situation of local government with regard to foreign residents

The Local Government Law in Japan stipulates that local authorities must maintain the security as well as the health and general welfare of the residents who live within their administrative areas.[12] The Law defines 'residents' to include not only Japanese, but all individuals who have their addresses within a given administrative area. Therefore, in principle, local governments are obliged to provide sufficient services for foreigners who have completed their alien registration (which is equivalent to the resident registration required of Japanese citizens) in the same way as for Japanese residents living within their jurisdiction.

Initially, the sharp increase in the number of migrant workers resulted primarily from strong and consistent demands for manual workers in industrial sectors suffering from labour shortages. It was in response to pressure from these sectors that the government revised the Immigration Control Law, thus providing a legal framework for the importation of a flexible and low-cost workforce in the form of the *Nikkeijin*. But, neither the government nor those industrial sectors most affected were prepared to shoulder the burden of the concomitant long-term social costs. Various problems resulting from the employment of these workers – such as provision of accident compensation for labour accidents, medical care and welfare, Japanese language courses, accommodation, and facilitating the integration of these foreigners into their areas of residence – remain unresolved. At the same time, infringements of human rights and discrimination against migrant workers have become commonplace. As a result, the development of specific policies to deal with these issues has been left to local governments in areas of migrant worker residence.

Social expenditure created by foreign workers

In terms of social expenditure, the problems associated with medical provision for foreign workers have become extremely serious. This is particularly true in the case of illegal migrant workers, the majority of whom are unable to pay medical bills in full, since they are not under the protection of the public health insurance system. As a result, many hospitals have refused to treat foreign patients in order to avoid unpaid medical bills. In Tokyo, for example, it is estimated that unpaid medical fees owed by foreigners to seventeen Tokyo metropolitan hospitals alone, in the five years leading up to 1994, amounted to about ¥68 million ($728,550) (*Tokyo Yomiuri Shinbun* 1994a: 31). Several local governments, such as the Tokyo metropolitan government, and those representing Gunma, Chiba, Saitama and Kanagawa prefectures, have created a system which provides partial compensation to foreign workers who are unable to meet medical payments (*Tokyo Yomiuri Shinbun* 1994b: 3).

Educational provision for the children of *Nikkeijin*, in particular, has become an important issue, as increasing numbers of *Nikkeijin* have come to Japan with their families. It has been estimated that in 1992 around 18 per cent of the total number of *Nikkeijin* workers were accompanied by children of school age. The same survey noted that approximately 20,000 *Nikkeijin* children lacked knowledge of the Japanese language (Miyajima 1992: 224). Despite efforts by various local authorities to provide Japanese-language instructors and Japanese-language textbooks, under-attendance of older foreign children remains at significant levels. To address this and other related problems, the Ministry of Education initiated a trial programme to foster Japanese language acquisition among foreign workers and their children in April 1993 (*Daily Yomiuri* 1993b: 2). While there are no legal obstacles to the education of foreign children through junior high school, educational provision is not guaranteed. The enrolment of foreign children in public sector elementary and high schools falls within the discretionary authority of local educational councils.

A fundamental dilemma for teachers and parents is whether *Nikkeijin* children should be educated with a view to permanent settlement in Japan (Miyajima 1992: 226). If the number of *Nikkeijin* who reside in Japan long term and eventually wish to settle in Japan increases in the future, the problem of older children seeking to enter senior high schools and universities will arise. In Kanagawa Prefecture, a small number of high schools have already been designated as 'receiving schools' for *Kikokushijo* (Japanese children who have returned to Japan after spending time abroad with their families). Some of these schools have also been accommodating *Nikkeijin* children who possess sufficient knowledge of the Japanese language and who wish to enrol in high school. By comparison, *Nikkeijin* children with little or no understanding of Japanese have little chance of enrolment in high school.[13] If educational access remains limited, their future occupational opportunities will also be severely constrained and this, in turn, may lead to a high unemployment rate among *Nikkeijin*. Effective long-term policies and educational facilities need to be established by local educational councils to ensure adequate levels of education for *Nikkeijin* children.

Local governments which attract Nikkeijin

Although most local authorities have only reluctantly acknowledged the social costs associated with integration of foreign workers, some local governments have provided various facilities and services as part of a campaign to attract *Nikkeijin* in particular. These local governments are normally located in areas where there are heavy concentrations of subcontractors and/or sub-subcontractors of the giant manufacturing companies. Since these companies regularly experience labour shortages, local governments in the areas where they operate are generally enthusiastic about accepting *Nikkeijin* as a means of stabilizing the local labour market. Since local governments in these areas also receive substantial tax revenues from the local manufacturing companies and their subcontractors, they are able and willing to provide a range of facilities for *Nikkeijin* workers and their families. This in turn acts as a magnet, encouraging other *Nikkeijin* to migrate to the area.

Hamamatsu City in Shizuoka Prefecture is home to the largest *Nikkeijin* community in Japan, including 6,313 Brazilian and 698 Peruvian *Nikkeijin*. The municipal authorities have shown considerable initiative in making special facilities available to *Nikkeijin* residents. These include the publication of information packs and newsletters containing information about National Health Insurance, traffic rules, emergency services, etc., for the *Nikkeijin* community. Spanish- and Portuguese-speaking staff have been assigned to the alien registration section in the town hall, while Japanese language classes for *Nikkeijin* residents (including their children at school) have been provided by the city (Hamamatsu Local Government 1993: 16; *Shizuoka Shinbun* 1992: 30).

The possibility of Nikkeijin settlement in Japan

While the majority of *Nikkeijin* currently regard themselves as temporary 'target earners', an increasing number of *Nikkeijin* have brought their families with them to Japan. Dependent upon their length of stay, it is highly probable that younger members of these families will develop a greater sense of attachment to Japan than to their countries of birth. Table 7.4 shows the number of Brazilian nationals entering Japan between 1986 and 1993 broken down into new entrants and re-entrants. Owing to the current recession that started in the autumn of 1991 and the decrease in the *Nikkeijin* workforce available from Brazil, the number of Brazilian entrants has been decreasing since 1991. In contrast, the number of re-entrants, or so-called 'repeaters', has been on the increase. This trend indicates that

Table 7.4 The number of Brazilian nationals entering Japan, 1986–93

	Total number	%*	New entrants	Repeaters
1986	13,434		12,918	516
1987	12,126	−9.7	11,479	647
1988	16,789	38.5	15,968	821
1989	29,241	74.2	27,819	1,422
1990	67,303	130.2	63,462	3,841
1991	96,337	43.1	83,785	12,552
1992	81,495	−15.4	57,574	23,921
1993	70,719	−13.2	44,804	25,915

Source: Ministry of Justice.

Note: * Percentage change on previous year.

migration to Japan has become a substantial income source and a recognized part of the survival strategy for an increasing number of *Nikkeijin* families in Brazil. According to statistics published by the National Bank of Brazil, total annual bank remittances from *Nikkeijin* migrant workers in Japan to Brazil was estimated at $2 billion in 1994 (*Sankei Shinbun* 1994: 8). A large number of those *Nikkeijin* families in Brazil with relatives working in Japan have also become financially dependent on such remittances as a means of supplementing the family income (Boyasbeck 1994: 82–3). The experience of life in Japan also appears to have provided a disincentive for *Nikkeijin* to take up poorly paid employment in their home countries. Indeed, many prefer to return to Japan and, when an opportunity arises, many do so, often accompanied by their families. According to a survey by the Association of *Nikkeijin* Abroad, of those *Nikkeijin* who have dependants, the proportion intending to settle in Japan reached 25.7 per cent in 1993 (Komai 1993b: 192). In economic terms, it appears as if a significant number of *Nikkeijin*, having cut their financial ties with their home countries, are now more inclined to settle in Japan. Their ability or willingness to integrate into Japanese society, however, remains unresolved. To a great extent this is due to the fact that most second- and third-generation *Nikkeijin* do not understand the Japanese language. Both socially and culturally they identify with their country of origin rather than with Japan. For third-generation *Nikkeijin* in particular, it is only weak ancestral ties that bind them to Japan. Moreover, the *Nikkeijin* in general do not normally have close contact with their relatives in Japan (except in the case of those who emigrated from Okinawa Prefecture).[14] Even when seeking employment, the majority tend to rely on brokers or local networks in preference to their Japanese relations.

Although many *Nikkeijin* undoubtedly expect to return to their home countries after a stint of working in Japan, it is reasonable to assume that an increasing number may choose to settle in Japan (as a result of the huge income differentials between Japan and their home countries), while still maintaining strong bonds with their own culture. Networks among the *Nikkeijin* that will stimulate further migration and make the process of migration much easier have already been established. As the number of networks increases, the psychological and financial costs of migration will fall and the potential benefits rise, inducing others to migrate.

In areas of relatively high *Nikkeijin* density, social networks have become well established. They have created a new environment that includes South American restaurants and supermarkets, as well as Portuguese-language newspapers (which also have some Spanish pages), Portuguese weekly magazines, and Portuguese radio programmes, while Hamamatsu City boasts a local branch of the National Brazilian Bank. At the same time, *Nikkeijin* tend not to have much contact with local Japanese residents, since *Nikkeijin* workers are normally housed in company accommodation and rely on company operated mini-bus services for commuting to work. In addition to these networks, facilities and services, the proliferation of global communications, including the expansion of satellite television, has reduced the 'emotional distance' for migrants by enabling them to keep in touch with their home country. For the modern migrant, his or her family is only a telephone call away; a significant proportion of international calls from Japanese public telephones are made by migrant workers. The number of such calls has been increasing by roughly 20 per cent a year and now constitutes around 20 per cent of all international calls made from Japan (Stalker 1994: 32).

The discount air fare from Japan to Brazil is currently around ¥160,000 (approximately $1,800). Though a significant outlay, this is an expense which most *Nikkeijin* could accommodate after several years' work in Japan. The speeding up of global communications and transport combined with the repeat flow of *Nikkeijin* using established networks in Japan suggests that the *Nikkeijin* may become 'circular immigrants', repeatedly moving between their home countries and Japan (Kajita 1994a: 161–3). Indeed, this kind of settlement pattern may become commonplace in the future in countries other than Japan which also suffer from labour shortages.

In relation to *Nikkeijin* permanent settlement, schooling for the children of *Nikkeijin* will be a key determinant. One of the most obvious problems confronting *Nikkeijin* children in Japan is the acquisition of the Japanese language. If the *Nikkeijin* keep moving between Japan and their home countries with a 'circular period' of, say, three years, both the acquisition of the Japanese language and native language maintenance will become difficult for their children (Kajita 1994b: 5). Japanese society attaches great importance to a person's educational background, while the certification provided by schools is the main determinant of work opportunities in both Japan and the home countries of the *Nikkeijin*. In this sense, access to higher education in Japan may well emerge as the primary factor determining whether *Nikkeijin* families will settle permanently in Japan. On the other hand, poorly educated *Nikkeijin* may be absorbed within the Japanese criminal underclass as has been the case with members of the outcast and Korean communities.

THE IDEOLOGICAL SIGNIFICANCE OF *NIKKEIJIN* MIGRATION

The presence of *Nikkeijin* also provides an opportunity to reconsider what it means to be 'Japanese'. It also raises questions about the ideological boundary which separates the Japanese from certain national minorities within Japan (Fukuoka 1994: 4). The commonsense definition of 'Japaneseness' encompasses both culture and pseudobiological notions of a Japanese 'race'. Although *Nikkeijin* are descendants of Japanese emigrants and therefore share the same lineage as the Japanese, their languages, culture, customs and behaviour derive from South America. The physical appearance of some *Nikkeijin* might be indistinguishable from that of indigenous Japanese, but it has been claimed that *Nikkeijin* are easily identified by their social behaviour (Stalker 1994: 77). Thus, while they may be regarded as Japanese in their countries of origin, in Japan they are identified as Brazilians or Peruvians

In Japan, lineage or 'race' are regarded as the primary determinants of Japaneseness. Following on from this, regardless of an individual's cultural or social background, they are treated as Japanese or 'semi-Japanese', as long as they share the same lineage, i.e. 'Japanese blood'. If the stereotypical image of a Japanese is 'someone who has Japanese lineage, has Japanese nationality, lives according to Japanese culture, speaks the Japanese language freely, and makes a living in Japan', people such as *Nikkeijin*, *Kikokushijo*, Japanese orphans left behind in China after the Second World War, and even Japanese permanent residents abroad must be considered somewhat different from 'real' Japanese (Kajita 1994a: 169). If we further compare the stereotypical image of an indigenous Japanese with that of third-generation Korean and Chinese permanent residents in Japan (who do not share Japanese lineage or Japanese nationality but share Japanese culture and language and are, therefore, sociologically 'Japanese') or the Ainu (an indigenous people who, as a result of a long process of assimilation, share the same nationality and language as majority Japanese, but maintain a separate cultural identity), the boundary markers which distinguish between Japanese and foreigners become extremely ambiguous.

Of course definitions of what constitutes a 'foreigner' are based on provisional criteria which vary depending on how national governments regulate their nationality laws. Nevertheless, the decision of the Japanese government to accept nearly 200,000 *Nikkeijin*, while excluding all other migrant workers, has reinforced assumptions of racial homogeneity (Ōnuma 1993: 10).

Japan grants citizenship according to the principle of *jus sanguinis*, the 'law of blood' or parental nationality. This in contrast to the option of granting citizenship on the basis of *jus soli*, the 'law of soil', whereby citizenship is the right of everyone born within a state's borders. The latter embodies an inclusionary concept of the nation: if immigration policy allows someone to become a member of the civil society, then citizenship policy allows that individual to become a member of state and of the nation (Castles and Miller 1993: 115–17).

This fundamental difference affects all aspects of public policy towards immigrants and minorities in any society. If Japan had adopted the principle of *jus soli*, the majority of Korean residents, for example, would have obtained Japanese nationality. From its inception, discussion of the issue of foreign migrant workers has assumed the existence of an absolute distinction between Japanese and foreigner. But, since this distinction is subject to interpretation under the Nationality Law, it is essential that we examine how the government has interpreted the Immigration Control Law in its attempts to legalize the status of residence of *Nikkeijin*.

Nikkeijin have been among the main beneficiaries of the recent changes (since 1985) to Japan's immigration and nationality laws; in particular those regarding the visa status of the 'spouse or child of a Japanese national'. Prior to 1985 this status was only issued when both the parents and the grandparents of the person applying for the visa were Japanese. Under the Revised Immigration Control Law, however, visas of this type are now relatively easy to obtain if a relative in Japan within the sixth degree of consanguinity guarantees the applicant's status. This has clear implications for *Nikkeijin* on this visa who subsequently apply for naturalization as Japanese citizens. Under the current Nationality Law, naturalization requires that the applicant shall have resided in Japan for a minimum period of five years. In the case of aliens whose residential status is defined as 'spouse or child of Japanese national', however, the residence requirement is reduced to three years.[15] In effect, the government's decision to redefine this status (which has the potential to influence the future form of the Nationality Law) reinforces the notion of lineage, however fictive, as the basis for Japanese nationality.

As a result of this expansion of the interpretation of lineage, a clear demarcation has been created between the *Nikkeijin* and other foreign workers. The possession of a *Nikkeijin* background has become a lineage-based 'qualification' for work in Japan (Kajita 1994a: 168). As a consequence, some Brazilians and Peruvians have applied for this status on the basis of falsified birth certificates, while others have undergone plastic surgery in an attempt to acquire Japanese facial characteristics. Screening of applicants has become more rigorous during the recession, and the government has rejected numerous applications for *Nikkeijin* status, mainly from Peruvians who had submitted false documents attesting to their Japanese ancestry (*Tokyo Yomiuri Shinbun* 1994e: 31).

The privileged position of *Nikkeijin* has also caused some to question Japan's overall policy towards foreign migrant workers. Even the Brazilian government has criticized the Japanese position on the grounds that discrimination in employment based on race or ethnicity is prohibited under Brazilian law (Fujisaki 1991: 235–6). Not only has the Japanese government adopted a policy that appears overtly discriminatory from a Brazilian perspective, but one which, with its emphasis on blood lineage, is increasingly at odds with trends in other advanced industrial states.

At first glance, the position of *Nikkeijin* in Japan is comparable to, for example, the *Aussiedler* (ethnic Germans) living in parts of Eastern Europe which were formerly German territory, who can claim residency and citizenship rights in Germany. Similarly, certain European states, notably Italy, Portugal, Germany and Spain, permit Latin American descendants of European immigrants to take up employment since they can claim citizenship in the mother country. Nevertheless, the *Nikkeijin* do differ from these other ethnic immigrants. Compared with immigrants of European origin, the relationship between *Nikkeijin* in South America and their nominal ancestral home was extremely remote until the revision of the Immigration Control Law came into effect in Japan. Until that time, the government had shown little interest in *Nikkeijin* emigrants once they had left Japan (Fujisaki 1991: 49–50). The *Nikkeijin* generally have had less contact with relatives in Japan than has been the case with Latin Americans of European origin. Adoption of Latin American culture has also created a larger cultural difference between the *Nikkeijin* and the Japanese than it has for those of European origin. Moreover, the massive influx of *Nikkeijin* into Japan was triggered by a political decision in the form of the revision of the Immigration Control Law. A revision which implied that *Nikkeijin* were to be introduced as 'functional equivalents' for illegal migrant workers. For the *Nikkeijin*, as well, the main motivation to come to Japan has been to earn income rather than to re-establish family or ethnic ties. In this sense, the *Nikkeijin* are basically 'foreign workers' rather than ethnic immigrants returning to their home countries.

Despite the obvious fact that unskilled foreign labour has continued to enter Japan, the official view has remained unchanged; that the country has not accepted any foreign workers employed in the unskilled job sectors. In the case of the *Nikkeijin*, the initial official line, dating from 1990, has been that they have come to Japan because 'they would like to see the country where their ancestors grew up and they wish to visit their relatives in Japan'. Since 'it will cost money for a *Nikkeijin* to stay with relatives in Japan, the government should allow them to work in Japan in order to recover the cost of their visit. The Immigration Control Law was not specially revised for the purpose of promoting their employment in Japan.'[16] What the government did not anticipate was that its encouragement of *Nikkeijin* through the revision of the Immigration Control Law would result in a massive influx of *Nikkeijin*. Eventually, the government began to provide some support for the *Nikkeijin* in Japan, while the Ministry of Labour has established an overseas vocational counselling office for potential *Nikkeijin* immigrants (*Daily Yomiuri* 1990b: 2). Although *Nikkeijin* were initially welcomed as a response to the severe labour shortage of the 'bubble' years, their status, too, has been undermined by the current recession. The Immigration Bureau has become much more rigorous in its screening of potential *Nikkeijin* immigrants, and visa renewals are no longer issued without question (*Tokyo Yomiuri Shinbun* 1994c: 15). None the less, provided the demand for low-cost labour in undesirable industries continues, foreign workers, including *Nikkeijin*, will never disappear entirely.

CONCLUSION

Although the *Nikkeijin* are a largely invisible minority and their numbers small in relation to the total population, their presence is significant in social, economic, and ideological terms. Firstly, as labourers they have offered themselves as a flexible and convenient workforce for employers, and have stimulated the emergence of an extensive network of brokers and recruiters. The *Nikkeijin* have also given rise to a stratified structure in the foreign labour market by demanding and receiving higher wages than illegal migrant workers. Their privileged position within the labour market is not, however, a function of either the skills they possess or a high degree of linguistic competence. Rather, their status has been secured by notions of blood and lineage alone. None the less, once fees have been paid to labour brokers or recruitment agencies, their net wages are comparable to those of illegal migrant workers. Similarly, during the current recession, they are being treated as surplus labour in the same way as illegal migrant workers. Secondly, the presence of the *Nikkeijin* represents a growing challenge to local governments in Japan. Unlike other minority populations, the *Nikkeijin* have the possibility of becoming an ethnic minority – that is, on the one hand, 'Japanese' by virtue of lineage; on the other, distinctively 'non-Japanese' in terms of cultural allegiance. Furthermore, the existing *Nikkeijin* population can be expanded through the arrival of new *Nikkeijin* immigrants who can claim a legal access to Japan, despite the fact that they are cultural 'aliens'. In the longer term, the government's attempt to shape immigration and nationality law on the basis of lineage alone may backfire. Instead of preventing the appearance of foreign ethnic enclaves with related social and economic problems, the government may have unwittingly acted to encourage their formation. Much will depend on whether local governments develop effective social and educational programmes for the *Nikkeijin*, whether Japanese society provides *Nikkeijin* with the opportunity to assimilate into the larger community or confines them to ghetto occupations, and whether the future economic development of Japan attracts more *Nikkeijin*. Thus, although relatively few in number, the *Nikkeijin* and their treatment in Japan can be taken as indicators of the degree to which Japan is prepared to meet the challenges that arise from its status as an affluent, maturing industrial state within an increasingly globalized, international society.

NOTES

1 Henceforth in this chapter the 'Immigration-Control and Refugee-Recognition Act' will be referred to as the 'Immigration Control Law'.
2 Under the existing system all foreigners must meet one of the residency status criteria stipulated in Article 2-2-1 of the Immigration Control Law, and work incompatible with residential status is, in the absence of special permission, prohibited (Article 19-1). There is no category that accommodates 'unskilled workers'.
3 These employers and brokers are fined up to a maximum of ¥2 million (about £14,280 at ¥140 = £1), or are imprisoned for up to three years (Japan Immigration Association 1990: 36–7).

4 According to the arrival statistics for 1994, 92.3 per cent of all the first-time visitors to Japan were temporary visitors who stay for less than three months. Less than 8 per cent of them managed to obtain status of residence which allowed them to work in Japan (Japan Immigration Association 1995b: 40–1).

5 According to an investigation with regard to the employment situation of foreign workers which was carried out by the Ministry of Labour in November 1994, the number of foreign employees employed in the manufacturing industry decreased by 7.3 per cent in 1994 compared to the previous year (*Tokyo Yomiuri Shinbun* 1994d: 2).

6 The first contracted emigrants, numbering 787, arrived in Peru in 1899; and in the case of Brazil, the first contracted emigrants, numbering 791 in total, arrived in 1908 (Watkins 1994: 58).

7 According to an investigation conducted by the Association of *Nikkeijin* in São Paulo in 1937, 85 per cent of Japanese emigrants wished to go back to Japan in the future (Suzuki 1992: 168–9).

8 Officially, there were 82,489 Brazilians in the United States in 1990, 7,325 in Canada in 1991, and around 20,000 in Portugal (Stalker 1994: 227).

9 The current Japanese nationality law, issued and enshrined in 1950 and amended in 1952 and 1984, retains the principle of nationality by descent or blood (*jus sanguinis*). A Japanese national who was born in a foreign country and has acquired foreign nationality by birth loses Japanese nationality retroactively as from the time of birth, unless the Japanese national clearly indicates his/her desire or volition to preserve his/her Japanese nationality. A Japanese national who was born in a foreign country and has acquired both foreign nationality and Japanese nationality by birth normally must adopt only one of these nationalities before he/she reaches twenty-two years of age. Therefore, if a parent who has Japanese nationality does not think that his/her child who was born in a foreign country will reside in Japan, he/she does not normally apply for Japanese nationality for that child. See Articles 12 and 14(a) of the Nationality Law in Moriki (1991: 219). By contrast the current Brazilian nationality laws retain the principle of nationality by place of birth (*jus soli*) so that any children born in Brazil may acquire Brazilian nationality.

10 The expression 'New Comers' usually indicates foreign residents who began residing in Japan during approximately the last fifteen years. This group includes, for example, returnees from China, Indo-Chinese refugees, foreign students, foreign pre-college students, foreign trainees, Asian brides, and migrant workers including *Nikkeijin* and illegal migrant workers. This phrase contrasts with 'Old Comers' which is used to describe Korean and Chinese permanent residents. See Kanagawa Zainichi Gaikokujin Mondai Kenkyūkai (1992: 3).

11 In 1991, the average hourly wage for a full-time *Nikkeijin* was ¥1,250 for males and ¥800–900 for females, whereas the hourly wage for Asian illegal male workers was ¥600–700 (Inagami *et al.* 1992: 25).

12 Article 3, paragraph 3(1), and Article 10 of the Local Government Law (Miyajima 1992: 218).

13 In this case, a very small number of high schools designated as 'schools which promote the education for international understanding' can permit enrolment after giving an interview to a child who wishes to study at

that school. The child attends the same classes as Japanese students, but is also required to attend special Japanese-language courses (Kanagawa Zainichi Gaikokujin Mondai Kenkyūkai, 1992: 86–7).

14 The weak bond between *Nikkeijin* and their relatives might be explained, at least in part, by the fact that Japanese do not attach importance to ancestry in a pure sense. Instead, they put emphasis on the continuation of a (fictitious) family system. In addition, since most emigrants from Japan are second and third sons from poor regions, they have been cut off from their families (Kajita 1994a: 156–7).

15 See Article 7 of the Nationality Law in Moriki (1991: 142).

16 This is an explanation offered by the Immigration Section of the Ministry of Foreign Affairs (Kura 1992: 249).

BIBLIOGRAPHY

Asahi Shinbun (1993) 'Nezukuka Gaikokujinkoyō, Fukyō no Nami, Chokugeki Senzai Juyō Otoroczu' (Will employing foreigners become common in Japan? Recession hits foreign workers, but the potential demand still exists), *Asahi Shinbun*, 14 May: 13.

Boyasbeck, A.C. (1994) 'Nippon Dekasegi Kiroku' (Record of Migration to Japan), *Sekai* 592 (March): 76–85, Tokyo: Iwanami Shoten.

Castles, S. and Miller, M.J. (1993) *The Age of Migration – International Population Movements in the Modern World*, London: Macmillan.

Daily Yomiuri (1990a) 'Japan jobs draw S. American immigrants', *The Daily Yomiuri*, 1 August, p. 2.

—— (1990b) 'Gambling on success far from home', *The Daily Yomiuri*, 16 August, p. 2.

—— (1993a) 'Quest for jobs sends migrants west', *The Daily Yomiuri*, 1 January, p. 3.

—— (1993b) 'Japanese courses for foreigners set', *The Daily Yomiuri*, 12 January, p. 2.

Fujisaki, Y. (1991) *Dekasegi Nikkei Gaikokujin Rōdosha* (Nikkeijin Migrant Workers), Tokyo: Akashi Shoten.

Fukuoka, Y. (1994) *Zainichi Kankoku Chōseniin* (Korean Permanent Residents in Japan) Chūkō Shinsho no. 1164, Tokyo: Chūōkōronsha.

Hamamatsu Local Government (1993) *Hamamatsu-shi ni okeru Gaikokujin no Seikatsu Jittai, Ishikichōsa* (An Investigation of the Actual Living Conditions of Foreign Residents in Hamamatsu City), Hamamatsu: International Exchange Group of the Planning Section of Hamamatsu Local Government.

Inagami, T., Kuwahara, Y. and Kokumin Kinyūkōko Sōgō Kenkyūjo (1992) *Gaikokujin Rōdōsha o Senryokukasuru Chūshōkigyō* (Small and Middle-sized Enterprises Using Foreign Migrant Workers), Tokyo: Chūshō Kigyō Research Centre.

Itō, R. (1992) 'Japayuki-san' Genshō Saikō (Re-examination of the Japayuki-san Phenomenon), in T. Iyotani and T. Kajita (eds) *Global Approach, Gaikokujin Rōdōsharon* (Global Approach, the Theories of Foreign Migrant Workers), Tokyo: Kōbundo.

Japan Immigration Association (1990) *A Guide to Entry, Residence and Registration Procedures in Japan for Foreign Nationals*, Tokyo: Nihon Kajoshuppan.

—— (1994a) 'Zairyū Gaikokujin notameno Sōdan, Annai' (Guidance and Advice for Foreign Residents), *Kokusai Jinryū*, January: 7–16.

—— (1994b) 'Ginō Jisshū Seidō no Jisshi Jōkyō' (The Current Situation of 'The Work Training Programme'), *Kokusai Jinryū* 7, 1: 32–4.

—— (1994c) 'Heisei 5 nen ni okeru Shutsunyūkokusha Tōkei – Gaikokujin oyobi Nihonjin' (The Number of Foreigners Admitted into Japan and the Number of Japanese Departed from Japan in 1993), *Kokusai Jinryū* 7, 5: 36–56.

——(1994d) 'Heisei 5 nen ni okeru Nyūkanhō Ihan Jiken' (The Number of Violation Cases Against the Immigration Control Law in 1993), *Kokusai Jinryū* 7, 7: 36–45.

—— (1994e) 'Heisei 5 nenmatsu genzai ni okeru Gaikokujin Tōrokusha Tōkei' (Foreign Residence Statistics for December 1993), *Kokusai Jinryū* 7, 10: 36–55.

—— (1994f) 'Honpō ni okeru Fuhō Zanryūshasū' (The Number of Over-stayers in Japan), *Kokusai Jinryū* 7, 10: 13–18.

—— (1995a) 'Nihongo Shūgakusei no Zairyū Jōkyō to Kongo no Ukeire Hōshin' (The Residential Situation of Pre-college Students Studying Japanese and the Governmental Policy with Regard to the Future Acceptance of Pre-college Students), *Kokusai Jinryū* 8, 2: 18–21.

—— (1995b) 'Heisei 6 nen ni okeru Shutsunyūkokusha Tōkei – Gaikokujin oyobi Nihonjin' (The Number of Foreigners Admitted into Japan and the Number of Japanese Departed from Japan in 1994), *Kokusai Jinryū* 8, 5: 38–42.

Kajita, T. (1994a) *Gaikokujin Rōdōsha to Nippon* (Foreign Migrant Workers and Japan), NHK Books 698, Tokyo: Nippon Hōsō Kyōkai Shuppan.

—— (1994b) 'A three-layered structure of foreigners in Japan – the challenge of incorporating long-term foreign residents in Japan', Conference paper prepared for Japan–US joint symposium regarding migrant workers in Japan held at MIT, Boston, US, 1995.

Kanagawa Zainichi Gaikokujin Mondai Kenkyūkai (1992) *Tabunka Taminzoku Shakai no Shinkō to Gaikokujin Ukeire no Genjō – Kanagawaken no Jirei ni sokushite* (The Movement Towards a Multi-cultural and Multi-racial Society and the Current Situation in Respect of the Acceptance of Foreigners – The Case of Kanagawa Prefecture), Kanagawa Prefecture: Kanagawa Prefectural Government Office.

Komai, H. (1993a) *Gaikokujin Rōdōsha Teijū e no Michi* (The Road to Permanent Residence by Foreign Workers), Tokyo: Akashi Shoten.

—— (1993b) 'Iminshakai no Iriguchi ni Tatte' (Standing at the Entrance to the Immigrants' Society), *Sekai* 580 (April): 185–99, Tokyo: Iwanami Shoten.

Kura, S. (1992) 'Gaikokujin Rōdōsha Jittai Chōsa Hōkokusho – Latin America' (An Investigative Report in Respect of the Situation of Foreign Migrant Workers – Latin America), pp. 246–69 in *Gaikokujin Rōdōsha no Shūrō Jittai* (The Real Employment Situation of Foreign Migrant Workers), Tokyo: Akashi Shoten.

Maeyama, T. (1990) 'Nikkeijin Gaikokujin Rōdōsha no sonogo' (The Situation of *Nikkeijin* Migrant Workers Since Entering Japan), pp. 4–5 in Japan Immigration Association (eds) *Kokusai Jinryū* 3, 7.

Mainichi Daily News (1992) 'Japan like blind date for Japanese-Brazilians', *Mainichi Daily News*, 11 July.

Miyajima, T. (1992) 'Gaikokujin Rōdōsha to Chiiki Shakai' (Foreign Migrant Workers and Local Society), in K. Tezuka *et al.* (eds) *Gaikokujin Rōdōsha to Jichitai* (Foreign Migrant Workers and Local Governments), Tokyo: Akashi Shoten.

Mori, H. (1995) 'Structural changes in Japan's labour market and its attraction of foreign migrant workers', *Journal of International Economic Studies* 9: 41–66 (Tokyo: The Institute of Comparative Economic Studies, Hōsei University).

Moriki, K. (1991) *Kokusai Kekkon Guide Book* (A Guide Book for International Marriage), Tokyo: Akashi Shoten.

Ōnuma, Y. (1993) *Tanitsu Minzoku Shakai no Shinwa o Koete* (Beyond the Myth of a Homogeneous Society), Tokyo: Tōshindō.

Sankei Shinbun (1994) 'Nikkeijin Dekasegisha no Sōkin, Nenkan 1940 Okuen ga Brazil ni Wataru' (Remittances from *Nikkeijin* Migrant Workers – ¥194 billion go to Brazil annually), *Sankei Shinbun*, 5 November, p. 8.

Sellek, Y. and Weiner, M.A. (1992) 'Migrant workers – the Japanese case in international perspective', in G.D. Hook and M.A. Weiner (eds) *The Internationalization of Japan*, London: Routledge.

Shizuoka Shinbun (1992) 'Buraziiru kara Nikkei-shin-shimin' (New Citizens from Brazil), *Shizuoka Shinbun*, 1 January, p. 30.

Stalker, P. (1994) *The Work of Strangers: A Survey of International Labour Migration*, Geneva: International Labour Office.

Suzuki, J. (1992) *Nihonjin Dekasegi Imin* (Japanese Emigrants), Tokyo: Heibonsha.

Tokyo Yomiuri Shinbun (1994a) 'Gaikokujin Iryōhi Taisaku, Zeishūgen ni Katezu Hoten Sakiokuri, Tokyoto' (Contribution Towards Medical Expense for Foreigners by the Tokyo Metropolitan Government: Compensation for Outstanding Medical Payments of Foreign Workers is Postponed Owing to a Decrease in Tax Revenue), *Tokyo Yomiuri Shinbun*, 14 January, p. 31.

—— (1994b) 'Gaikokujin Rōdōsha no Iryōhi Daiega Futan, Jichitai no Katagawari ya Kōseishō no Kikinkōsō mo Fuhatsu' (Who is Going to Carry the Burden of Medical Expense for Foreign Workers?: Neither Compensation by Local Governments nor a Plan to Establish a Compensatory Foundation by the Health and Welfare Ministry are Working), *Tokyo Yomiuri Shinbun*, 12 May, p. 3.

—— (1994c) 'Nikkeijin Shiendantai ga "Baratsuki Nyūkan" o Hihan, Ukeireta noni Musekinin' (Civil Groups Supporting *Nikkeijin* Criticize the Immigration Bureau for its Inconsistent Response and for not Showing any Sense of Responsibility, Even Though it Once Welcomed *Nikkeijin*), *Tokyo Yomiuri Shinbun*, 24 October, p. 15.

—— (1994d) 'Gaikokujin Rōdōsha ni mo Endaka no "Kage", Koyō, Seizōgyō de Rokugatsu genzai 7.3% Heru' (High Yen Hits Foreign Workers, too – June Figures Show 7.3% Fall in Manufacturing Industry and Employment), *Tokyo Yomiuri Shinbun*, 18 November, p. 2.

—— (1994e) 'Sashō, Hyōryū suru Nikkeijin' (Wandering *Nikkeijin*), *Tokyo Yomiuri Shinbun*, 24 November, p. 31.

—— (1995) 'Gaikokujin Rōdōsha, Usuragu Kanshin, Mondai wa Shinkokuka, Fueru Hanzai, Taizai Chōki ni' (A Lack of Concern Towards Foreign Workers – Problems Worsen, Crime Rises, More Stay Longer), *Tokyo Yomiuri Shinbun*, 21 February, p. 15.

Watkins, M. (1994) *Hikage no Nikkeijin* (The Troubles of the *Nikkei*), Tokyo: Sairyūsha.

Yamamoto, K. and Chiba, T. (1995) 'Job change of foreign workers in contemporary Japan – the case of Japanese Brazilians', *Journal of International Economic Studies* 9: 67–78.

Yamanaka, K. (1993) 'New immigration policy and unskilled foreign workers in Japan', *Pacific Affairs* 66, 1: 72–91.

Yoshimen, M. (1992) 'Nikkeijin no Wagakuni ni okeru Shūrō no Genjō to Taisaku' (The Employment Situation and Measures Relating to South American–Japanese Descendants), pp. 114–24 in *Kikan Rōdōhō* 164 (Tokyo: Sōgō Rōdō Kenkyūjo).

8 *Soto* Others and *uchi* Others

Imaging racial diversity, imagining homogeneous Japan[1]

Millie Creighton

INTRODUCTION

In a recent essay on Asian American history and experience, Gary Okihiro (Okihiro 1994) asks the provocative question, 'Is yellow black or white?' The question reveals the persistent racial conceptualizations underlying ideas of mainstream and minorities in American society. These racial constructs are, of course, not so much biological as social categories. As Blauner points out, 'Physical anthropologists who study the distribution of those characteristics we use to classify "races" teach us that race is a fiction because all peoples are mixed to various degrees' (Blauner 1994: 24; see also van den Berghe 1978: 9 and Essed 1991: 43). Although a biological fiction, these racial categories have sociological reality. As constructed concepts they tend to be collapsed categories. What, in US society for example, appears to be a simplistic false colour trichotomy – white, yellow, black – into which everyone can presumably be somehow made to fit, is an even more simplistic colour dichotomy where life is either black or white, while yellow mediates the spaces in between (and Native Peoples tend to be dismissed, rendered invisible and unheard). Blauner shows that American consciousness of race is more powerful than class or ethnicity, and that it tends to be defined 'along the black–white dimension' (Blauner 1994: 24).[2]

These race-designating colours are more than social categories. They are also symbolic spaces where individuals inhabiting the landscape of America's cultural pluralism are located. Okihiro answers his question by asserting that yellow is neither black nor white, but also by suggesting that even though assimilation practices and stereotypes of the 'model minority' have allowed Asian Americans to become wealthy and bright, almost white, they occupy a symbolic space closer to American Blacks given their historical experiences of racial discrimination and ongoing struggles against white hegemony.

This chapter looks at the images surrounding racial categories projected in Japan, particularly through advertisements. These images are part of the process through which Japaneseness is constructed as normative, in contrast to foreigners who represent universal 'Otherness'. The imagination of Japaneseness is strongly tied to notions of *uchi* and *soto*, inside and outside. *Uchi* defines the boundary of an inside group or space; that is, a primary locus of membership and belongingness. Although interacting networks of relationships in Japan are also conceptualized in *uchi/soto* terms, such that the indexical framework of *uchi* and *soto* is situational and shifting, there is a general sense that all of Japan creates an *uchi*, a national inside boundary of affiliation, in contrast to everything that is *soto* or outside of Japan (see Bachnik and Quinn 1994; White 1988). Foreigners reaffirm the *uchi/soto* dialectics that are one foundation of Japanese identity because they embody *soto*. The Japanese word, most commonly translated as 'foreigner', is *gaijin*, which literally means 'outside person'. The first ideograph in the word is also read *soto*. A foreigner is an outside person, a *soto* Other.

The Otherness of foreigners, however, has multiple loci. Definitions of these *soto* Others, or 'outside Others', is often differentiated along sociological categories of race, conforming to the white, yellow, black continuum. Although the word *gaijin* can be applied to any non-Japanese person it is most commonly only used for white foreigners, who are conceptualized as 'pure *gaijin*', or 'true *gaijin*' (Creighton 1994: 233). Research by Manabe *et al.* (1989) reveals that Japanese tend to use the word *gaijin* only for Whites, while the term *gaikokujin* (person from an outside country) is used for Blacks and non-Japanese Asians. Blacks are also called *kokujin*, while other Asians are called *Ajiajin*, or referred to by the country of their origin (i.e *Chūgokujin* for a Chinese person).

Images of foreigners are prevalent in Japanese advertising. By providing an oppositional contrast, these images help construct and perpetuate an imagined Japanese self-identity. In a semiotic analysis of advertising images, Williamson claims that advertisements 'are selling us something else besides consumer goods: in providing us with a structure in which we, and those goods are interchangeable they are selling us ourselves' (Williamson 1978: 13). I would add that by providing representations of 'not us' advertising images also create and sell Otherness. In Japan, this creation and representation of Otherness is a large part of the construction of Japanese self-identity. Roy

Andrew Miller asserts that 'any facet of Japanese life or culture is thrown into sharp relief when it is brought into direct confrontation with a similar or parallel foreign phenomenon' (Miller 1977: 77). Images of foreigners in Japanese advertising function to underscore Japanese identity by visual citations of what Japan and Japanese are not. The Japanese self is thus created in juxtaposition with *soto* Others.

The imaging of foreigners and the corresponding, highly managed, imagining of the Japanese cultural self has implications for Japan's minorities. I speak of the Japanese as imagining 'self' in the singular for a reason. It is likely that for human individuals there is no unitary self, but a harmony of selves. As Fitzgerald explains, 'There is no *one* self, only a cluster of *many selves*, both culturally and situationally specific' (Fitzgerald 1993: 34; see also Spinelli 1989). It is in this sense that Kondo (1990) refers to the Japanese in the work communities she studied as 'crafting selves'. I agree with Kondo that Japanese personhood is multiple and complex. However, I use the word 'self' to underline that the imagination of a national Japanese identity has emphasized, indeed insisted upon, a homogeneous, unified self. Gordon asserts that, 'the concept of Japan as a homogeneous and cohesive middle-class society was a powerful ideological force in postwar history' (Gordon 1993: 461). This powerful ideological force has been capable of denying the realities of those on the margins, Japan's minorities, including Burakumin, Okinawans, resident Koreans, indigenous Ainu. Gordon adds that the 'imagery or ideology of the inclusive harmonious society was amplified in the face of persisting difference', while mass-culture industries helped manage 'the way individuals could imagine their society' (Gordon 1993: 462).

The imagination of Japan as a homogeneous society despite enduring difference and the presence of minorities was accomplished in part through the transposition of difference (Kelly 1993). To explain this transposition of difference, Kelly utilizes Dale's concept of 'cultural exorcism' (Dale 1986: 40) by which 'internal tensions are projected onto an external and inauthentic Other' (Kelly 1993: 194). The prevalent image statements surrounding foreigners in Japanese advertisements serve not only to define Japanese identity traits, but ultimately to project heterogeneity onto the outside world, reaffirming Japan's self-assertion of homogeneity, while symbolically negating diversity within Japanese society (Creighton 1995a: 155).

Japan's self-assertion of an imagined homogeneous self, maintains its minorities in a living contradiction. While denying these people exist as minorities, since they have supposedly been incorporated into Japan's harmonious and all-encompassing 'middle-mass', they are not granted social equality, and are strongly discriminated against by many mainstream Japanese individuals, institutions, and social structures. They exist within Japan's borders as *uchi* Others, 'inside Others'. Ironically, although their existence as specific minority groups is denied in the imagination of homogeneity, like foreigners, they also serve as a contrasting Other in opposition to which mainstream Japanese identity is constructed; where foreigners represent 'not us', minorities are 'not quite us' (Harrell 1995: 28). Japan's minorities cannot for the most part be defined according to 'race' categories. However, I discuss the possibility that majority and minority groups in Japan occupy analogous *symbolic spaces* of yellow, black and white in the Japanese mindscape. I also suggest that there is a linked association of *soto* Others and *uchi* Others such that Japan's modern goal of 'internationalization' which has prompted Japan to reconsider its images of *soto* Others (foreigners), may also be prompting greater reflexivity about *uchi* Others (Japan's minorities).

MOOD ADVERTISING: FANTASY AND FOREIGNERS

Japanese advertisements, like the advertising catalogues analysed by James Carrier, are 'collections of images that professional image-makers have found to appeal to people' (Carrier 1990: 702). Japanese advertisements do not emphasize providing information about products, but instead have an essentially symbolic focus. Images of foreigners appeal to Japanese interest in foreign people and foreign places, but they also fit into the Japanese advertising industry's offerings of 'fantasy excursions'. Many Japanese advertisements contain little information about products or persuasive arguments, providing instead pleasant or unusual imagery and playful excursions into a fantasy world. Images of foreigners become fantasy vignettes, representations of exoticism, visual quotations of Otherness, while foreigners are rendered *misemono*, things to look at, and not quite real.

Japanese advertising has been characterized as 'mood advertising' since it does not attempt to explain much about the products being sold, or position them as superior to competitors. Instead, it predominantly attempts to communicate a special mood or elicit a particular emotional response. Advertising that focuses on images rather than informational content is not unique to Japan, but such advertising tends to be overwhelmingly abundant in Japan. There are commercial and economic reasons for the abundance of mood advertising which cultural predispositions strengthen. Competition is in conflict with espoused Japanese social values, and advertising is a means of competition. Although competition does exist in Japan, overt expressions of competition should be avoided. Thus advertisers are left in an enigmatic position; they must compete without appearing to be overtly competitive. Cultural expectations of humility, or at least the outward expression of humility, create another problem. Advertisements that extol the virtues of items being sold, or that even provide extensive information about them, violate expectations of formalized humility. This creates a second contradiction for advertisers: how to brag about products while appearing humble.

To circumvent these conventions, fantasy vignettes and startling visual imagery, often divorced from any logical association with the product being sold, have come to dominate the Japanese commercial advertising industry. At the heart of this industry is what has been designated in Japan as the *'no miiningu ado'* (no meaning ad). People I interviewed in the advertising industry frequently referred to the 'no meaning ad' as a partial explanation for the prevalent images of foreigners. A creative director from Dentsu,[3] now the world's largest advertising agency, explains:

> Japanese commercials and advertisements are not really trying to be realistic like Western ones; instead they are more image-provoking. It does not seem strange to have so many foreigners, because the goal is just to create a nice or different feeling. It is all part of the advertisement's goal to build a dream world. . . . In order to capture the market you need to create a different image, a better fantasy feeling.

The idea that images of foreigners are used to create fantasy moods is also emphasized by a section chief at the Osaka Yomiuri Advertising Agency:

> Japanese advertisements are not so realistic. . . . Instead they create a mood. Something is wanted to help create that mood, or a fantasy feeling. Pictures of foreigners and foreign places help create this.

As foreigners are transformed into images of fantasy and exoticism, they are rendered *misemono*, spectacles, or 'things to look at'. Although this is true to some extent with the imaging of foreigners generally, significant differences occur in the representations of Whites, Blacks, and other Asians.

'IT'S A WHITE WORLD'

Throughout Japanese cultural history foreigners have been accorded a dual nature, as bearers of highly valued innovation and style and as an intrusive threat (Ohnuki-Tierney 1987: 145). From the Meiji era (1868–1912) on, white Westerners became the foremost outsiders in relation to whom the Japanese dialectically defined self. The Meiji era, which marked Japan's reopening to the outside world after two and a half centuries of self-enforced isolation, was characterized by intense curiosity about the West combined with a strong consciousness of Western power, technological expertise and economic dominance. From the beginning of Japan's modern history the white Western world thus became the model to emulate, the standard by which to gauge Japan's progress and modernization. The impact of these economic, political, and historical processes is recognized by those in Japan's modern advertising industry. A creative director at Dentsu explains the extensive imagery of white Westerners this way:

> Another reason for the abundance of *gaijin* is that for a long part of Japanese history, from Meiji at least, we have always been looking at Western countries as progressive ones. These were places that Japan had to catch up with. From this there developed sort of a complex – 'it's a white world'.

Whites have also become a standard of beauty. The shift from kimono as everyday clothing to *yōfuku*, or 'Western-style clothing', accentuated this. Japanese people accepted the idea that 'Western-style clothing', because it originated abroad, would be better suited to Western body types. Therefore it was consistent with popular expectations for fashion and beauty products to portray foreigners in these advertisements.

If white Westerners became a standard of progress and beauty since Meiji, the popular culture of post-war Japan reinforced this. The American occupation of Japan brought with it American popular and consumer culture. In the early post-war period the prominence of American-made movies created the feeling that seeing white imagery in such media was *atarimae*, 'natural'. Average households began to obtain television sets during or soon after the American occupation in the 1950s. Many early television programmes were either dubbed or side-titled American productions involving white middle-class Americans. This reinforced the feeling that images of Whites on screen was 'natural'. These conditions persisted long after the occupation because of the continuing international economic and political dominance of Western countries, in particular the United States. *Gaijin* became not all or any foreigners, but an essentialized projection of white Westerners. Images of foreigners in advertising also involved a sexual projection of the Other, particularly the allure of the white woman.

A combination of this projected sexual allure and the rendering of foreigners as 'unreal' accounts for the frequent use of nudity in advertising imagery of foreigners. A few examples of such advertisements should suffice. An advertisement for the Japanese wedding hall, 'Marriage', depicts a white woman standing in the rounded doorway of a white wall. Her long blondish-white curly hair drapes to one side providing some minimal coverage. A white cloth is draped around her body from the waist down. While she is naked from the waist up, her arms cross her breasts slightly, so that her nipples are concealed even though most of her breasts are visible. The advertisement's imagery repeatedly merges the themes of whiteness, nudity, sexuality. In a jewellery commercial a white woman, naked except for her jewels, plays in a fountain with her back to viewers. She does not remain motionless, but turns back and forth in her play, often coming tantalizingly close to a full frontal view. Parco, a prominent retailing chain, featured a frontal view, from below the navel up, of a white woman standing naked for one of its theme campaigns. In contrast to the above two advertisements, there was no attempt to mask or subvert her nudity in any way – she simply stands completely naked before a viewing public. In an earlier Parco theme campaign a white female American celebrity, clothed in white, slowly peels an egg next to two bare-chested pre-pubescent girls.

Such nude representations of white foreigners are common in advertisements for products and services where naked presentations of Japanese would be considered inappropriate. It is true that naked presentations of Japanese, particularly Japanese women, appear on late-night television broadcasts defined as erotic viewing, in *manga* ('comic books'), and in advertisements for products and services defined as part of the sex trade. However, naked presentations of Japanese for everyday, mainstream products and businesses – such as a major retailing store chain – are uncommon, whereas nude depictions of Whites for these are commonplace. Commenting on the prevalence of naked or near-naked white women in advertisements, a member of Osaka Dentsu's advertising branch says, 'advertisements can't use Japanese women for such nude scenes because it is too realistic, so *gaijin* are used'. Colonialism has involved the white gaze viewing the bare-breasted women of societies lower down the political and economic hierarchy. Modern Japanese advertising inverts this hierarchy and shifts the gaze; now it is bare-breasted white women on view for an economically advanced Japanese consuming public. The white male body is similarly used to image sensuality. For example, a Zephyr lotion commercial highlighted the heavily muscled and sweat-glistening torso of a white male (Abe and Yamakawa 1990: 166).

In addition to providing a fantasy mood and exotic sexuality, images of foreigners are used to break Japanese social conventions. For example, images of white foreigners are consciously used by advertisers to portray romance while evading a long-standing cultural expectation of public restraint in such matters. A creative director for Dentsu confirmed that:

> There are a lot of love scenes in ads – like kissing. In Japan for a long time there has been an idea that kissing, even holding hands, is something that people shouldn't do in public. But having *gaijin* kiss is one way to portray romance, and it's OK, because, after all, they are *gaijin*.[4]

Japanese society has extensive concepts of classificatory status (Lebra 1976) involving expectations for appropriate forms of dress depending on gender, age, and social rank. Red is considered a colour for little girls but too bright and conspicuous for adult women. White models are frequently presented in red dresses or outfits to circumvent this convention in the fashion industry.

In contrast to Japanese expectations of *enryō* (restraint), including good grooming and controlled body posturing, *gaijin* are much more likely to be shown with free body posturing, or with hair and clothes in total disarray. One advertisement for an English school shows young white teachers in dishevelled clothing, laughing uproariously, with bodies sprawled across a park bench. In the 1990s humorous, and somewhat patronizing, portrayals of Arnold Schwarzenegger swinging kettles and punching dough while buried in flour for *ramen* commercials became a common sight.

Images of white foreigners also provide a safer means to express selfish sentiments in a culture that has long disapproved of *wagamama*, or self-centred, concerns. This can be related to the prevalent use of the English word 'my' in advertising, and Japanese product names rather than the Japanese equivalents *watakushi no, watashi no*, or *boku no*. Advertisements and products frequently refer to 'my car', 'my jeans', 'my home', 'my trip', 'my peanut butter', and 'my toilet paper'. Applbaum argues that the proliferation of the English 'my' in such usages reflects greater exposure to Western values that are 'in marked contrast with the earlier generation's critical attitude towards individualism' (Applbaum 1992: 24). I argue instead that what is most important is the code-switching from Japanese into English to make such individualistic assertions. By switching to the English 'my', egoism and individualism persist as foreign projections, while core values of conformity, collectivism, and self-abnegation remain intact. In September 1990, the autumn theme poster for My City, a large retailing complex (and itself another example of the use of 'my') in the central Shinjuku district of Tokyo, did use the Japanese word *watashi*. However, this self-centred assertion was made by the white female depicted, not by a Japanese. The substitution of Whites for Japanese represents a form of visual code-switching, similar to code-switching in language use.

Another example of this visual code-switching is an advertising campaign conducted by Lotteria, a fast-food chain. In the theme campaign promoting Lotteria's new Kaiser Sandwich, a white woman appears, exclaiming, *'Suki na mono shika, tabetakunai'* ('I don't want to eat anything that I don't like'). A Japanese person may frequently wish to express such sentiments, but Japanese values define such an assertion as overtly egoistic, ungrateful, and immature. Kondo explains the expected Japanese cultural attitude towards food as she learned it at an ethics retreat:

> Even our food held a lesson for us. . . . Cleaning our plates, even if we didn't like what was served, would prevent selfishness and lead to a grateful, gentle heart. Giving in to likes and dislikes, on the other hand, was the beginning of selfish, egocentric behavior.
>
> (Kondo 1990: 91–2)

In all of these examples, images of white foreigners are used to break with Japanese social conventions. They allow the expression of sentiments, or posturing, once avoided but at the same time they reinforce concepts of Japanese identity by oppositional statements of what Japanese identity is not. *Gaijin* are also frequently shown pursuing 'traditional' Japanese arts or habits, but are often presented as somehow inept at these pursuits. In the 1980s Woody Allen appeared wearing a kimono and wielding a calligraphy brush in Seibu Department Store's *'Oishii Seikatsu'* (Delicious Life) campaign (Nishioka

1989: 131). 'Delicious Life' combines two words, not normally put together in Japanese, to break with conventional language use, providing an interesting, catchy idea which captured the public imagination. However, the advertisements played on the additional incongruity of the clumsy white foreigner inept at a traditional Japanese pursuit.

A shift has occurred in recent advertisements, whereby white foreigners, once the standard of what Japanese wanted to become, are now used to highlight the economic dominance and world prominence of Japan. A Japanese report on advertising suggests that 'desire requires something unreachable' (*'akogare ni wa kyori ga hitsuyō'*), and Japanese are beginning to feel that they have not only caught up with Westerners, but have surpassed them. A resulting trend is commercials making fun of white foreigners (*Asahi Shinbun*, 2 June 1990). If for decades advertisements reflected a *'gaijin* complex' that 'it's a white world', with Japan's new assurance in its own cultural identity and world prominence, images of the white Other are now used to suggest that maybe it is, or should be, a Japanese world after all. Several recent commercials make fun of beautiful and elegantly dressed white women trying to tell jokes in Japanese but stumbling inadequately with the language. A commercial for the Osaka Keihin shopping mall shows a white foreigner repeating the statement, 'I can't keep up with the Japanese' (*Asahi Shinbun*, 2 June 1990).

An advertisement by the National Rice Council is another example of the use of *gaijin* to assert the centrality and merit of Japaneseness. According to this advertisement it is no longer the Japanese trying to 'catch up' with the West. Instead a white businessman in Japan is trying to determine why the Japanese are the front runners. The white businessman sits, holding a bowl of rice in his hands, and says to himself, 'I wonder what makes Japanese business so successful. It must be the rice they eat' (Ashkenazi 1993: 168). In order to understand the impact of this advertisement fully, it is important to realize that rice is both a metaphor and metonym for the collective Japanese self. It is not just any rice, but short-grained Japanese rice (in contrast to other long-grain forms of Asian rice or rice grown in Western countries) that serves as a dominant symbol of Japanese identity. Ohnuki-Tierney claims that as a metaphor of identity, Japanese rice suggests purity, asserts a 'natural' link between the Japanese and their land, and reaffirms a Japanese myth of cultural homogeneity (Ohnuki-Tierney 1993).

As these examples suggest, the imagery of white foreigners in Japanese advertising is twofold. For a long time they have been objects of glorified attention, symbols of progress and beauty, but have also been used to show traits considered negative by Japanese values. Projections of their awkwardness with Japanese customs, or in using the Japanese language, reinforce a sense that there is something about these cultural identity markers that is solely for the Japanese. In recent advertisements there is a new trend towards ridiculing Whites and having them proclaim the cultural superiority of the Japanese. This suggests a shift from the idea that 'it's a white world' to Japan's assurance of its own place alongside other industrialized Western countries. It also suggests the possibility that mainstream Japanese have moved into the *symbolic space* of 'white', the cognitive space of prominence and ascendancy.

IMAGING THE BLACK OTHER

In his analysis of the social perception of skin colour in Japan, Wagatsuma (1967) points out that Japanese have long associated the colour 'white' with purity and positive traits, while 'black' has symbolized that which is ugly and impure. He gives examples to show how this colour symbolism has through time led to an association of white skin with motherhood, spiritual purity, beauty, refinement, advanced civilization, economic wealth, and urban life, and of black skin with dirt, impurity, ugliness, poverty, debasement, animality, and lower-class rural life. As one Japanese respondent explained:

> When something becomes dirty and smeared, it gets black. White skin in our minds symbolizes purity and cleanliness. Then by an association, black skin is the opposite of purity and cleanliness. . . . Black skin after all suggests something unclean. It is not the natural state of things.
>
> (Wagatsuma 1967: 431)

This symbolism might help account for the problematic representations of Blacks in modern Japanese advertising. Images of Blacks tend to be highly caricatured, comic, low-class or foolish figures. Depictions of Blacks are few relative to Whites. This is often attributed in the industry to a ranked association of racial groups in which Blacks are looked down upon. An interesting distinction between the use of Whites and Blacks in advertising imagery is that Whites appear in large numbers and can either be so-called *tarento* ('talents'), who are famous celebrities, or anonymous 'nobodies'; usually for

Blacks to be featured they must be famous. Featured black *tarento* (including Sammy Davis, Jr., Carl Lewis, Whitney Houston) are nearly always famous athletes, singers, or performers. Although representations of famous Blacks are often positive, or at least not degrading, they do not help the Japanese conceptualize dignified adult Blacks in other occupations or forms of human endeavour.

Most Japanese have had little actual exposure to, or experience with, Blacks; their encounters with Blacks have mostly been through stereotyped imagery. A cartoon called 'Adventurous Dankichi', serialized for many years in a children's magazine in the 1920s and 1930s, provided such imagery. Dankichi was a Japanese boy who fell asleep on a fishing outing and drifted to the South Pacific. Through his cleverness, he continually outwits the black natives of this island and eventually becomes their king. After this he commands his black servants, while wearing a crown and majestically riding a white elephant (Wagatsuma 1967: 433; Russell 1991a: 87). From 1958 to 1960 Japan was rocked by a *Dakko-chan* doll fad. *Dakko-chan* was a highly caricatured jet black figure with big eyes and huge red lips, sold with a pole. When inflated, *Dakko-chan*'s arms extended in such a way that, with prompting, the figure would scurry up the pole. *Dakko-chan* became Japan's top-selling toy and a common household item in its first year. Takara, the manufacturer, made the *Dakko-chan* image its corporate logo; a logo which was only dropped, under pressure, in the 1980s. However, the Japanese continue to buy 100,000 *Dakko-chan* dolls a year (Jones 1988).

In the mid-1980s, *Chibikuro Sanbo* (Little Black Sambo) dolls produced by the Japanese toy company Sanrio, became a huge fad. The dolls were manufactured even though scholars and human rights activists outside Japan had long complained about the dehumanization of Blacks through the Sambo archetype (Lyman 1994: 161–3). The Japanese doll version of the Sambo family included Sambo, Hanna and Bibinba, all wide-eyed, large-lipped characters who were depicted as silly, clumsy, foolish, and uneducated.[5] For example, a Sambo image on products such as T-shirts proclaimed, 'When I'm hungry there's no stoppin' me, I'll be up in a palm pickin' coconuts before you can count to three. An' I can count way past three, too!' (Shapiro 1988). After criticism of these products appeared, the manufacturers defended them, saying they were 'humorous' and 'friendly' and that therefore Japanese children who wore the T-shirts or played with the dolls would 'not grow up to be racists'. After continued public outcry, mostly from non-Japanese, the dolls were finally removed from the market.

Another controversy arose over a line of black mannequins featured at Sogo Department Store, which were also caricatured large forms, with crossed eyes and large lips. A Foreign Ministry representative, Okamoto Yukio, admitted that the mannequins were 'disgusting and offensive', but he defended the suppliers and the store by saying there was no intention of racism. This defence fails to recognize that discrimination includes acts with intended or unintended negative consequences for a group. As Essed states, 'It is important to see that intentionality is not a necessary component of racism' (Essed 1991: 45).

There was also a debate surrounding the trademark character used for years by the Japanese drink Calpis (*Carupisu*). This trademark character was a stereotyped image of a black man, with large lips, dressed in hillbilly clothing and a straw hat. He was shown consuming the white drink, accompanied by the phrase '*hatsu koi no aji*' ('the taste of first love'). Echoing the Foreign Ministry official referred to above, an employee of Japan's largest advertising agency whom I interviewed claimed there was no racist intent behind any of these images, but that the problem stemmed from Japanese lack of experience with racial diversity. He did, however, acknowledge that:

> There is a long way to go before most people have direct experience of Whites. Right now they are still just '*misemono*', a curiosity. Something to be seen. Japanese have had even less experience with Blacks and are even less likely to understand them. I think there is no desire to be discriminatory. It is just not understood that such problems arise. I think we must take greater care with these things.

These controversies over images of Blacks in advertising and on commercial products occurred around the time of then Prime Minister Nakasone's infamous *faux pas* against American minorities. Nakasone stated that the average Japanese IQ was higher than that of Americans, attributing this partly to the presence of Blacks and other American minorities pulling down the general IQ level. The remarks were racist and were soundly criticized as such by foreigners, including both black and white Americans. However, such remarks do not necessarily indicate that the Japanese are more racist than people in other societies even if there is less caution in expressing such attitudes. Pettigrew contends that one of the major components of modern racism is its subtle and indirect expression (Pettigrew 1994), whereby many people, instead of learning not to be prejudiced, have learned to mask any direct expression of such prejudice in keeping with contemporary social norms. What was frequently over-looked in Nakasone's statement was that it also served, again, to project heterogeneity and the existence of minorities outward, to American society, while re-asserting that Japan was a homogeneous society with no minorities, and further surrounding this assumed homogeneity with value.

Despite the loud criticism aimed at the Japanese because of the racism and discriminatory nature of these representations, the white Western world shares the blame for helping to create demeaning stereotypes of Blacks in Japan. When Japan was first re-opened to the outside world by Commodore Perry in 1854, it was also intro-duced to the Western world's comic use of black representations by Perry's crew who, with blackened faces, produced a minstrel show for their Japanese hosts. The first Japanese diplomatic envoy to the United States in 1860 encountered the clear hierarchical separation of Whites and Blacks. Since southern Blacks were slaves at that time, the Japanese concluded that they must be the American ana-logue to Japan's Eta, or untouchable class (Thorton 1989). Since this is the group from which one of Japan's minorities, Burakumin, are descended, it created the symbolic association of Blacks with Burakumin. Many Japanese have gained their only understanding of Blacks through literature produced by Whites, or popular foreign films.[6] Goosen explains how such films create or reinforce racial stereotypes in Japan:

> [T]he economic and cultural dynamism of the American monolith has projected 'domestic' stereotypes about Blacks into the outside world, where they have taken on a life of their own. To watch the film version of Margaret Mitchell's undying epic *Gone With the Wind* in a Tokyo theatre, for example, is to witness the subtle reinforcements of a whole set of stereotypes about Blacks in an audience most of whose members have likely never talked to a Black in their lives.
>
> (Goosen 1989: 138)

In the 1980s a collection of racial jokes degrading Blacks was written and published in Japan by a well-known white person who was the host of a television English education programme. The book, *It's Only a Joke* (Spector 1984), which the foreword justified as an affirmation of the tradition of ethnic humour, was sold to Japanese as an educational guide to the study of English. Japanese continue to learn other racial stereotypes from white Westerners, based on images they bring to Japan which are often no longer tolerated in their home countries. In 1985, a voice command computer was displayed at the American pavilion at Expo '85, an international fair held in Tsukuba, Japan. The computer system and software program, designed by Texas Instruments, presented five American scenes which fair visitors could colour-in by voice command. The scene of Texas showed a broad stately man wearing a large cowboy hat and riding a horse, about to lasso the scrawny, slouching figures of two half-naked native Americans. Nearly all Japanese fair visitors had learned their lesson well; they coloured the cringing looking natives red, and the stately cowboy on the horse white.

Like images of Whites, images of Blacks in Japanese advertising seldom allow Japanese to have a greater understanding of black culture or individual Blacks; they too are rendered 'not really real'. However, in contrast to the frequent glorified projections of Whites, Blacks tend to be either denigrated as inferior and low class, or seen as comic, foolish and clumsy. Like Nakasone's comments, which more than anything else suggested that America's problems resulted from its homogeneity, these negative depictions of Blacks reinforce a belief in the value of Japan's presumed homogeneity.

OTHER ASIANS/THE ASIAN OTHER

In discussing Japanese identity in relation to both other Asians and Western societies, Wagatsuma writes:

> It remains a curious fact of Japanese identity that there is relatively little kinship expressed with any Asian countries other than China, toward which present-day Japan feels less and less cultural debt. Japanese eyes, despite cases of plastic surgery, may keep their Oriental look, but through these eyes Japanese see themselves as part of the modern Western world conceptualized in Western terms.
>
> (Wagatsuma 1967: 435)

In keeping with these suggested attitudes, depictions of non-Japanese Asians in advertising are rare in contrast to the prevalence of white imagery. Other Asians are not considered similar enough to spark a kindred identity, nor distant enough to provide an appropriate contrasting Other. The marginality of other Asians makes them problematic and contributes to a Japanese tendency to look down on them. A Japanese researcher explains it this way:

I think there are not so many advertisements with other Asians. The idea of imitating other Asian peoples does not appeal to the Japanese so much. In truth there is still much discrimination against these people and Japanese look down on them. I myself do not understand this, why Japanese tend to discriminate or look down on other Asians like ourselves. But still, it is true.

Other Asians do appear in advertisements for designated ethnic products, such as speciality Chinese foods, or for cleaning products, suggesting stereotyped labour roles. A CM (commercial) creator for Dentsu indirectly suggests that in these cases non-Japanese Asians are stereotyped into lower-class positions or roles:

There are almost no Asians in advertisements. Maybe for things like Duskin, which are cleaning agents or cleaning products. Things conceptualized as not clean work.

Presentations of foreign scenery also illustrate this diminished interest in other Asian countries. Japanese advertisements respond to the public interest created by particular events, and the Olympics is a notable example. In most cases the host country of the Olympics, rather than the Olympics itself, becomes a featured focus of advertisements. For example, commercials featured scenery of Spain for two years preceding the 1992 Barcelona Olympics. Department stores hosted exhibits of Spanish artists and architects, while the travel industry promoted Barcelona and other Spanish areas as vacation destinations. The situation was notably different for the 1988 Olympics held in Seoul. When I asked people in the industry whether the 1988 Olympics coincided with a similar increased interest in Korea, I got responses such as, 'No, it didn't happen at all', and 'There was no Korea boom at all'. The rare commercials invoking Olympic symbolism that year tended to ignore the host-country location. One commercial showed legs of unidentified runners racing around a track, highlighting an association with the Olympics as an event, but removing it from any association with its location that year in Korea.

JAPAN'S MINORITIES AND THE SYMBOLIC SPACES OF WHITE, BLACK, YELLOW

This review of advertising images of foreigners has suggested that mass culture industries, like other aspects of Japanese society, have helped manage how Japanese imagine national identity, by projecting heterogeneity, in part represented by racial differences, onto an out-side world. Since racial categories are often associated with ideas of 'minorities' this in turn helped project the existence of minorities to an outside world, reinforcing the self-construction of Japan as a homogeneous society. Japan has on occasion more boldly denied the existence of minorities within its borders. The Japanese government's response to the United Nations' call for the elimination of discrimi-nation against minorities was an official statement that no minorities exist in Japan and that therefore there is no discrimination against minorities in Japan. (The statement added that Japan believed minor-ity groups should not be discriminated against in those countries where they did exist.) The pretence of homogeneity is bolstered by the circumstance that minority groups are not differentiated from the Japanese mainstream by 'race'. (The only possible exception to this are the indigenous Ainu. According to some theories this indi-genous people were also originally of Asian background, but other theories suggest they originally came from Siberia and were of Caucasian extraction.) Since minorities often deny their own status, and attempt 'passing' as mainstream Japanese, population figures are difficult to verify, but include about 600,000 resident Koreans, 50,000 resident Chinese and Taiwanese, 50–60,000 Ainu, over 1 million Burakumin who are descendants of the earlier Eta-Hinin outcasts, and over 1 million Okinawans. In total, these comprise about 3 mil-lion people belonging to Japan's 'non-existent' minorities (Thomas 1989: 224).

Despite the denial of diversity and the assertion that these groups have been assimilated, they are *uchi* Others. Even if members of these groups wish to 'pass' as mainstream Japanese it is not easy to do so, and the psychological costs are high. Discrimination against these groups remains strong, along with persistent mainstream Japanese attitudes that define these people as different, and usually inferior. Japan's minorities, which not only exist but have never been rendered fully 'invisible' (DeVos and Wagatsuma 1966), are not defined along conventional colour lines, but it is possible to sug-gest that white and black and yellow are present in Japanese society as symbolic spaces marking the cognitive boundaries dividing Japan's mainstream and marginals.

The earlier quote from Wagatsuma (p. 225) indicates that the Japanese have for some time seen themselves not as orientals, but as part of the Western world in Western terms. However, the feeling that the white Western world embodied a symbol of progress and advancement, a state to which Japan aspired but had not yet attained, created a gulf between Japanese and white Westerners. With the post-war attainment of fully modernized nation status, a high level of economic affluence and some of the world's most efficiently run business institutions, mainstream Japanese have entered the symbolic space of 'white', a space suggesting privilege, economic and political prominence, and cultural dominance. This transition has even on occasion been officially recognized by white governments, such as when the apartheid government of South Africa designated Japanese honorary Whites. Japanese self-projections sometimes suggest this transition as well, imaging mainstream Japanese as white. One example is a Japanese newspaper article that warns Japanese travellers about problems they might encounter abroad because of their ignorance regarding interracial issues. In the article a cartoon illustration depicts the experience of a young Japanese woman studying in the United States who was stopped on an American street by two black men irritated by the Sambo representations on her clothing. Although it is the Japanese woman who is wearing the objectionable images, the cartoon perpetuates stereotypes by posing the black men as hostile, threatening and frightening. What is most interesting about the cartoon, however, is that the young Japanese woman is depicted with stereotypical white features and hair colouring (Russell 1991a: 100).

In contrast to the above, there are ways in which Okinawans and Burakumin are assigned to the symbolic space of black. In suggesting that Okinawans are symbolically equated with black, Wagatsuma points out that according to Japanese colour symbolism the white/black opposition also correlates with the conceptual oppositions of urban/rural, core/periphery, higher economic status/lower economic status. Mainstream Japanese are thus more likely to occupy the valued symbolic space of white associated with urban core centres and higher economic well-being. Okinawans, living at a distance from the four main islands of the Japanese archipelago, and generally having a lower economic status, are Japanese citizens but excluded from a mainstream Japanese identity. It has been suggested that Okinawans internalized this assigned identity, and experienced skin colour accordingly. Wagatsuma cites a Japanese social psychologist who believed that 'many Okinawans become self-conscious of their "black" skin when they meet Japanese from Japan. To Okinawan eyes, the Japanese appear to have "whiter" skin' (Wagatsuma 1967: 418–19). Since Wagatsuma conducted this research minority groups, including Okinawans, have attempted to recapture a positive identity based on their own heritage, and fewer would hold these conceptions than twenty to thirty years ago. By contrast, mainstream attitudes towards them have not changed to the same extent.

The Burakumin have also developed a new, positive self-awareness, and no longer define themselves as inferior. However, the majority society still defines them in an inferior position. According to Donoghue the Burakumin reflect 'the persistence throughout a long history of a class of people considered "base" or "defiled"' (Donoghue 1978: 107). They occupy a black symbolic space defined by the correlating oppositions of white and black with purity and impurity. In this instance social psychological factors maintain the division between mainstream and marginal. The white space of superiority, ritual righteousness and cleanliness is occupied by mainstream Japanese, while Burakumin are assigned to the black space of inferiority, defilement and impurity.

In the summer of 1994, while conducting field research among the Ainu, I also accompanied a group of Burakumin on a bus tour through Hokkaidō. This group consisted of high-school and first-year university students who were involved in an ongoing discussion group about Burakumin issues, and three members of the city office (two of whom were Burakumin and one mainstream Japanese) who worked with the youth group. They were travelling through Hokkaidō meeting with Ainu, in attempts to mutually explore their positions and identities as minorities in Japan. I sat through their sessions in the evenings at the inns we were staying at, listened to their stories, took notes on their discussions. What for me was anthropological data, I soon realized, was for these 16-, 17-, and 18-year-olds a continuing struggle to cope with the reality of their lives and their negative definitions within Japanese society.

One of these youths enunciated the problematic positioning of Burakumin in Japanese society in terms of *kegare*, pollution. He said that in order for majority Japanese, and in particular for the emperor as a symbol of the Japanese, to remain pure the society required a scapegoat, something to represent the opposite aspect of impurity. There has to be a group of people who absorb the possible impurity of the emperor and the majority, allowing them to remain symbolically clean. In the feudal period, the Eta absorbed this impurity by fulfilling those tasks defined as defiling, such as butchering animals or tending the dead, sparing majority Japanese from defilement. They symbolically continue to exist in Japanese society as an oppositional Other, occupying the symbolic loci of impurity and inferiority that provides the necessary contrast for the mainstream's self-projection of symbolic superiority and purity. Although this

Burakumin youth described the social position of Burakumin in terms of Japanese symbolic concepts of pollution, many mainstream Japanese, who contend that these concepts were erased following the acquisition of formal equal status, instead identify poverty and poor living conditions as the primary causes of continued exclusion. The lower educational achievements and impoverished living conditions of many Burakumin are often seen as justification for the continuing discrimination against them, rather than recognized as the results of this discrimination.

In discussing images of foreigners, internal relations between mainstream and minorities, and the symbolic spaces of black and white in Japan, Russell asserts that, 'In some ways the black other occupies the same symbolic space and function as Burakumin and Koreans, two categories of other with which Blacks are often equated' (Russell 1991b: 13). I would agree with Russell that the analogy extends to Burakumin, but believe there is something categorically different about Burakumin and resident Koreans. Despite the problematic positioning of both groups, and their current existential search to construct a more positive and self-affirming identity, Burakumin at least know they are Japanese, while resident Koreans are constantly reminded that they are not.

The marginality of Korean residents of Japan is greater because they straddle the division between *uchi* and *soto* (inside and outside). The president of a Japanese trend-watching and consulting firm revealed the Japanese conceptual links between *soto* Others and *uchi* Others by suggesting that there are three distinct types of foreigner: white foreigners, non-white foreigners, and people designated as foreigners who are not foreigners:

> We have three *gaijin*. The pure *gaijin* is white. The second *gaijin* is non-white, people from Asia, people from Africa and South America. In fact, my generation don't really think of these as true *gaijin*. The third kind of *gaijin* are Korean-Japanese and Chinese-Japanese. Still, at present these people are not considered Japanese at all.

Although referred to as Korean-Japanese and Chinese-Japanese by this interviewee, these minorities are usually not referred to in this way, and the Japanese government does not recognize them as such. These 'non-foreign foreigners' living in Japan are largely descendants of people brought to Japan as labourers from other Asian countries, particularly Korea, before or during the Second World War. Although they were born in Japan, have lived their entire lives in

Japan, and speak Japanese as their first language, the government does not grant them citizenship. They are considered to be basically discontinuous with the Japanese. They exist within Japanese society occupying a symbolic space analogous to the Asian Other living outside Japan. In this case the myth of Japanese homogeneity is maintained by the legal and psychological designation of these permanent residents as 'foreigners'.

It is possible for Korean or Chinese residents of Japan to become citizens, but doing so normally requires taking a Japanese name and giving up all aspects of ethnic identity. Japan's assertion of homogeneity does not allow its members to inhabit hyphenated spaces. These *uchi* Others sometimes attempt to pass as mainstream Japanese, but often at great psychological cost. The extent of psychological pain involved in attempting to bridge the divide between mainstream Japanese and resident Korean through denial, was brought home to me during an interview with a young woman I, until then, had not known was a resident Korean. In 1985, while conducting research on department stores in Japan, I enrolled in a tuition-free Korean language class offered by a local municipal office. Among the students in the class were two women, both of whom had Japanese names, were acquainted with one another, but did not particularly resemble each other. Members of the class would occasionally socialize afterwards at nearby coffee shops. On one such occasion I asked the older of the two women, who always seemed to be the best student in the class, how she got interested in studying Korean. She said she happened to see an NHK Korean language programme on television one day, found it interesting and decided to enrol.[7] On another occasion, I explained my research and the younger of these two women mentioned that she had once worked at a department store. I asked if I could interview her and, after some moments, she agreed.

The interview itself was rather ordinary. However, what was unforgettable was her reaction and comments to something I asked after finishing all my 'official' interview questions. Thinking to end the interview on more of a social note, I asked how she had become interested in studying the Korean language as a hobby. She was visibly shaken and soon on the verge of tears. She began to fidget, and then started making comments – it was not clear whether they were directed at me or whether she was talking to herself – that at first were incomprehensible to me. 'My older sister kept telling me not to come and do this interview. She said there would be questions like this. My sister told me not to talk about anything like this.' I was totally confused. I did not know that she had a sister, and if she did what possible relationship this could have to our interview. Suddenly the floodgates of hesitation broke and this young woman told me about her life. Although they never allowed anyone to know it, she and the other woman in the class were sisters. They were Korean on their father's side, but both were trying to pass as majority Japanese. Although their mother was Japanese, until the Japanese family law changed in 1985, citizenship could only be passed through the father. Children of a Japanese mother and foreign father were not granted citizenship, although children of a Japanese father and foreign mother were. Officially, the two women existed in Japan as resident Koreans, legal aliens. Their family had been living in Korea when both of the women were born, and moved back to Japan when the older daughter was six and the younger daughter not quite two years old. The younger woman said she envied her older sister's fluency in Korean, resulting from their age difference when they returned to Japan. Here was a very different account of why the older woman was the best student in the Korean language class. Her interest was not happenstance, awakened one day while watching a language programme on TV, instead she had been born in Korea and raised there until the age of six. Korean was her first language. Now that their father was dead, the younger woman said she longed to return to Korea someday and visit the places where her father's relatives live, but felt it would be better if she could speak some Korean. She also indicated that her elder sister intensely desired to regain her Korean language ability. At one point, she said:

> My older sister wants to study Korean, but she is very apprehensive about it. She says that if you are able to speak Korean everyone will think that you must be Korean or part Korean, so she is afraid of this.

Just as these two women felt a need to keep their identities as sisters a secret, even their desire to learn Korean was experienced as problematic given the desire to 'pass'.

There are internal divisions in Japanese society; different symbolic spaces that separate mainstream and minorities. Projecting heterogeneity outward by defining it as characteristic of *soto* Others is one means of perpetuating the imagination of a homogeneous Japanese society. Denying the inclusion of resident Korean or resident Chinese by declaring them foreigners, or denying the differential realities of Ainu, Burakumin and Okinawans is also necessary to the imagination of homogeneous Japan, given the presence of these *uchi* Others.

CONCLUSIONS

This chapter has discussed images of foreigners in Japanese advertising, suggesting that representations of these *soto* Others provide an oppositional contrast for the construction of Japanese identity. It has also discussed the symbolic positioning of different categories of foreigners, and how imaging the differences among *soto* Others serves as a means of projecting heterogeneity outward, reaffirming the imagination of a self-asserted homogeneous Japan. The association of the concept of 'race' with minorities helps bolster the belief that minorities exist outside Japan. Minorities do exist in Japan, but the divisions in Japanese society are not along racial lines. Instead symbolic and socio-psychological divisions prevent minorities from obtaining full and equal participation in the society, despite proclamations of homogeneity.

There are indications that Japan may have entered a transitional period both with regards to *soto* Others and *uchi* Others. Changes in attitudes and representations are occurring. Responding to negative criticism regarding both images of Whites and Blacks, Japanese advertisers have begun to review their advertising strategies. In particular, they have had to consider the criticism of earlier representations of Blacks. Now some advertisements are encouraging Japanese to reflect on their own degree of awareness and acceptance of others. In 1990, Isetan Department Store ran an advertising campaign showing a black woman, a white girl, and a non-Japanese Asian man. The theme slogan for the advertisement was written in *kanji* (ideographs) which could be read either as '*nannin made ai saseru ka*' ('Up to how many people are you able to love?') or '*nanbito made ai saseru ka*' ('Up to what kind of people are you able to love?').

The construction of Otherness creates boundaries between Japanese and foreigners, but also marks divisions within the society. I believe there is a profound link between *soto* Others and *uchi* Others, such that the explicitly stated goal of *kokusaika* (internationalization) may have implications for Japan's minorities. Internationalization prompts an acceptance of social and cultural diversity, something at odds with the value Japan currently places on social and cultural homogeneity. The linked association of *soto* Others and *uchi* Others means that as Japan reconsiders its identity in relationship to foreigners it must also reflect on its own minorities and assertions of homogeneity.

Many Japanese have gained greater acceptance and appreciation of the world's cultural diversity because of internationalization campaigns and increasing travel abroad, which in turn creates a new way of viewing minority groups within Japan. With its well-publicized interest in internationalization, Japan is very concerned with world opinion and pays attention to foreign criticism of its treatment of minorities. When foreign human rights leaders such as Jesse Jackson came to Japan protesting representations of Blacks, but also protesting treatment of Burakumin, it drew greater attention to minority issues in Japan. After the United Nations recognized the Ainu as an indigenous people, and an international forum was held in the Ainu area of Nibutani to mark the United Nations declaration of 1993 as the 'Year of Indigenous Peoples', there has been greater pressure for Japan to recognize the Ainu as a distinct minority and an aboriginal people. With growing international pressure, the annual speeches commemorating the atomic bombing of Hiroshima in the 1990s began to mention the particular suffering of resident Koreans.[8]

Ohnuki-Tierney (1993) argues that the adoption of rice as a dominant symbol of Japanese self-identity used to assert homogeneity, involved a twofold process of constructing Japanese identity in contrast to foreigners, or *soto* Others, *along with* the taming of minorities in Japan, *uchi* Others, and relegating them to the margins. Hutcheon (1988: 35) calls people who have been marginalized in such ways by dominant groups, 'ex-centric'. Lebra claims there has been 'an ironic by-product of internationalization: namely, the worldwide exposure of historically persistent fissures between dominant and marginal Japanese' (Lebra 1993: 12). Internationalization therefore poses a threat to the Japanese imagination of self by calling into question assertions of national homogeneity. Discussing the relationship between imagination and the self, Kiowa[9] author N. Scott Momaday says:

> We are what we imagine. Our very existence consists in our imagination of ourselves. . . . The greatest tragedy that can befall us is to go unimagined.
>
> (Vizenor 1978: epigraph)

It is also threatening for the cultural self to go unimagined. By questioning assertions of homogeneity, Japan's 'ex-centrics' are proposing a new vision for the imagination of Japan. Minorities in Japan are currently striving for a more positive self-identity and greater official recognition of Japan's diversity. Issues concerning minorities are earnestly being reconsidered the world over. Japan's modern international prominence means it must reconsider its conceptions of, and relationships with, *soto* Others – foreigners. However, it also means Japan must reflect upon the internal divisions that create *uchi* Others, and in the process reconsider issues concerning Japan's minorities.

NOTES

1 *Acknowledgements*: The research presented here was conducted under a Nakasone grant issued by the Japanese government to support research related to internationalization.
2 For example, the Kerner Commission report of 1968 suggested that America was two societies 'one white and one black' without explaining where other minorities fit (Blauner 1994: 21).
3 In keeping with the company's romanized version of its name, the word 'Dentsu' appears without a macron.
4 After my preliminary research on Japanese advertising revealed this possibility (Creighton 1994, 1995a), Nariko Takayanagi (1995) designed a research project to test for this in Japanese women's magazines. Her research revealed a high quantitative correlation of whites presented in scenes with kissing or hand-holding.
5 At the time the Sambo images were popular in Japan I was working at Expo '85, held in Tsukuba, Japan, where I had the opportunity to watch the reaction of a black American co-worker when she first saw the images. After a group of Japanese entered our pavilion with Sambo T-shirts, she left the floor on her break period, entered the staff room and expressed her disgust with the images to all present, along with her irritation that the Japanese visitors wearing them did not realize they were offensive.
6 Although much of the earlier representations of Blacks came through films and literature translated and introduced from abroad, contemporary Japanese writers also create images of Blacks for Japanese. Oe Kenzaburo, who won the Nobel Prize for Literature in 1994, used a black male character as the central motif in his first story, 'Catch'. A popular contemporary writer, Yamada Emi, focuses her work nearly exclusively on erotic relationships between Japanese women and black men. In both of these cases certain stereotypes of Blacks prevalent in Japan suggesting animality and heightened sexuality are perpetuated.
7 NHK is a non-commercial broadcasting station in Japan that shows educational, documentary, and other programmes. It presents television language classes in several languages.
8 An excerpt from one of the speeches in 1993 that mentions the suffering of resident Korean victims and *hibakusha* (atom bomb survivors) appears on a video presentation at the Hiroshima Peace Memorial Hall. Large numbers of resident Koreans died in the blast and Korean *hibakusha* often faced particular problems because of their marginal status. Many Koreans in Japan returned to Korea after the Second World War. Programmes to deal with the medical treatment of *hibakusha* set up between Japan and

the United States were designed to deal with survivors in Japan and did not consider the medical problems of Koreans living in Korea.
9 The Kiowa are a native people of the North American southern plains. Allan Ryan brought this reference to my attention.

BIBLIOGRAPHY

Abe, T. and Yamakawa, H. (eds) (1990) *The CM kanpanii: jidai o bijinesu suru imeeji komyunikeeshon*, Tokyo: Daiyamondosha.
Applbaum, K. (1992) '"I feel coke": why the Japanese study English', *Asian Thought and Society* 17: 18–30.
Asahi Shinbun (Yukan) (1990) 'Datsu "akogare" "imeeji": Dajyare renpatsu no bijo ya nansensu Nihongo gakkō', 2 June.
Ashkenazi, M. (1993) *Matsuri: Festivals of a Japanese Town*, Honolulu: University of Hawaii Press.
Bachnik, J.M. and Quinn, C.J. Jr. (eds) (1994) *Situated Meaning: Inside and Outside in Japanese Self, Society, and Language*, Princeton: Princeton University Press.
Blauner, B. (1994) 'Talking past each other: black and white languages of race', in F.L. Pincus and H. Ehrlich (eds) *Race and Ethnic Conflict*, Boulder: Westview Press.
Carrier, J.G. (1990) 'The symbolism of possession in commodity advertising', *Man* 25: 693–706.
Creighton, M. (1994) 'Images of foreigners in Japanese advertising', in J. Kovalio (ed.) *Japan in Focus*, Toronto: Captus Press.
—— (1995a) 'Imaging the Other in Japanese advertising campaigns', in J.G. Carrier (ed.) *Occidentalism: Images of the West*, Oxford: Oxford University Press.
—— (1995b) 'The non-vanishing Ainu: a damning development project, internationalization and Japan's Indigenous Other', *American Asian Review* 13, 2: 69–96.
Dale, P.N. (1986) *The Myth of Japanese Uniqueness*, New York: St Martin's.
DeVos, G. and Wagatsuma, H. (1966) *Japan's Invisible Race*, Berkeley: University of California Press.
Donoghue, J.D. (1978) *Pariah Persistence in Changing Japan*, Washington, DC: University Press of America.
Essed, P. (1991) *Understanding Everyday Racism: An Interdisciplinary Theory*, London: Sage.
Fitzgerald, T. (1993) *Metaphors of Identity: A Culture Communication Dialogue*, New York: State University of New York Press.
Goosen, T. (1989) 'Caged beasts: black men in modern Japanese literature', in K. Tsuruta (ed.) *The Walls Within: Images of Westerners in Japan and Images of the Japanese Abroad*, Vancouver: The Institute of Asian Research, University of British Columbia.
Gordon, A. (1993) 'Conclusion', in A. Gordon (ed.) *Postwar Japan as History*, Berkeley: University of California Press.
Harrell, S. (1995) 'Introduction: civilizing projects and the reaction to them', in *Cultural Encounters on China's Ethnic Frontiers*, Seattle: University of Washington Press.

Hutcheon, L. (1988) *A Poetics of Post Modernism: History, Theory, Fiction*, London: Routledge.

Jones, T. (1988) 'Racial gaffe rekindles criticism from overseas: black mannequins, toys seen as sign of same attitudes as Watanabe's remark', *Japan Times*, August 2.

Kelly, W. (1993) 'Finding a place in metropolitan Japan: ideologies, institutions, and everyday life', in A. Gordon (ed.) *Postwar Japan as History*, Berkeley: University of California Press.

Kondo, D.K. (1990) *Crafting Selves: Power, Gender, and Discourses of Identity in a Japanese Workplace*, Chicago: University of Chicago Press.

Lebra, T.S. (1976) *Japanese Patterns of Behavior*, Honolulu: University of Hawaii Press.

—— (1993) *Above the Clouds: Status Culture of the Modern Japanese Nobility*, Berkeley: University of California Press.

Lyman, S.M. (1994) *Color, Culture, Civilization: Race and Minority Issues in American Society*, Urbana and Chicago: University of Illinois Press.

Manabe, K., Befu, H. and McConnell, D. (1989) *An Empirical Investigation of Nihonjinron: The Degree of Exposure of Japanese to Nihonjinron Propositions and the Functions these Propositions Serve*, Nishinomiya: Kwansei Gakuin University.

Miller, R.A. (1977) *The Japanese Language in Contemporary Japan: Some Sociolinguistic Observations*, Washington, DC: American Institute for Public Policy Research.

Nishioka, F. (1989) *Jishin o mochitai anata no imeeji seisan no geijutsu*, Tokyo: JICC Shuppankyoku.

Ohnuki-Tierney, E. (1987) *The Monkey as Mirror: Symbolic Transformations in Japanese History and Ritual*, Princeton: Princeton University Press.

—— (1993) *Rice as Self: Japanese Identities Through Time*, Princeton: Princeton University Press.

Okihiro, G.Y. (1994) *Margins and Mainstreams: Asians in American History and Culture*, Seattle: University of Washington Press.

Pettigrew, T.F. (1994) 'New patterns of prejudice: the different worlds of 1984 and 1964', in F.L. Pincus and H.J. Ehrlich (eds) *Race and Ethnic Conflict*, Boulder: Westview Press.

Russell, J.G. (1991a) *Nihonjin no kokujinkan: mondai wa 'Chibikuro Sanbo' dake de wa nai*, Tokyo: Shinhyōron.

—— (1991b) 'Race and reflexivity: the black Other in contemporary Japanese mass culture', *Cultural Anthropology* 6: 3–25.

Shapiro, M. (1988) 'Old black stereotypes find new lives in Japan: marketers defend Sambo toys, black mannequins, insist racism was not intended', *Washington Post*, July 22.

Spector, D. (1984) *It's Only a Joke*, Tokyo: ARK.

Spinelli, E. (1989) *The Interpreted World: An Introduction to Phenomenological Psychology*, London: Sage.

Takayanagi, N. (1995) 'A cross-cultural comparison of women's magazines in Japan and North America', Unpublished MA thesis, University of British Columbia.

Thomas, R. (1989) *Japan: The Blighted Blossom*, Vancouver: New Star Books.

Thorton, M.C. (1989) 'Collective representations and Japanese views of African-descent populations', *International Journal of Sociology and Social Policy* 6: 90–101.

Van den Berghe, P.L. (1978) *Race and Racism*, New York: John Wiley and Sons.

Vizenor, G. (1978) *Wordarrows: Indians and Whites in the New Fur Trade*, Minneapolis: University of Minnesota Press.

Wagatsuma, H. (1967) 'The social perception of skin color in Japan', *Daedalus* 96: 407–43.

White, M. (1988) *The Japanese Overseas: Can They Go Home Again?*, New York: The Free Press.

Williamson, J. (1978) *Decoding Advertisements: Ideology and Meaning in Advertising*, London: Boyars.

Index

aboriginality 11, 39; *see also*
Australian Aborigines; indigenous
peoples
activism xv, 30–4, 57, 58, 60, 61,
67–8; *see also* student unrest
activist organizations 30; Ainu 43;
see also Ainu Liberation
League; Utari Kyokai
Act of Annexation (1910) 84
advertising 212–13, 215, 221, 226,
233; foreign imaging of 212–13;
mood xvii, 214–16; self-identity in
212, *see also* identity; white
female nudity in 217–18
aggression, colonial 80–1; *see also*
colonialism; colonization
agriculture 21, 194
aid 64, 95, 99, 162; for healthcare
97–100; for Hibukusha 102;
for Ryukyuans 149–50; *see also*
Special Measures Law
Ainu, the xi–xiii, 9, 11, 17–49, 143,
144, 145, 167, 201, 213, 227, 229,
232, 234; Ainuness 34, 44;
assimilation of xv, 22, 24–5, 28,
40, *see also* assimilation;
civilization of 22; dilution of
26–7; dispossession of 17, 23;
exclusion of 24, 28, *see also*
exclusion; exploitation of 20, 22,
31; inferiorization of 10, 12, 18,
23, 24, 27, 30, 35, *see also*
inferiorization; isolation of 24;
Japanese relations with 18–25;
marginalization of 18, 28, 29, *see*

also marginalization; New Law
Campaign 40–2; relocation of 17,
22, 23; in post-war Japan 25–8
Ainu: activism 31; alliances 39;
consciousness 34, 37; Council 31;
culture 18, 36, 43, 44; history 29,
37, 41; elderly 35; identity 26, 28,
34, 35, 44, *see also* identity;
Liberation League 30; 'problem'
28, 31, 34; trade 22, *see also*
trade; unity 25; welfare 28, 33–4,
35, 41, 45, *see also* welfare
Ainu Kaihō Dōmei 30–2
Ainu Kyōkai 24–5, 27, 33, 34
Ainu *minzoku* 37, 41
Ainu Moshiri 25, 37, 39, 41, 43
Ainu nationhood 34–40, 42, *see also*
nationhood
Ainu politics 25, 28–34, 42, 44, *see*
also ethnopolitics
Ainu population 18, 23, 24, 45
Ainu shinpō 28, 40–3; rights 35, 40,
see also human rights; civil rights;
rights
Ainu Protection Act 23, 28, 42, 43;
abolition of 41; revision of 24,
29–30
aji 148–9
Ajiajin *see* Asians
Akan 29
Akinaiba 20
Akita Prefecture 131
Alaskan Native Claims Settlement
Act (1971) 39